Visual Antietam Vol. 3: Ezra Carman's Antietam Through Maps and Pictures: The Middle Bridge To Hill's Counterattack

Ezra A. Carman

Edited and Illustrated by

Brad Butkovich

Copyright © 2020 Historic Imagination LLC

www.historicimagination.com

All rights reserved.

ISBN: 978-1-7325976-2-4

Dedication

This book is dedicated to Anya, Lexi, and Jack. They have had to endure my absence on may trips to the various battlefields across the country over the years. And even gone on a few battlefield walks, which I'm sure thrilled them to no end.

BRAD BUTKOVICH

VOL. 3: THE MIDDLE BRIDGE TO HILL'S COUNTERATTACK

CONTENTS

	Introduction	vii
20	The Middle Bridge: The V Corps and the Advance of Pleasonton's Cavalry Division	1
21	The Burnside Bridge	43
	Appendix 1: Order of Battle	171
	Bibliography	187
	Index	189

BRAD BUTKOVICH

Introduction

In the early 1900s Ezra A. Carman wrote a sweeping and detailed manuscript chronicling the Maryland Campaign of 1862. As the colonel of the 13th New Jersey Infantry, he was a participant in the battle. He "served as a trustee on the Antietam National Cemetery Association Board from 1866 to 1877 and as an 'historical expert' and member of the War Department's Antietam Board for Antietam National Battlefield Site from 1895 to 1897." Drawing from extensive interviews with fellow veterans, including numerous walks on the battlefield, the manuscript provided a unique and detailed history of the campaign. Unfortunately, it was never published. However, it has served as a starting point for most books written about the battle ever since.

I first became acquainted with the manuscript when it was included in the 1999 release of the computer game *Sid Meier's Antietam!*. I was fascinated by the detail presented in the document, but soon set it aside as I read other accounts, most notably John M. Priest's *Antietam: The Soldier's Battle* and Stephen W. Sears' *Landscape Turned Red: The Battle of Antietam*. However, it wasn't until farther along in the digital age, when I discovered and downloaded the Carman/Cope maps in high resolution from the Library of Congress, that I was able to fully appreciate Carman's work.

My Civil War interests have always centered on maps and visual context. My website www.civilwarvirtualtours.com details several battles with maps, videos, and photos. For my previous battle studies on Pickett's Mill and Allatoona Pass I created all the maps myself. After a discussion with friends, I decided that instead of researching and writing my own text, I would use Carman's manuscript. In my opinion, it is still the most detailed and readable study of the battle currently available. Thus was the genesis for this three volume set.

The *Visual Antietam* series is intended for both readers who visit the battlefield, and those, perhaps overseas, who will never have the chance to see it. On every opposite page of the Carman text is an image to help the reader visualize the battlefield. The maps detail the movement of the men and units far more often than in most other works. There are pictures of the landscape, both period and modern, to help the reader understand the terrain and "lay of the land." And finally, where appropriate are pictures, not just of the generals, but also of the common soldiers and line officers that fought on the battlefield that day. Given the graphics heavy nature of the work, a single volume would have been too large. The series is divided into three volumes. Those wishing to visit the battlefield with the books can do so with individual volumes in a convenient carry size.

This series is not envisioned to be a detailed, heavily annotated study of the campaign or battle. The full, proper title of Carman's manuscript is *The Maryland Campaign of September 1862*. However, since I am focusing on only the battle itself, I have altered the title. Campaign chapters and those that do not relate directly to the battle have been omitted. There are few footnotes in the text. My purpose was to bring his book, and more specifically the battle, to life with an emphasis on visual context. For those wishing to read comprehensive versions of the Carman manuscript, digging into his source material and methods, I highly recommend Thomas Clemens' *The Maryland Campaign of September 1862. Volume II: Antietam* (and Volumes I and III of course) and Joseph Pierro's *The Maryland Campaign of September 1862: Ezra A. Carman's Definitive Study of the Union and Confederate Armies at Antietam*. Both are thoroughly researched and noted.

Very few editing changes were made to the manuscript. Some changes are for readability, some to bring the text up to modern standards. These include standardizing times by adding colons between the hour and minutes instead of periods, adding commas consistently to numbers between the thousands and hundreds, indenting large quotes, and changing book titles to italics. As stated, footnotes are minimal. I only used them to highlight important changes in the text, such as misspellings, as well as sections where Carman added large clippings from the *Official Records of the Rebellion*. Otherwise, Carman's idiosyncrasies have been left alone, such as using recrossed instead of re-crossed. Or Louisianians instead of Louisianans.

Volume 3

The Visual Antietam series is divided into three volumes. *Visual Antietam Vol. 1: Ezra Carman's Antietam Through Maps and Pictures: Dawn to Dunker Church* opens the battle on the evening of September 16th, and continues through the opening fighting in the infamous Cornfield and East Woods, ending with the Confederates ultimately being expelled from both. *Visual*

Antietam Vol. 2: Ezra Carman's Antietam Through Maps and Pictures: The West Woods To Bloody Lane continues the narrative by focusing on the struggle for the West Woods and the Sunken Road. *Visual Antietam Vol. 3: Ezra Carman's Antietam Through Maps and Pictures: The Middle Bridge to Hill's Counterattack* brings an end to the trilogy by focusing on the fighting around the Middle Bridge, Lower Bridge (Burnside's Bridge), and Ambrose P. Hill's defense and counterattack.

Most of the pictures in this work were taken as close as possible to the hour they occurred in 1862, even taking modern daylight savings time into account. For *Volume 3*, this means plenty of late afternoon photographs.

I hope the reader will enjoy the numerous maps and photos throughout the book. The afternoon fight south of Sharpsburg does not receive as much attention as the struggle for the Cornfield, Sunken Road, or even Burnside's Bridge. These maps and pictures should help form an idea of what went on there and help bring the fight into perspective.

Carman's manuscript spans the entire Maryland Campaign. The Battle of Antietam falls in the middle. This is reflected in the unusual chapter numbering in this book. It only contains chapters 20-21. In the original manuscript Chapter 21 is very large, containing both the fight for the Lower Bridge and the later fight between the Ninth Corps and Hill. Several modern studies break this large chapter into two sections. I have left them in its original format.

Acknowledgments

I wish to extend by gratitude and thanks to the many people who have helped bring this third and final volume to print. Their contributions are many and varied, but each one helped further along the release of this book and for that, I give my thanks.

Scott Felsen, a good friend and experienced professional photographer and videographer, agreed to accompany me on one of several trips to the battlefield to take pictures. His tips helped me improve my photography skills, and produced several great photos for this trilogy. Several of the images are credited to him. A voracious learner, he has enthusiastically come along on several battlefield tours throughout Georgia, Tennessee, Maryland, and Pennsylvania. I wish to thank his immense contribution in helping bring the "visual" part of this volume and series to life.

I also wish to again thank my proofreaders Andy Papen, Patrick McCormick, and Scott Felsen for reading over the manuscript and pointing out all those little details and layout errors that escape the eye when you've stared at the same words for months at a time. Their help was invaluable, and I hope they enjoy the three volumes on any future Antietam battlefield visits.

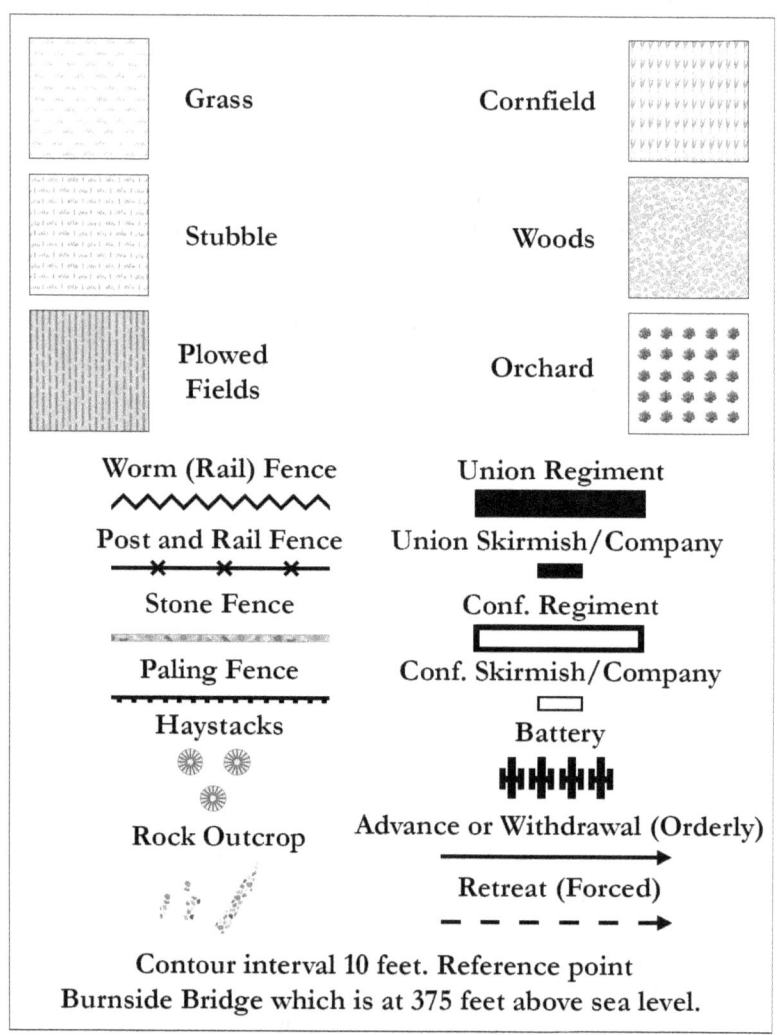

Chapter 20

The Middle Bridge:
The V Corps and the Advance of Pleasonton's Cavalry Division

At daybreak of the 17th the bold bluff bordering the east bank of the Antietam was crowned with 46 heavy, long range guns. North of the Keedysville road were the batteries of Wever, Langner, and Kusserow—20-pounder Parrott guns—and soon after daybreak Hazlett's Battery of Parrott guns was placed in the position occupied on the preceding day by Taft's, von Kleiser and Weed. Durell's Battery was put on Weed's left early in the morning and Benjamin's was still farther to the left and rear, overlooking Sharpsburg and the country below it. They swept most of the ground between them and the Union troops. They were well-served, especially the guns of Benjamin's Battery, whose field of fire was extensive, reaching as far as the Dunker[1] Church. From early morning until late in the day these batteries engaged the enemy's guns and fired upon their infantry, and their fire was very destructive upon the divisions of Ewell, Jackson, Hood and D. H. Hill, and inflicted much loss on the Confederates who were contending against the advance of French and Richardson at the Sunken Road. The batteries on the extreme left were supported by Burnside's Ninth Corps, those in the center and on the left by Porter's Fifth Corps.

---

[1] Carman used the alternate spelling Dunkard throughout the manuscript instead of Dunker. Dunkard now reflects a more conservative sect split from the church post-war. I have kept the more accurate lineage spelling of Dunker.

Sykes' Division held the line and supported the artillery south of the Keedysville road, three batteries of reserve artillery—Graham's, Miller's and Van Reed's—being in rear of Buchanan's Brigade, which was on the right of the division; Lovell's Brigade was on the left of Buchanan's, Warren's small brigade of two New York regiments and Randol's Battery were to the left and rear, covering the approaches in the direction of Harper's Ferry and connecting with the right of Burnside. About 9 a.m. Morell's Division relieved Richardson, on the right of Sykes. Waterman's and A. P. Martin's batteries were thrown forward, onto the bluff, the former joining in the fire of the heavy guns. Not including Humphrey's Division which did not reach the field until the morning of the 18th, Porter's strength as reported by McClellan was 12,930, and, including the Reserve Artillery, he had 78 guns.

Pleasonton's cavalry division bivouacked on the night of the 16th in the west suburbs of Keedysville. While the battle was raging on the right the heavy batteries were already engaged, but Pleasonton's cavalry and Porter's infantry were idle. One of McClellan's staff says:

> During these operations the clamor of the artillery along the whole line of battle was incessant. We could hear the distant muttering of musketry from the flanks, but Sumner's movement had evidently come to a stand. This produced a lull in the battle within our sight, and I had leisure to remark upon the headquarters group immediately about me. In the midst was a small redan built of fence rails, behind which sat General Fitz John Porter, who, with a telescope resting on the top rail, studied the field with unremitting attention, scarcely leaving his post during the whole day. His observations he communicated to the commander by nods, signs, or in words so low toned and brief that the nearest by-standers had but little benefit from them. When not engaged with Porter, McClellan...was intently watching the battle...and conversing with surrounding officers and giving his orders in the most quiet undertones.... Everything was as quiet and punctilious as a drawing-room ceremony.

From this position McClellan viewed the progress of the action at the Sunken Road, with a studied calmness of manner that scarcely concealed the underlying excitement, and, when affairs seem to [sic] going well, exclaimed: "By George, this is a magnificent field, and if we win this fight it will cover all our errors and misfortunes forever." Up to this time not an infantry soldier or cavalryman had crossed the middle bridge that morning, nor had a demonstration been made beyond it, nor any action taken to relieve the pressure on the right, but Pleasonton had been ordered forward,

VOL. 3: THE MIDDLE BRIDGE TO HILL'S COUNTERATTACK

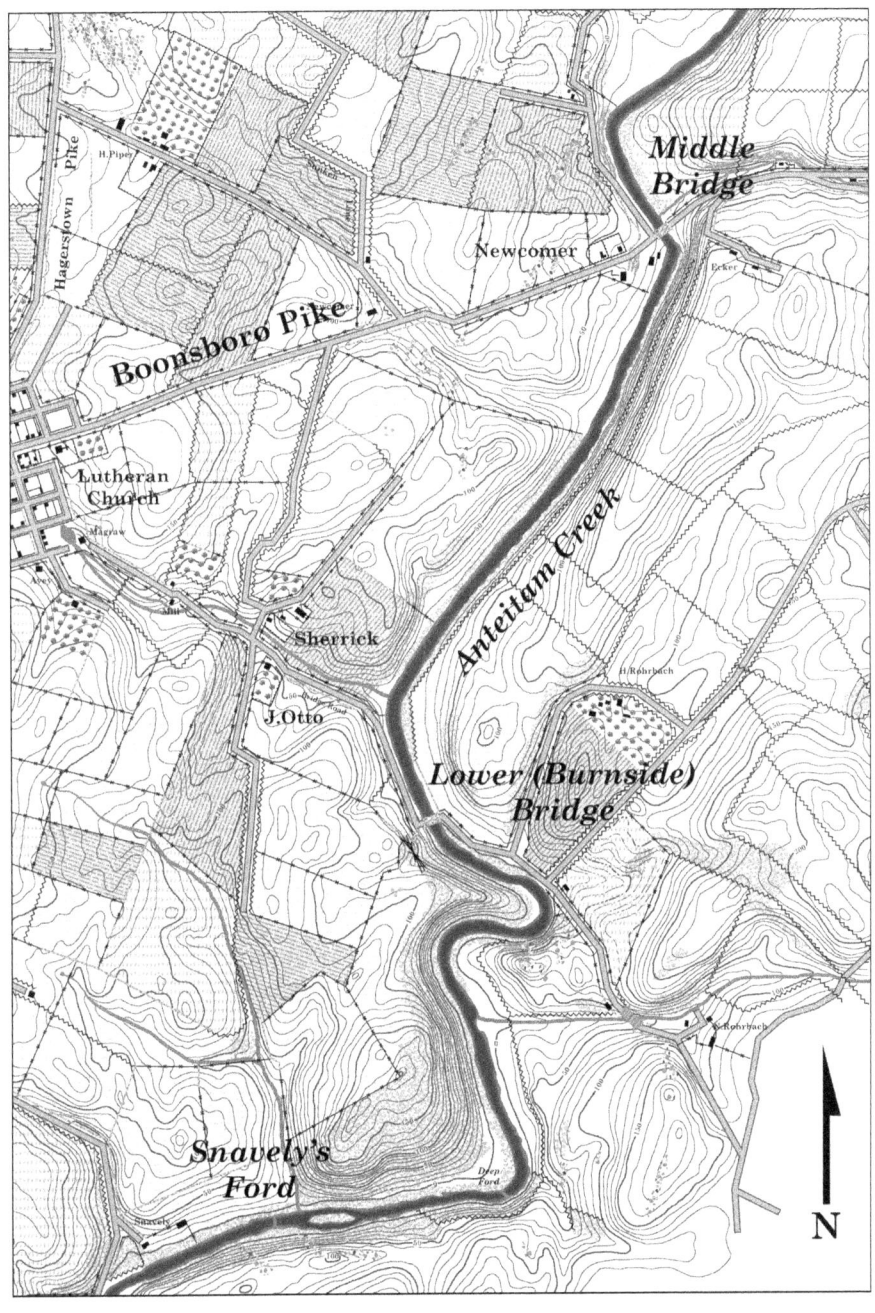

and was then moving on the road in the direction of the bridge with six regiments and a squadron of cavalry, and the batteries of Gibson, Tidball, Hains, and Robertson. He was under orders to take position beyond the bridge and support the left of Sumner's line. Finding the enemy had a crossfire of artillery on the bridge, and sharpshooters covering it, he first threw forward cavalry skirmishers, and then advanced Tidball's Battery by piece to drive off the sharpshooters with canister.

The advance was led by Captain S. B. M. Young, with a squadron of the 4th Pennsylvania Cavalry, followed by Lieutenant W. N. Dennison's section of Tidball's Battery. On nearing the bridge the column came under the fire of the Washington Artillery on Cemetery hill, and of H. P. Jones' batteries on the ridge, north, but Young pushed on, dashed across the bridge, passed the pickets of the 12th U. S. Infantry, that had crossed the night before, and charged up the long hill to its crest, 675 yards from the bridge, and, as he reached this point, still in the road, a shell was exploded in his ranks, killing and mortally wounding four men. Young immediately deployed on either side of the road and engaged the Confederate infantry near the west foot of the ridge, under cover of the stone fences lining the road.

This body of infantry was a detachment of Colonel George T. Anderson's Brigade, under command of Captain H. D. D. Twiggs, 1st Georgia Regulars. Late in the afternoon of the 16th Twiggs had been ordered to take charge of this detail of 85 to 100 men, and do picket duty between Sharpsburg and the Antietam. He took position to the east of the town, on a rise of ground about midway between the Antietam and the Keedysville road, and threw out skirmishers. He was not recalled to join his brigade, when it moved to the left, on the morning of the 17th, and when an officer of the advanced picket post reported the approach of cavalry and artillery, he selected 20 of his best sharpshooters and hastened to the road, placing his men behind the stone fences on either side of it, at the foot of the hill, and when Young appeared opened fire upon him with such effect as to drive him back. Young again advanced and attacked. By this time Dennison's section of artillery came up and was pushed forward to the highest point of the road; it had scarcely unlimbered when Twiggs, who had now called up his reserve and assembled his entire force behind the stone fences, drove the cannoneers from their guns, and it was with much difficulty that they were withdrawn from their exposed position and, while withdrawing, the Confederate batteries on Cemetery hill dropped shell and solid shot among the men and guns.

Meanwhile, Young was skirmishing with Twiggs, whose men were well protected, and Colonel Childs came up with the main body of the 4th Pennsylvania, which he halted before reaching the crest of the ridge, while he went forward, on the right of the road, to reconnoiter. He immediately saw that the place was not proper for cavalry and was returning to report

VOL. 3: THE MIDDLE BRIDGE TO HILL'S COUNTERATTACK

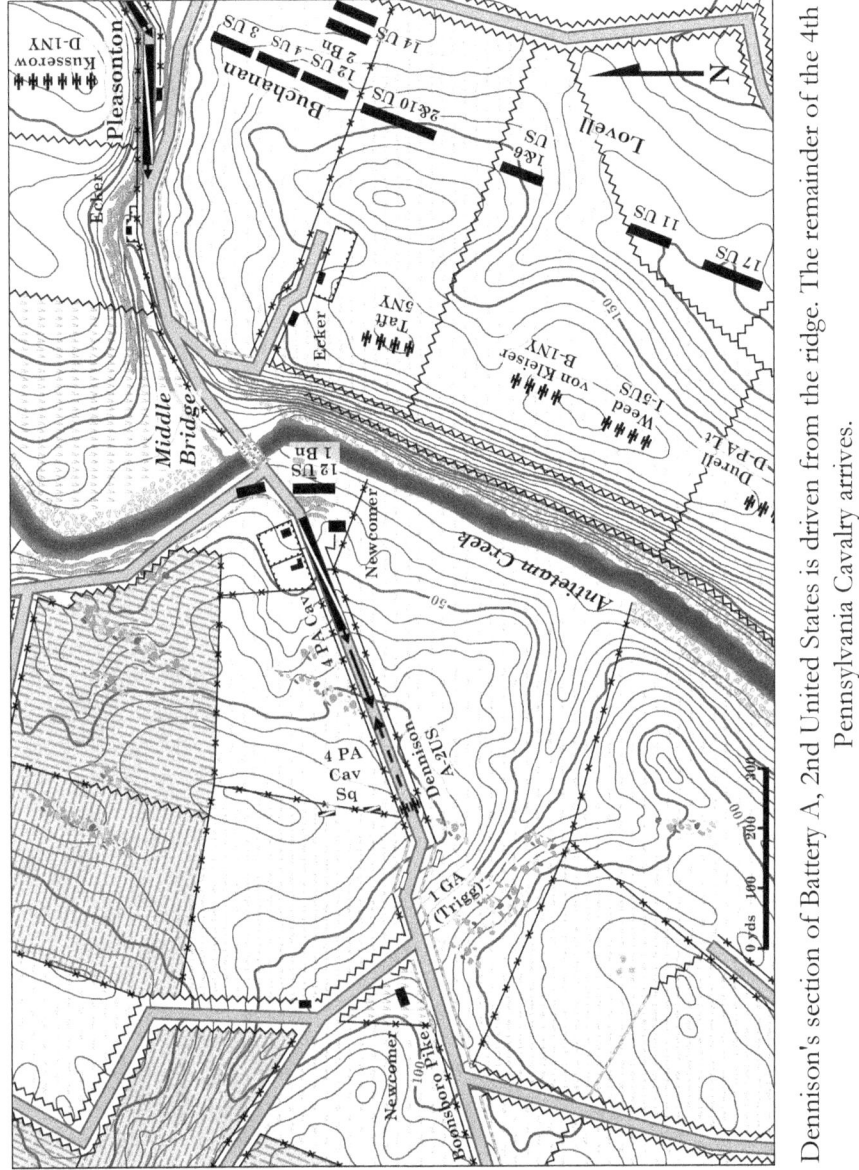

Dennison's section of Battery A, 2nd United States is driven from the ridge. The remainder of the 4th Pennsylvania Cavalry arrives.

the fact to Pleasonton and to bring up support to Young and the artillery, and, when on or very near the road, a few yards east of the crest, was struck by a cannon shot, fell from his horse, and died within an hour.

The other two sections of Tidball's Battery had already followed Childs and his regiment and, turning to the right were run by hand up the ridge, to a point about 160 yards from the road and immediately opened fire upon the enemy's batteries on the ridge beyond; Dennison's section following. Hains' Battery followed Tidball and formed on his left, one section north of the road, the other on its left.

It came into action under a heavy fire of artillery, directed particularly upon the right section, and was annoyed by Twiggs' men, who were in good rifle range. Robertson's Battery followed Hains and went into position 80 yards to his left and rear, coming immediately under fire of the guns on Cemetery hill. Gibson's Battery followed Robertson and took position between him and Hains. Pleasonton says the plan of sending forward cavalry skirmishers and advancing Tidball's Battery by piece "in a short time succeeded in clearing the front sufficiently to obtain positions for Gibson's, Robertson's, Tidball's and Hains' batteries, who opened upon the enemy with good effect, having a direct fire in front and an enfilading fire in front of Sumner's Corps on the right, and supporting the left of Burnside's Corps, the distance to Sumner's Corps being nearly a mile, and something greater to that of Burnside, my force being the only one in front, connecting the two corps."

Meanwhile Twiggs was keeping up his fire upon the batteries, especially Tidball, which, from its advanced and more exposed position, presented a good target, until a battery beyond the Antietam, probably Weed's, enfiladed his position and he retreated precipitously, some of his men halting under cover of some haystacks and a stone fence near the position from which he had advanced, where, joined by some of the 17th South Carolina, they renewed their fire and remained until driven back by the advance of the 2nd and 10th U. S. Infantry.

The cavalry followed the artillery across the bridge under a terrific fire of artillery, by which many saddles were emptied, and formed in rear of the horse batteries. The 4th Pennsylvania until relieved by the advance of the regular infantry, remained on the right of the road, and the 5th U. S. Cavalry formed on its left. On the left of the road were the 6th and a squadron of the 8th Pennsylvania, 3rd Indiana, 8th Illinois and 1st Massachusetts. Some of the regiments were beyond the Newcomer barn and close up to Robertson's Battery; others on the left and rear of the barn within a few yards of the Antietam. All were under fire; shell and spherical case exploded over them and solid shot, directed at the batteries, skipping over the elevation in front, dropped among them. One of the officers thought the round shot were endowed with military intelligence: "As they

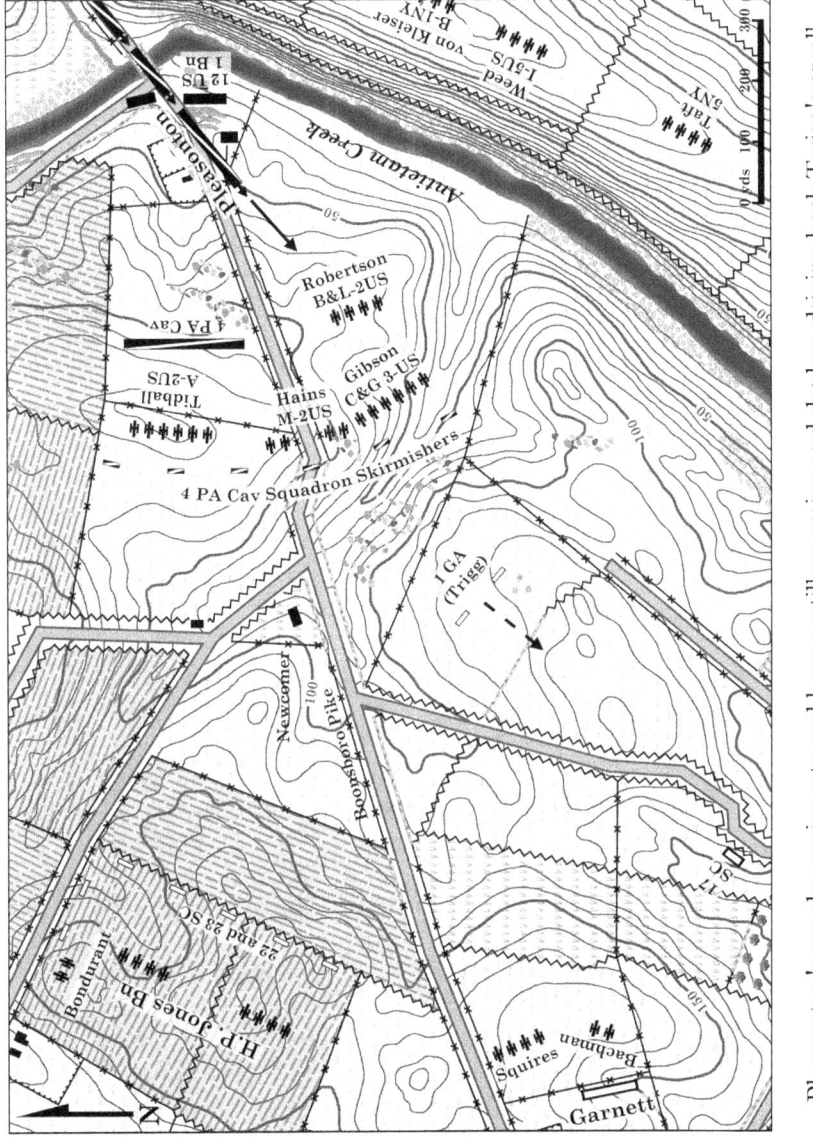

Pleasonton's cavalry regiments and horse artillery arrive and deploy, driving back Twigg's small group of skirmishers.

came to a certain point of the ridge in front and missed their mark, they evidently saw the cavalry under the hill and began to descend into the ranks, and everybody ducked their heads."

The position of the cavalry was certainly an uncomfortable one. Most of the shot and shell directed at the batteries in front, flew over the heads of the artillerymen and dropped into its ranks, while it could do absolutely nothing, not even see the enemy; and the nature of the ground, fences, and ravines was such as to have made efficient action as cavalry very difficult, if it had been called upon to repel an attack on the guns. Several times during the day the men mounted and drew sabers, as all supposed, to charge, but were dismounted again without attempting anything. The fire of Lee's artillery was fierce, and, together with that of the Union guns in the immediate rear, made a noise infernal and deafening. The historian of the 1st Massachusetts says: "the air was full of shot and shell, which had the curious effect of putting the men to sleep. Everywhere could be seen groups of men fast asleep."

General John C. Tidball, in the *Journal of the Military Service Institution*, Vol. 12 (1891), p. 955, says:

> The cavalry that had crossed the bridge, finding itself greatly exposed and without the power of acting, took shelter in hollows and under the banks of the creek. At this period of the war the cavalry had not yet fallen into the hands of those who knew the proper use to make of it."

Another, a gallant young cavalry officer later in the war, says: "It is one of the surprising features of this surprising battle that the Federal cavalry, instead of being posted, according to the practice of the centuries, on the flanks of the infantry, was used throughout the day in support of its own horse batteries, in rear of the Federal center, and in a position from which it would have been impossible for it to have been used as cavalry, or even to have emerged mounted."

The horse batteries crossed the Antietam and went into position on the ridge just after Lee had given directions to his chief of artillery to put his most powerful batteries along the crest in front of Sharpsburg, and engage those beyond the Antietam that were so annoying his infantry, but before this could be effected the 24 pieces of Pleasonton opened such a spirited and accurate fire, as not only to prevent the establishment of other batteries in their front, but to drive under cover those already there, and as occasion offered they directed their fire to the right upon the Confederates opposing Richardson and French and to the left upon the troops confronting Burnside.

Although Twiggs had been driven from their immediate front these batteries were still annoyed by sharpshooters of Evans' Brigade, that, under

Tidball's Battery A, 2nd United States looking toward Cemetery Hill and the Confederate position. The Boonsboro Pike bisects the hill in the center of the photo. *Author's collection.*

cover of the stone and rail fences, rock ledges in the fields and other protection, kept up a severe fire upon them, especially Tidball's, that the cavalry skirmishers were not able to silence, and Pleasonton called upon Captain M. M. Blunt of the 1st Battalion, 12th U. S. Infantry, then at the bridge, to advance a line of skirmishers and drive them away from Tidball's front, which was immediately done by Captain Frederick Winthrop. Soon after this General Sykes ordered Blunt's battalion to advance to Tidball's support and Winthrop deployed his company in skirmishing order down the road and in the fields south of it, to the left of the battery, the battalion moving in the field as a support.

When Sykes ordered Blunt forward from the bridge, he ordered the 2nd and 10th U. S. Infantry (consolidated), under command of Lieutenant John S. Poland, to cross the Antietam and support Blunt. Poland crossed over, filed to the left, and came up to Blunt's Battalion on the level near the stream. Advancing beyond Winthrop's skirmishers he deployed seven companies as skirmishers to the left of the batteries, holding five companies in reserve. The entire battalion was south of the road.

While Poland was doing this the horse batteries ran out of ammunition and were relieved by two batteries of Porter's Corps; Robertson and Gibson being relieved by Lieutenant A. M. Randol, commanding Battery E and G (consolidated), 1st U. S. Artillery. Gibson, after replenishing ammunition, took position on the bluff east of the Antietam and on the north side of the road, where he remained during the day. One section of Robertson's Battery, under command of Lieutenant Albert O. Vincent, moved northwest about 860 yards and took position on the left of Richardson's Division, where, as we have seen, it became engaged and remained until relieved by Graham's Battery, when it recrossed the Antietam. Battery K, 5th U. S. Artillery, Lieutenant William E. Van Reed, relieved Tidball and Hains, taking position about 75 yards north of the road. Sykes reports that it was against his judgment that he sent Randol's and Van Reed's batteries across the Antietam, and with them four additional battalions of regular infantry, under the command of Captain Hiram Dryer.

We give place to an incident along Morell's line east of the Antietam. The historian of the 118th Pennsylvania (Philadelphia Corn Exchange Regiment) says:

> At noon the combat raged in all its fierceness. It was near this hour when General McClellan, with his huge and imposing staff, rode upon the ground occupied by our division. The deep and abiding enthusiasm that habitually followed him, promptly greeted him. Shouts, yells, and cheers of appreciation rent the air. This unusual noise, so loud that it was borne above the din of battle, to the enemy's

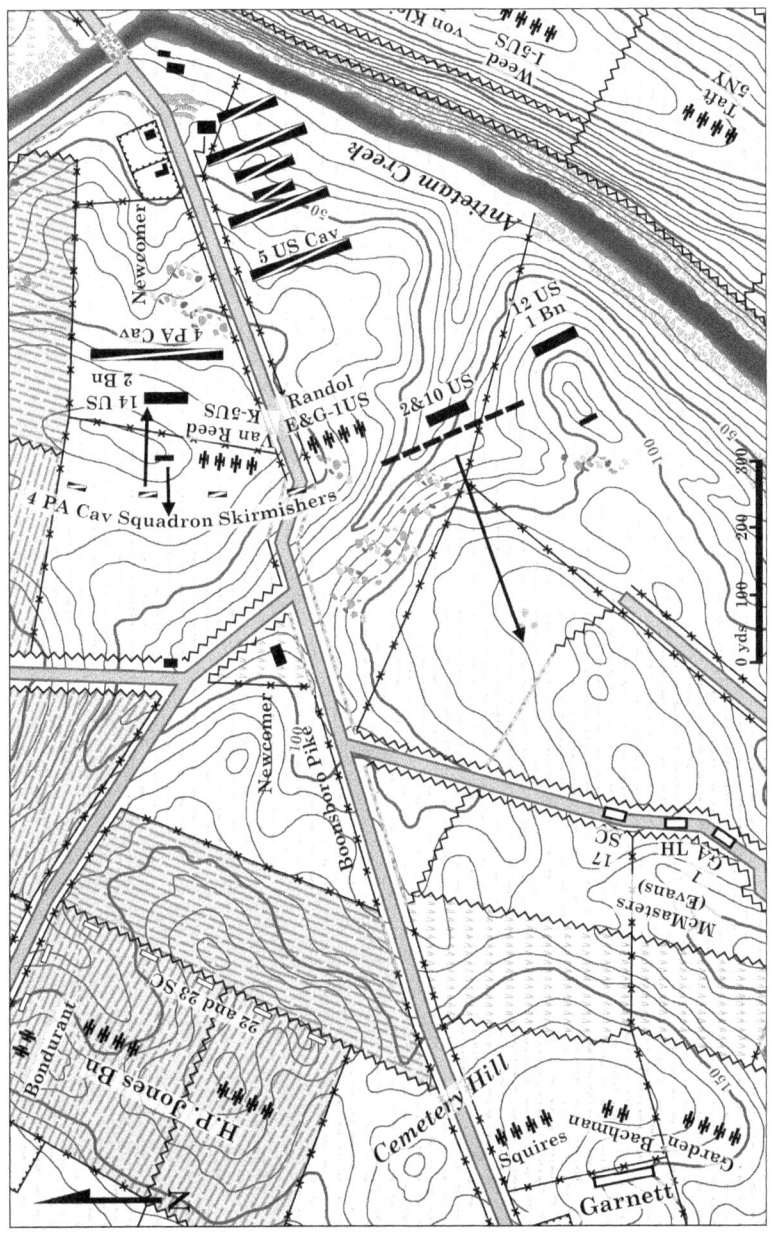

The United States Regulars relieve the cavalry skirmishers and move into position.

line, brought on a vigorous and persistent shelling. Regardless of the flying, bursting missiles, there he sat astride his splendid charger, glass in hand, calmly reviewing the mighty hosts, whose discomfiture with his trusted legions he was bent upon that day accomplishing. Intent, no doubt, on securing some permanent advantage at this particular point, he turned suddenly to Colonel Webb, of his staff, who subsequently won imperishable fame in command of the Philadelphia brigade at Gettysburg, and after a few moments of hurried instructions, dispatched him on his mission down into the valley—down into the very jaws of death. The smoke of the conflict soon engulfed him, and he was lost to view entirely.

Where Webb went on his mission, into the "very jaws of death," on the peaceful side of the Antietam is not of record, but it was soon thereafter, that Poland was seen leading his men down to the road from the left and thence across the bridge and expectations ran high that now the Fifth Corps was to advance and engage the enemy, and thus relieve the pressure on the right and pierce the center; but these expectations were not realized.

Poland was soon followed by the 2nd Battalion, 14th U. S. Infantry, Captain D. B. McKibbin. McKibbin says he was ordered to move at 1 p.m. to support some batteries. After crossing the stream he marched up the road some distance, filed to the right, halted his command under the crest of a knoll, relieving the 4th Pennsylvania Cavalry, in support of a battery in front, and sent one company, under Captain Horace K. Thatcher, as skirmishers, to relieve those of the 4th Pennsylvania Cavalry, under Captain Young, and these became engaged with the skirmishers of Twiggs and those of Evans' Brigade. Upon being relieved by McKibbin the Pennsylvania Cavalry fell back to the Newcomer barn.

As the advance of the regular infantry practically relieved the cavalry from any further duty on this part of the field we shall here dispose of it and dismiss it from our narrative. At 1 p.m. the squadron of the 8th Pennsylvania recrossed the bridge, marched up the east bank of the Antietam, recrossed to the west side at Neikirk's and took position with a squadron of the 12th Pennsylvania Cavalry on high ground southwest of Kennedy's, near where Richardson formed for his advance. The two squadrons were here engaged in gathering stragglers, upon which duty they remained until night, when they rejoined their division near Keedysville. At 3 p.m., the 1st Massachusetts moved across the road to the right and marched about 500 yards to the cover of a ridge where it remained free from casualty or any apparent duty until late in the day when it recrossed the upper Antietam. Under McClellan's order of 4 p.m., to send two squadrons to report to Meade, the 3rd Indiana and 8th Illinois moved up the west bank of the Antietam and bivouacked in rear of the right wing of

David B. McKibbin, commanding 2nd Battalion, 14th United States Infantry. Photographed as colonel of the 158th Pennsylvania Infantry in 1863. *United States Army Heritage & Education Center.*

the infantry. The 5th United States, 4th and 6th Pennsylvania remained until the horse batteries were withdrawn and accompanied them to the bivouac near Keedysville.

The cavalry was not as usefully employed as it should have been, and Pleasonton was disgusted at the enforced inaction; McClellan gives it these few words, and they tell the whole story: "The cavalry had little field for operations during the engagement, but was employed in supporting the horse batteries in the center, and in driving up stragglers, while awaiting opportunity for other service." We return to the regular infantry.

At 2 p.m. Sykes ordered Captain Hiram Dryer, commanding 4th U. S. Infantry, to cross the bridge with his regiment and the 1st Battalion of the 14th, Captain Harvey W. Brown, and take command of the regular infantry on that side of the stream, consisting, in all, of the 2nd and 10th, 4th, 1st Battalion of the 12th, and the two battalions of the 14th. The command aggregated about 1,640 men; 400 in the 2nd and 10th; 320 in the 4th; 280 in the 12th, and 640 in the 14th. Dryer's orders were to "support the batteries and to dislodge the enemy from certain haystacks in a field on the right [left] of the road."

Meanwhile Randol's Battery had retired. As soon as it had taken position, relieving Gibson and Robertson, it opened a fire of spherical case upon the flank of a Confederate battery on Cemetery hill, which soon retired out of range. Being somewhat annoyed by the enemy's skirmishers, who were behind the stone fences and hidden in the cornfield in his front, Randol had Poland advance his skirmishers to the front of the guns, which was some relief. But as his position was an unfavorable one for the use of his guns he was directed by Pleasonton to retire; Sykes says he "very properly withdrew his battery." He was engaged but a short time, had no losses, and resumed his position with the reserve, beyond the Antietam.

Dryer had now come up, it was nearly or quite 3 o'clock when he crossed the Antietam, and Van Reed's Battery was the only one in position, but, in a very few minutes, Tidball, who had fed his men and horses and replenished his ammunition, returned to his former [position] on Van Reed's right, and both became engaged with such Confederate batteries as had the temerity to show themselves, and fired at such bodies of infantry as came within view, especially upon D. H. Hill's men, on the Piper farm, and those that were opposing Burnside, who had now crossed the lower bridge and was advancing on Sharpsburg. It was about 3 o'clock when Pleasonton asked McClellan for more infantry, and at 3:30 p.m., his request was thus answered by the chief of staff: "General McClellan directs me to say he has no infantry to spare. Confer with Major General Porter, and if he cannot support your batteries, withdraw them."

About 3:30 p.m., under Pleasonton's orders, the right section of Tidball's Battery, in charge of Lieutenant A. C. M. Pennington, advanced about 650

The Middle Bridge just a few days after the battle. The Newcomer barn is to the left, and the house is in the center on the right side of the Boonsboro Pike. *Library of Congress.*

yards to the right and front, and took position on the left and front of Richardson's Division and engaged a battery west of the Hagerstown road and a few yards north of where Piper's lane intersects it.

With the 4th U. S. Infantry and the 1st Battalion of the 14th Dryer advanced over the Newcomer ridge, in column, exposed to a severe fire, and halted on the right of Poland's command, which had been deployed as skirmishers, with the right resting on the road, between the crest of the hill occupied by the artillery and the end of the Sunken Road. Dryer ordered Poland to advance with his skirmishers to the front and left, and take possession of some haystacks in a field about 150 yards to the front and 300 yards to the left of the road. At the same time Lieutenant C. H. Carlton was directed to deploy to the three leading companies of the 4th Infantry, about 120 men, to the right of the road and advance near the crest of a ridge about 250 yards in front, Dryer using the remaining five companies of the regiment as a support. Poland and Carlton moved promptly to their allotted work and Dryer deployed his five companies on the right of the road and the 1st Battalion of the 14th on the left, its right resting on the road.

Before following the advance of this thin line, let us note what had been transpiring in its front and what it has to encounter. Early in the morning Cemetery hill was occupied by the batteries of Squires, Miller and Bachman, and, on the extension of the ridge, north of the road, were the four batteries of H. P. Jones' Battalion. These seven batteries were supported by the brigades of George T. Anderson, Garnett, and Evans. During the forenoon Miller's Battery and a section of Bachman's, with George T. Anderson's Brigade, were sent to the left, and Jones' guns, that could not cope with the heavier guns beyond the Antietam, were retired under cover of the ridge, and one battery was sent to the left. During the forenoon Jones again ascended the ridge with three batteries and at noon these were in position: Squires' Battery of four guns, one section of Bachman's, the three batteries of Jones, with Boyce's Battery farther to the left with D. H. Hill. This artillery was supported by Garnett's Virginia brigade of 260 men and Evans' South Carolina brigade of 280 men. Garnett was on Cemetery hill, in rear of the artillery. He says, "as far as practicable the command was sheltered in a hollow in rear of the artillery...where for four or five hours it was subjected to an almost uninterrupted fire of solid shot, shell, and spherical case, from the guns beyond the Antietam, by which a number of men were killed and wounded, which casualties were borne by the troops with remarkable firmness and steadiness." All this was before noon, after which he was ordered forward on the brow of the hill to annoy the artillery, and where he was more exposed than in his former position, and suffered considerably. "At length," says Garnett, "for some cause unknown to me, a

Lieutenant Caleb H. Carlton of the 4th United States Infantry. *Library of Congress*.

large portion of the pieces were withdrawn, and I moved my command farther back to a more secure place."

Evans' small South Carolina brigade was divided. On the evening of the 16th the Holcombe Legion and 17th South Carolina, both under command of Colonel F. W. McMaster, not numbering over 100 officers and men, were sent to the right and front of Cemetery hill, to Sherrick's lane, and Twiggs' detail from George T. Anderson's Brigade took post on their left and front. Everything was quiet until about 1 p.m. of the 17th, when Twiggs and the skirmishers were driven in and rallied on the left, some of Twiggs' men stopping at the haystacks and at a stone fence near them. Soon after this McMaster was informed by an officer of Squires' Battery that a Union battery had proved quite destructive to Squires, and that he would be compelled to discontinue firing unless it was silenced, upon which McMaster "immediately sent out about 25 volunteers, who silenced the battery of the enemy for some time." Three regiments of Evans' Brigade, the 18th, 22nd, and 23rd, under command of Colonel P.F. Stevens, were on the left of the road, supporting the batteries that, from time to time, were pushed forward to the crest of the ridge and almost as quickly obliged to fall back before the fire of the guns beyond the Antietam, and, later in the day, by those of the horse batteries. The 18th South Carolina, under command of Colonel William Wallace, was on the left, acting as a support to Boyce's Battery; the 23rd, Captain S. A. Durham, and 22nd, Major H. Hilton, were near the road and in front of the artillery, and for a great part of the time between the fire of the contending batteries, and exposed to the heavy and continuous shelling of the Union guns, but, being deployed in skirmishing order, sought cover and did not suffer much loss. When Pleasonton's horse batteries advanced and used canister upon them, the skirmishers fell back, but as the fire ceased they again went cautiously forward, but not as far as the advanced position from which the canister had driven them.

D. H. Hill says it was about 4 o'clock, Anderson says it was earlier, "and Burnside's corps was moving to attack our right. A heavy column was advancing up the Boonsboro Pike, and I ordered up some 200 or 300 men, under command of Colonel G. T. Anderson, to the knoll commanding Sharpsburg, but they were exposed to an enfilade fire from a battery near the church on the Hagerstown pike, and compelled to retire." The position on the ridge, vacated by Anderson, was soon occupied by portions of Colquitt's and Garland's brigades. It will be remembered that when Colquitt and Garland were disposed of by Greene's Division, early in the day, some of the men were rallied on Rodes' left, in the Sunken Road, but many of them continued their retreat to Sharpsburg. Captain Garrett, 5th North Carolina, went into town, hoping to get up with them, and met General Lee in the street, to whom he reported the misfortune that had befallen them,

VOL. 3: THE MIDDLE BRIDGE TO HILL'S COUNTERATTACK

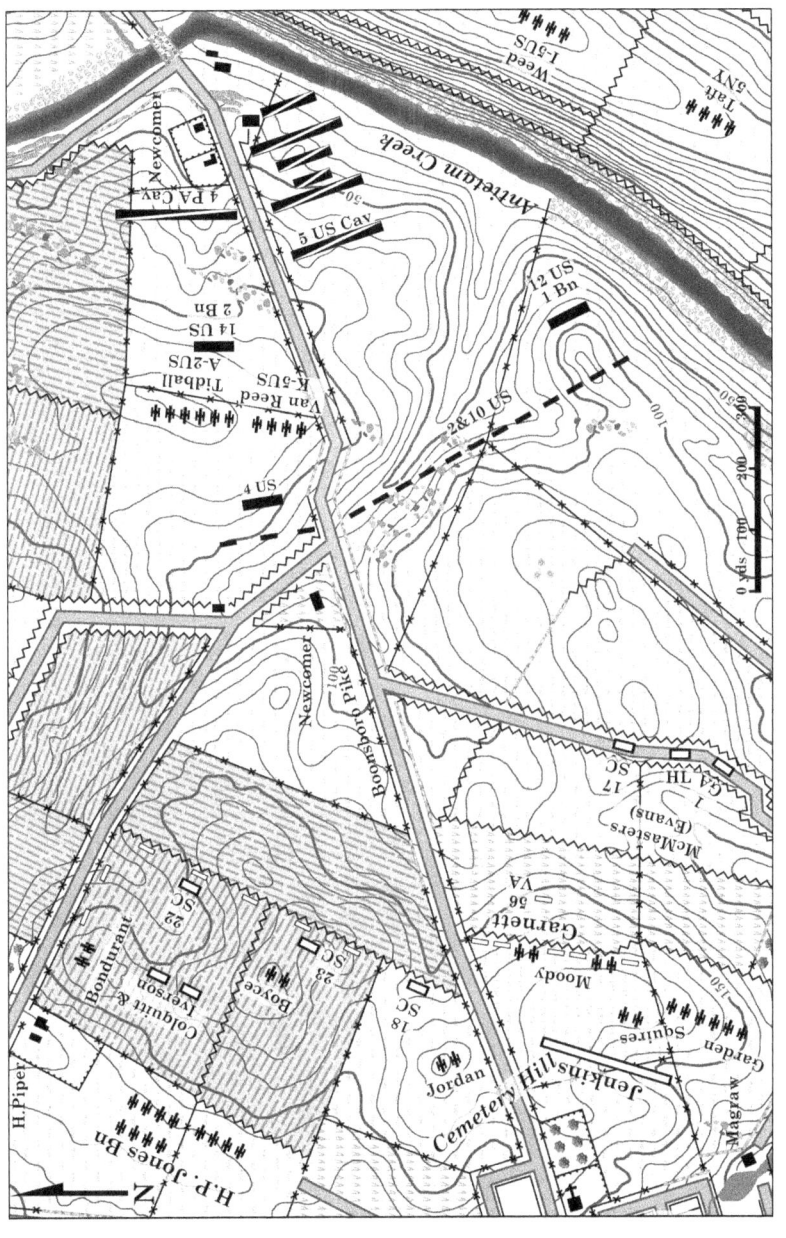

The Union and Confederate positions during the afternoon.

and asked for directions. Lee ordered him to rally all the stragglers he could, without regard to what command they belonged and report with them to General Evans. Only about 50 men of his own regiment could be found, but, with the assistance of others, about 150 men were rallied and carried up to Evans, on the ridge north of town. These were formed in line, under Garrett's command, along with other stragglers, and all placed under command of Colonel Alfred Iverson of the 20th North Carolina. Evans reports that, with the assistance of his staff and after considerable exertion, he succeeded in collecting about 250 men and officers, whom he formed into two commands, and placed them under the command of Colonels Colquitt and Iverson of D. H. Hill's Division. These small commands supported the three regiments of Evans' Brigade.

Meanwhile Bachman's two guns, running out of ammunition, had withdrawn from Cemetery hill, and the line of the ridge was held by Squires' Battery of four guns, south of the road, supported by Garnett's Brigade of 260 men and McMaster's command of about 190 men, including Twiggs. On the left of the road were twelve guns of H. P. Jones' Battalion; Boyce's Battery, now reduced to 2 guns, and 1 gun of Bondurant's Battery. These 15 guns were supported were supported by Colquitt, Iverson and Evans, with about 430 men. In all there were 19 guns and about 870 infantry in Dryer's front, when he was forming for an advance, but, before the advance was ordered, Colonel Stephen D. Lee, came up with 10 guns, under Longstreet's orders to take position on the right and left of the road, relieving Colonel Walton's Washington Artillery. Four guns of Moody's Battery were placed on the right of the road, between it and Squires' Battery; two guns of Jordan's Battery on the left of the road and about 150 yards from it, two guns of Parker's some distance to the left of Jordan's, and a gun of Rhett's Battery on a ridge of the Hagerstown road about 600 yards from the main street of the town. Parker's guns were somewhat late in coming up, and when moving to position some if not all of Jones' guns were retiring. Jones' 12 guns were not all on the ridge at the same time. During the afternoon his batteries had relieved each other by turns but all were available.

Before Lee's guns took position on the east slope of Cemetery hill, Captain Hugh P. Garden's South Carolina Battery of 6 guns crossed the Burnside bridge road. About the same time Jenkins' South Carolina Brigade of 755 officers and men, under command of Colonel Joseph Walker, crossed the Burnside bridge road from the west and was held in support of Squires' Battery and the right section of Moody's. Garden's Battery and Jenkins' Brigade were engaged principally, if not wholly, with Burnside's troops, and are not to be included among those who opposed Dryer's advance, but, by their presence on Garnett's right, they gave his men moral support.

Looking east from the approximate location of the 18th South Carolina toward the Union lines. The US Regular's skirmish lines advanced on both sides of the Boonsboro Pike in the center of the photo. *Author's collection.*

When Colonel Lee put Moody's guns in position, on the edge of a cornfield, Garnett sent the 56th Virginia, 40 men, to protect them from the Union sharpshooters. The Virginians advanced into the standing corn, and became immediately engaged with Poland's skirmishers, now advancing.

Captain Dryer had halted in the ravine separating the two parallel ridges and ordered the two commands of Poland and Carlton to advance, as skirmishers, on either side of the road. Poland had 400 men and Carlton 120, and it was this line of 520 men, that went forward over open ground, against 20 to 25 guns, favorably posted on a commanding ridge and supported by 870 infantry. The advance of Poland and Carlton was made at the same moment, but we first consider that of Poland. When Poland was ordered to take the haystacks on his left and front, five companies of his command were in reserve. These he deployed on his right, in skirmishing order, and the entire line, quite a long one, went forward, ascended the slope of a hill and, under a heavy fire of canister from Squires' and Moody's guns in front, and some guns beyond the road on the right, and from Garnett's skirmishers, pushed over the high ground, passed the haystacks, where some of Twiggs' men and others of the 17th South Carolina were captured, drove back McMaster, who, at the same time was attacked on the right by the advance of Burnside, and, reaching Sherrick's lane, halted under the cover of the fence and became closely and sharply engaged. He had advanced about 385 yards. The right of the line, not hearing the order to halt at the lane fence, went some distance beyond and, Poland reports, "by well directed fire compelled the enemy's cannoneers to leave their guns. At this juncture the fire from our own batteries compelled them to fall back to the fence, as their shells fell short." Referring to this advance on Moody's guns, Colonel S. D. Lee says: "At one time their infantry was within 150 yards of our batteries, when, by a charge of our supporting infantry, they were driven back." Poland's right rested on the road to Sharpsburg and extended to the left, along the lane fence, about 450 yards in the direction of Sherrick's house. After reaching this position the Confederates in his front were reinforced; Garnett advanced his entire brigade, its left in front and on the flanks of the two left guns of Moody's Battery, in the cornfield; and the 56th Virginia, then in front, was recalled to a position on the left of the brigade, close to the road. The fighting now became general along the entire line of the brigade, which was in very open order, covering ground around to the southern slope of the hill.

Carlton deployed his three companies of the 4th U. S. Infantry, as skirmishers on the right of the road, advanced through a small triangular shaped cornfield of about three acres, lying adjacent to the road, and, driving some of Evans' skirmishers before him, gained the crest of some high ground about 150 yards beyond the cornfield, and on a line with

View from Lt. Caleb H. Carlton's three companies of the 4th United States Infantry. Located on the north side of the road, this is what they saw looking toward the top of Cemetery Hill and the Confederate position. *Author's collection.*

Poland, who was on the left of the road. Here the skirmishers were immediately halted until Dryer could position his supports.

When Poland and Carlton had gained some distance Dryer advanced the five companies of the 4th Infantry to the west part of the triangular cornfield, and concealed them as much as possible in the tall corn, and Brown's Battalion of the 14th Infantry advanced in line to the protection of a deep ravine, on the south side of the road, opposite the mouth of the Sunken Road. The 2nd Battalion of the 14th advanced beyond the batteries and took position in a ravine, on the right of the 4th, with skirmishers thrown to the crest of the ridge in its front. It was under a heavy fire of shot and shell, but, being well sheltered, had one man only wounded. The 4th on its left, on higher ground, suffered some casualties. The 4th and the two battalions of the 14th made no farther advance, and the fighting was done by Poland's and Carlton's skirmishers, whom Dryer, with his three battalions had closely supported, and halted only when Poland was brought to a stand in front of the enemy's artillery and infantry.

When Evans saw the advance of Carlton's skirmishers, with a front of 300 yards, followed by their support, he ordered Colquitt, Iverson, and his own men forward. Captain Garrett of the 5th North Carolina, who was near the left of Iverson's line says, says D. H. Hill ordered the attack upon a regiment of the enemy "which was maintaining a doubtful contest with a small body of our own troops." They had not advanced far before the skirmishers of the 22nd South Carolina were driven in upon the main line, closely followed by Carlton's men, and the engagement became general. At first Carlton was forced to yield some ground, but quickly recovered it, and opened such a telling fire that Colquitt and Iverson were soon driven from the field. We again quote Garrett:

> We moved up in line and soon engaged them with spirit, and forced them, for a moment, to give back. Very soon, however, the left of the line, of which my command formed part, gave way, and being left with but few men from my regiment, I ordered them to retire and form behind a large rock in the field, about 50 yards distant. This was done, and, by determined conduct of those few men, the regiment of the enemy was held in check for twenty-five or thirty minutes. After feeling our strength, however, he began to advance, and I ordered the men to retreat.

They went entirely off the field and scattered in the streets of Sharpsburg, where the rest of Iverson's men and a part of Colquitt's had preceded them. Colquitt refers to a small party of his command, under Lieutenant Colonel W. H. Betts, 13th Alabama, who "was directed to deploy as skirmishers along the crest of a hill upon which the enemy was advancing and did so

VOL. 3: THE MIDDLE BRIDGE TO HILL'S COUNTERATTACK

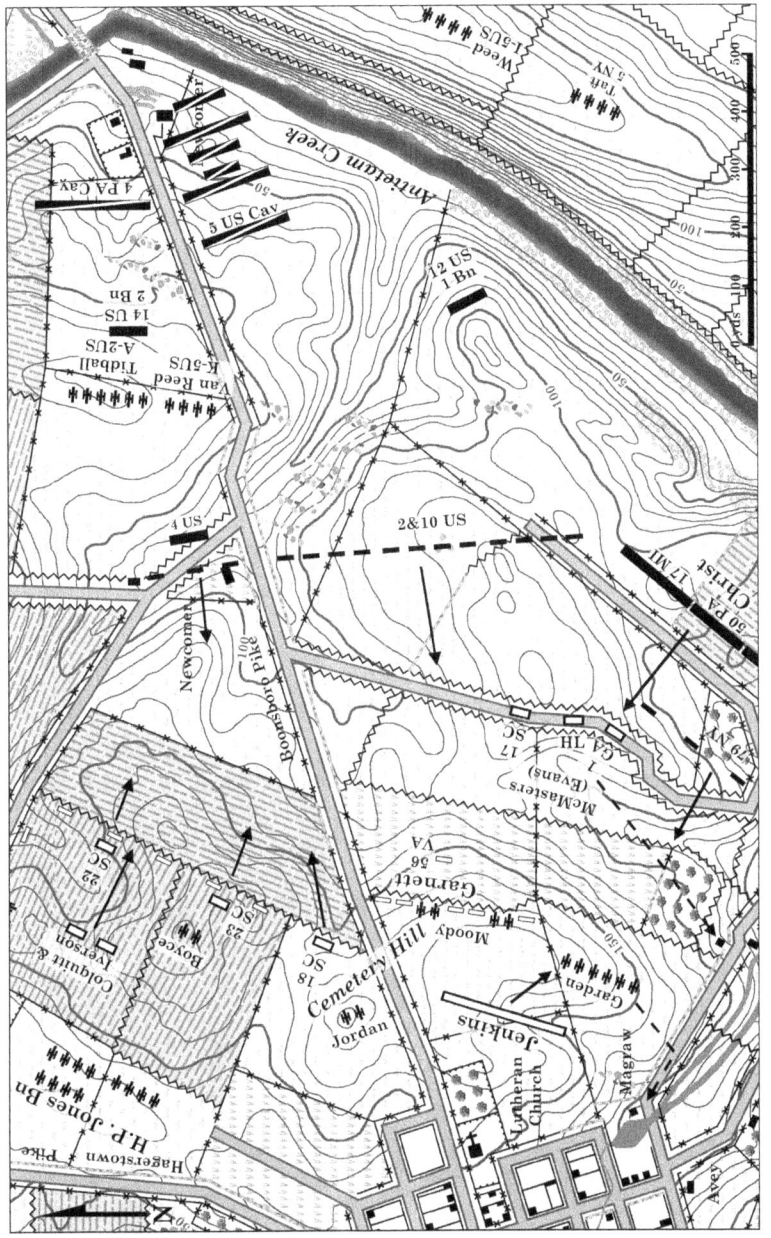

The United States Regulars begin their advance toward Cemetery Hill with Christ's Ninth Corps brigade moving with them on their left. Colonel McMaster's small detachment of Evan's Brigade is driven back.

with good effect, keeping back a large force by their annoying fire and the apprehension, excited by their boldness, that they were supported by a line in rear." Under the elastic pen and poetic license of D. H. Hill this statement of Colquitt's assumes these grotesque proportions:

> About 30 men under Lieutenant Colonel W. H. Betts, 13th Alabama, remained as support to my division batteries. The Yankee columns were allowed to come within easy range, when a sudden stream of grape and canister drove them back in confusion. Betts' men must have given them a very hot fire, as Burnside reported that he had met three heavy columns on the hill. It is difficult to imagine how 30 men could so multiply themselves as to appear to the frightened Yankees to be three heavy columns.

As a matter of fact Betts was detached on the left of Colquitt's line, in support of some guns, beyond the right of Carlton's advance, and opposed only by a few men, who faced in his direction. Carlton's right being refused to conform to the curvature of the hill over which he was advancing, and, connecting on the right with the skirmishers of McKibbin's battalion, one company of which was thrown forward from the ravine where it had halted and as McKibbin reports, under Captain Thatcher, "were actively engaged during part of the afternoon." As to Burnside he was entirely beyond the road and his right never came within canister range of Hill's guns.

The three South Carolina regiments of Evans' Brigade soon followed Colquitt and Iverson. Colonel Stevens, who was with these regiments, seeing his men falling rapidly, while Carlton was still advancing, and apprehensive of being flanked, ordered them to fall back to the stone fence on the Hagerstown road. Colonel Wallace, commanding the 18th South Carolina, reports that Boyce's Battery, which it had been supporting, having retired under orders from Colonel Stevens, his regiment was deployed as skirmishers, and advanced over the hill to repel the advance of a heavy body of skirmishers thrown forward by the enemy. The direction of his advance was toward the Sharpsburg road, and by a rapid movement he gained a rail fence running nearly parallel with the road. "This position," he says, "we held against a very largely superior force of the enemy for a considerable time, when Colonel Stevens, who was upon the left of our line, seeing the left was beginning to suffer severely, ordered the whole line to retreat to a stone fence some distance in our rear and upon the road running in a northwesterly (north) direction from Sharpsburg. This retreat was accomplished under a sharp fire of musketry and artillery, from which the regiment suffered some damage. Almost immediately the regiment was reduced to a handful of men." Boyce's Battery, as stated by Wallace, fell back before engaging the infantry; Jordan's two guns were well protected by

VOL. 3: THE MIDDLE BRIDGE TO HILL'S COUNTERATTACK

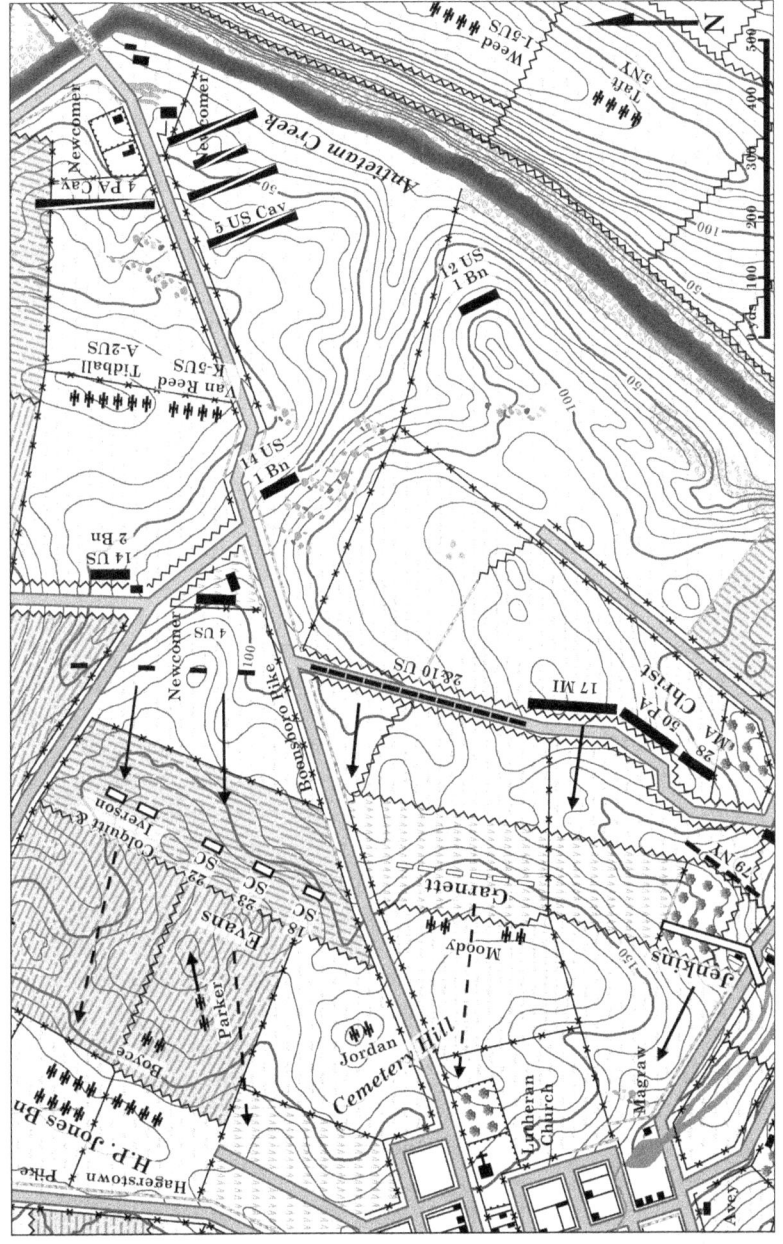

The Regulars and the 17th Michigan of Christ's brigade continue their advance. Most of the Confederates withdraw from Cemetery Hill.

the ridge and did not suffer from infantry fire, but were so severely shelled by artillery that they remained in action not to exceed 30 minutes and withdrew as Carlton's men were advancing and the Confederate infantry was giving way. Everything was now clear in Carlton's immediate front; he had advanced to with 450 yards of the Lutheran Church and partially crowned the crest of the ridge from which he could look into Sharpsburg, and was still advancing, when he was opened upon by a fire of canister and musketry, full upon his left flank, from two of Moody's guns and Garnett's infantry, south of the road. Garnett and S. D. Lee had been standing in the tall corn, observing Poland's advance and had not seen Carlton's approach on the left of the road and were not aware of it, until their attention was attracted to the rattling skirmishing fire, when, looking in that direction, they saw the blue-coated regulars directly on their flank and the Confederates in retreat. Lee turned Moody's two guns upon them and Garnett faced a few men of the 56th Virginia to the left and sent a few rifle shots down the line, and at the same moment Carlton received an order from Dryer to fall back, under cover, on a line with Poland, who was still holding his position in the Sherrick lane, and to whom and Garnett we now return.

When Garnett advanced his brigade to the support of Moody's guns the 56th and 28th Virginia, about 100 men, were placed in the corn, on the left and in advance of Moody's left section, which was on open ground, just in rear of the corn; on the right of this section were the 19th and 18th Virginia, about 120 men, also in the corn, and deployed four to five feet apart, in single line; in rear of Moody's right section, which was in the right and rear of the 18th Virginia, was the 8th Virginia, about 20 men only. The 56th, 28th and part of the 19th Virginia were faced east and engaged Poland's right and center, a part of the 19th and all of the 18th and 8th engaged Poland's left and the advance of Burnside. Reports agree that the entire was severely engaged and lost heavily. Garnett reports that he was "called upon to deplore the loss of many brave spirits." Colonel Hunton, 8th Virginia, says he lost one half his men. Major Cabell, 18th Virginia, reported a loss of over one third and that the "entire color guard was either killed or wounded." The losses in the other regiments was large.

Some of Poland's men were quite well sheltered in the lane, under cover of the fence and the inequalities of the ground, but the greater part of them were much exposed; all kept up a cool and constant fire, and Dryer was about to charge Moody's Battery in Poland's front, when he was ordered to withdraw.

Dryer had been ordered across the Antietam, against the judgment of Sykes, his division commander, to support Pleasonton's guns, drive the enemy from their front, and take the haystacks on the left of the road, and this was the extent to which it was intended his men should be employed.

Looking west from Sherrick lane where the left of the 2nd & 10th United States held their ground. The slope was a cornfield in 1862, held by Garnett's Brigade. The current wall to the National Cemetery is in the approximate location of the stone wall held by Moody's Battery. *Author's collection.*

"They were, however," says Porter, "diverted from that service, and employed to drive the enemy's skirmishers to their reserves." When it was seen that Dryer had exceeded his instructions, and advancing on either side of the road, with the evident intention of carrying the ridge, upon which could been seen from beyond the Antietam 18 guns and what appeared to be two full regiments; there was some apprehension, and at this moment came a note from Captain Blunt, commanding 1st Battalion, 12th U. S. Infantry. Dryer had ordered Blunt to move forward and support him in an advance, and Blunt sent the note to Sykes, stating that Blunt was about to make an attack and that he (Blunt) did not understand that he had been sent over the Antietam for that purpose, and asked for instructions. Sykes was very much annoyed and immediately ordered Lieutenant W. H. Powell of Buchanan's staff, to ride over to Dryer with orders not only to suspend assault, but to withdraw his troops to the ridge upon which were Pleasonton's batteries and maintain a defensive position. Powell rode fast and found Dryer in the road, at the intersection of the Sherrick lane, where he had just given an order to Poland to push forward, when he saw the troops on the right of the road advance, and was about the order the 4th Infantry forward. When Powell delivered his orders Dryer asked if there might not be something left to his discretion; when informed that the order was imperative, he ordered Carlton to withdraw, as we have seen, and wheeling his horse about, rode off after Poland, whose left had now been joined by Burnside's advance from the lower bridge.

When Powell gave the order for Dryer to withdraw the Confederates had abandoned the ridge north of the road and were then abandoning Cemetery hill. When Burnside's men approached from the lower bridge, Garden's Battery left its position and went through Sharpsburg; soon after, Squires' Battery, now coming under the fire of Burnside's skirmishers, went down a ravine southwest to the road leading to the lower bridge, and turning to the right went through the streets of Sharpsburg. Jenkins' Brigade was driven back from the apple orchard on the southeastern slope of the hill. All on Garnett's left and right had gone, and it was but a few minutes after he had seen Carlton fall back that he discovered that the extreme right had been turned and was giving way and that "a number of Yankee flags appeared on the hill in rear of the town and not far from our only avenue of escape." Deeming the brigade in imminent danger of being captured he ordered a retreat, and as the main street of the town was commanded by the Union artillery, his infantry passed, for the most part, to the north of the town along the cross-street, and in this direction he found "troops scattered in squads from various parts of the army, so that it was impossible to distinguish men of the different commands." Moody's left section was withdrawn without difficulty and retreated through the main street of the town, but the right section had some difficulty, was slow in getting under

VOL. 3: THE MIDDLE BRIDGE TO HILL'S COUNTERATTACK

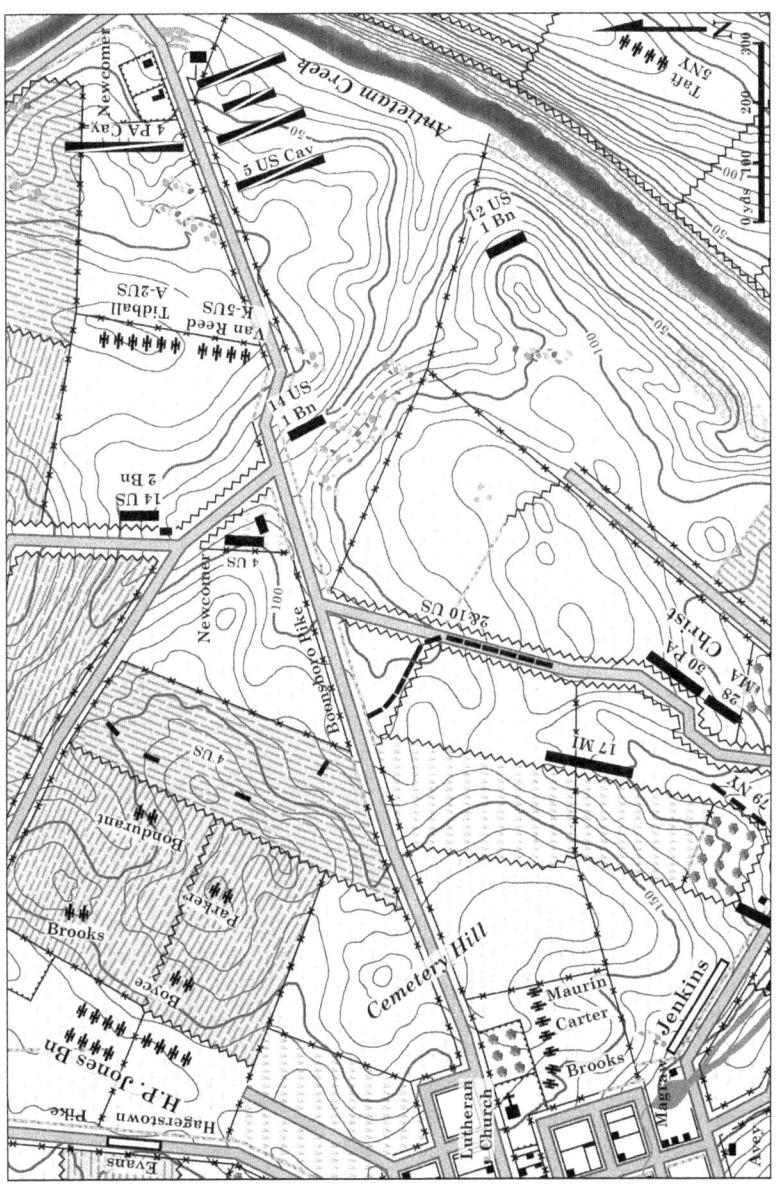

The Confederates have essentially abandoned Cemetery Hill. The position and movement of the Confederate batteries north of the Boonsboro Pike is more fluid than the map suggests.

way, and perceiving this and that the guns were in danger from Poland's men and the advance of Burnside's Corps, Major Cabell, commanding the 18th Virginia, who had moved back some 50 yards, halted his small regiment, faced it about, moved back into the corn and waited until the guns were moved off, then rejoined his brigade. It is this movement which is thus referred to by Poland in his report: "the enemy advanced a regiment to protect the withdrawal of their guns from the hill directly in front of our left. This regiment was driven back, but their object had been effected." While Poland was engaged with Garnett's retiring troops, the 79th New York and 17th Michigan of Willcox's Division, Ninth Corps, came up and fired a few shots at the retiring 18th Virginia, and the left of his line being relieved by the 17th Michigan, Poland assembled his regiment on the center files. It was while thus engaged that Dryer came up and ordered him to withdraw a short distance, halt his command under shelter of the ridge over which he had charged and await a supply of ammunition. He had lost 54 men killed and wounded. Carlton had lost about half that number—together their losses were about 85 of the 95 men killed, wounded and missing of the 5th Corps. Garnett's loss was 78 killed and wounded, about one third of the number he had engaged. The loss sustained by the Confederates opposing Carlton cannot be definitely stated.

As Pleasonton records it, it was nearly 4 o'clock, after his batteries with "renewed vigor and energy" had driven the enemy's batteries from their position in front that a heavy column of dust could be seen moving behind Cemetery ridge towards Sumner's left. He directed the fire of the batteries into the dust, and "soon the development of the enemy's line of battle, fully a mile long, could be seen bearing down on Richardson's Division, then commanded by Hancock." Hancock called for some guns to assist him; none could be spared at the moment, but Pleasonton "directed the fire of some 18 guns upon the enemy's line in front of him for twenty minutes, when he had the satisfaction of seeing "this immense line" first halt, deliver a desultory fire and then "break and run to the rear in the greatest confusion and disorder." A section (Pennington's) of Tidball's Battery was immediately advanced to the crest of a hill several hundred yards to the front, and in front of the infantry of Hancock's left.

We cannot identify this immense column of Confederates moving to the left, the drift, if any, at this hour, was in the opposite direction. We know that small bodies of D. H. Hill's men were keeping up a desultory affair with Richardson and about the time indicated by Pleasonton, George T. Anderson, with 200 to 300 men, moved from left to the right upon the ridge, but seeing, as he reports, no enemy, and being enfiladed by a battery on his left, moved back again to the ridge near Piper's barn, but we cannot identify any body "fully a mile long," bearing down on Richardson. However, Pleasonton's success in breaking this immense line; the additional

Brigadier General Alfred Pleasonton
Library of Congress

success of Dryer in advancing far to the front on either side of the Sharpsburg road, and Burnside's advance, driving the enemy back, convinced Pleasonton that the field was open for an advance to Cemetery ridge, to which point he desired to forward his batteries, to obtain an enfilading fire upon the enemy in front of Burnside and enable Sumner to advance to Sharpsburg. So satisfied was he that this could be done that, at 4 o'clock, he sent a request to Porter for a division to support his advance, accompanied by a report that both Burnside and Sumner were driving the enemy and that he desired to take advantage of the opening and advance to the ridge. Porter could not spare the division; in fact he did not have it. Earlier in the day Warren's Brigade had been sent to support Burnside and at 4 p.m., while Pleasonton was framing his request, the brigades of Griffin and Stockton of Morell's Division had gone to the right to support Sumner. Parts of two other brigades were already with Pleasonton. Moreover, Porter says:

> Between the dispatching and receiving of that call the tide of battle had changed. Our troops on the left, under Burnside, had been driven from the heights which they had so gallantly crowned, while those on the immediate left, under Sumner, were held in check. The army was at a stand. I had not the force asked for, and could not, under my orders, risk the safety of the artillery and center of the line, and perhaps imperil the success of the day by further diminishing my small command, not then 4,000 strong—then in the front line and unsupported, and protecting all our trains.

Palfrey justifies Porter's action in "not complying with the request of an officer who was not even a corps commander, who was his inferior in rank, and whose request had not received the approval of the general commanding." It appears, however, that Porter at 5 p.m. sent this dispatch to Sykes: "Burnside is driving the enemy. Please send word to the command you sent to Pleasonton, to support his batteries, and let him drive them."

Meanwhile Van Reed's Battery, which arrived on the field about 2 o'clock, relieving Hains', after expending 400 rounds of ammunition, was relieved in turn by Hains' at 5 o'clock, and recrossed the Antietam. Hains put all his guns on the right of the road, directing their fire against Confederate infantry, entirely, and principally against those on the Piper farm, who were then engaging the 7th Maine, by which fire they suffered severely, both in advancing and falling back. At dusk both Tidball and Hains recrossed the Antietam. The 5th United States, 4th and 6th Pennsylvania Cavalry followed the artillery and all joined their division near Keedysville. Dryer remained in his advanced position until the artillery had

Major General Fitz John Porter
Library of Congress

been withdrawn, when he marched back, waited until the cavalry had crossed and then went over the bridge at 7:30 p.m., carrying with him his dead and wounded. Sykes reports that Dryer's troops "behaved in the handsomest manner, and had there been an available force for their support, there is no doubt he could have crowned the Sharpsburg crest." Before Dryer retired the Confederates re-occupied the ground from which they had been driven.

It will be remembered that early in the action, in fact before Carlton's and Evans' men had become engaged, Boyce's two guns had been retired under cover of the ridge and between it and the Hagerstown road, but commanding the crests of the two hills in front. It appears that when Stevens, with his South Carolinians, was driven back to the Hagerstown road he had forgotten Boyce and his guns, but he soon recalled the fact. He says:

> Perceiving that my retreat had left unsupported a section of Boyce's artillery, which I had not before seen, I again resumed my position, and, bringing up Boyce's battery, opened fire with musketry and artillery upon a line of the enemy advancing on the right of the road. The line was broken and driven back. Colonel Walker, of Jenkins' brigade, having sent for artillery, I ordered Captain Boyce to his support. It was now late in the evening, and my men having nearly exhausted their ammunition, I left general instructions and sought the ordnance officer. Before I could get more ammunition my men had fallen back, in accordance with instructions, and, finding them scattering in town, I marched to the rear and bivouacked for the night.

Captain Boyce reports:

> Colonel Stevens advanced...with a few skirmishers to the crest of the hill, and, finding the ground not occupied by the enemy immediately beyond, signaled me to advance. I went forward and placed my guns on the hill within canister range of the enemy. A few shots drove him beyond the range of canister. I afterward used solid shot, cutting down his flag and driving him back. Having occupied this important position but a few minutes, an order came, from some source, for me to recross the road near the place occupied by me when I received my first order in the morning to go into battle. I crossed over the road, as ordered, but could find no one there to give me any information as to who gave the order or what was required. This was late in the afternoon, and the battle soon after ended.

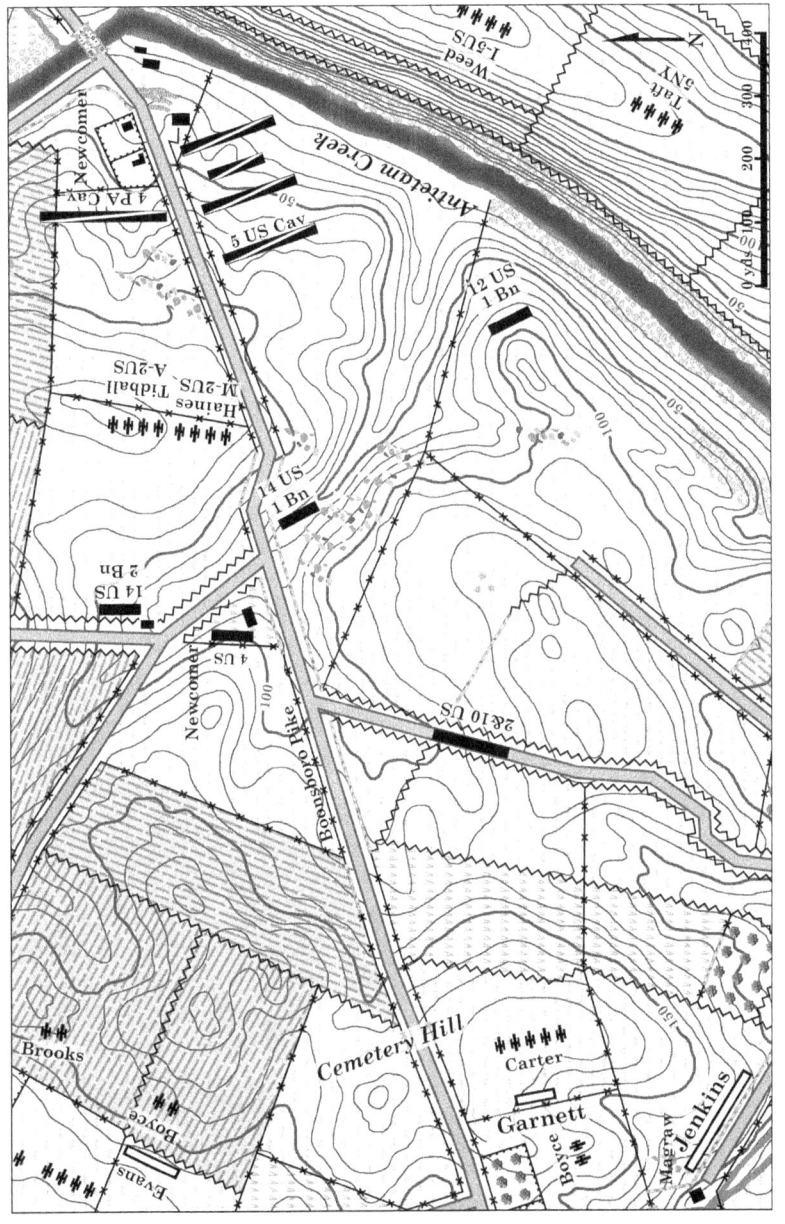

The two lines along the Boonsboro Pike during the late afternoon.

Boyce went through the town and bivouacked with his (Evans') brigade. Evans says his little command gallantly drove the enemy, 4th U. S. Infantry, from his cover in the cornfield and caused him to retreat in confusion, leaving a number of dead and two stands of colors, the latter having been shot down by a well directed fire of Captain Boyce's Battery. It is difficult to reconcile this statement with the fact that the 4th Infantry did not leave their colors and that Dryer reported he carried off his dead and wounded.

Parker's Battery of 2 guns, under Lieutenant J. Thompson Brown, appears to have come on the field about the time the infantry and some artillery were in retreat. Brown says he went about 500 or 600 yards north of the road and passed the major of two batteries, who had been unable to hold the hill and was retiring. The officer inquired where he was going, and having been informed, he ordered him back saying that he had not been able to hold the hill and it would be folly for his section to attempt it. Thompson [sic] replied that he was under orders from Colonel Lee and passed on, taking position in a depression of the ground between two trees, an old excavation or ice-house in the ground, and firing over the hill at the 4th Infantry. "I remember," he writes, "seeing the standard bearer shot down and the staff shot off near the colors, and while he was lying down he raised the colors up on a corn-hill."

When Dryer recrossed the Antietam, the 18th Massachusetts of Morell's Division crossed to the west side, established headquarters and a reserve at the Newcomer Mill, and advanced a strong picket line to the ridge where the batteries had been engaged during the day.

In the *Century Magazine* for October 1886, Lieutenant Colonel Thomas M. Anderson writes that, late in the afternoon of the 17th, he was talking with his brigade commander, Colonel Buchanan, when an orderly brought a note from the senior officer in command of the regular infantry beyond the Antietam, stating in effect that there was but one Confederate battery and two regiments in front of Sharpsburg, connecting the wings of Lee's army, that he proposed to charge the battery, but asked instructions. Buchanan sent the note to Sykes, who, at the time, was talking with McClellan and Porter, some yards away, sitting on their horses between Taft's and Weed's batteries. After the war Anderson asked Sykes why an advance was not made upon Dryer's report. Sykes replied that he remembered the circumstances very well and that he thought McClellan was inclined to order in the Fifth Corps but that when he spoke of doing so, Porter said: "Remember, general, I command the last reserve of the last army of the Republic."

In the *Century* for January, 1887, Porter says that no such note as Captain Dryer's report was seen by him and no such discussion for using the reserves took place between him and McClellan.

Mount Calvary Lutheran Church along the Boonsboro Pike. Looking west from the top of Cemetery Hill into the town of Sharpsburg. *Library of Congress.*

In a private letter of January 31, 1899, Anderson says the incident occurred at sunset, two hours after the Pleasonton report and request and recalls that while he was talking with Buchanan, in front of his battalion, a shell exploded in a pile of cracker boxes, when Buchanan remarked that it was "the quickest distribution of hard-tack he had ever seen," and that at the time they were watching the movement of a body of Confederate troops from their center to left to attack Burnside and Buchanan received the note and, after reading it, said: "Dryer reports center very weak and wants leave to attack," then sent the note to Sykes, and he saw the note delivered to Sykes, and Buchanan said: "Fall in your men, our turn has come at last," but no order was given to advance. Anderson further says that when Dryer returned that evening he blamed Blunt for not making the attack with him, as he proposed, without orders.

There is no record of such a paper being sent by Dryer, either in his own report or in those of his brigade or division commander, nor elsewhere in the official records. Colonel W. H. Powell, then a lieutenant and adjutant-general of Buchanan's Brigade, intimates that such a note may have been received by Buchanan, but, if so, it was after Sykes had ordered the withdrawal of Dryer and while he was carrying the order of withdrawal. In the *Century* for March 1887, Powell writes:

> Gallant and impetuous as Dryer always was, he could not remain idle, and it was observed that he was pushing forward on each side of the pike towards the crest occupied by the enemy, with a view, as afterwards understood, to charge and take a battery there. Having observed this, and knowing it was not the intention, nor could we afford, at this particular time, to make any forward movement on center, I reported this to General Sykes and Buchanan, who were together at the time, and I was directed by General Sykes to proceed at once to the advanced position which Captain Dryer had obtained (being within 300 to 400 yards of the enemy's batteries) and direct him to withdraw his troops immediately to the original position at the head of the bridge, and then report in person to General Sykes. During my absence at the front, I believe, the note in question was received. When Dryer reported, those who were present know that the interview was in no wise a subject of consultation....It was confidently believed, however, by the two brigades of regular infantry that if they had been thrown forward at any time towards the close of the day, supported by Morell's Division, they could have carried the center, and thus could have enabled General Burnside to drive the enemy from the field on the left.

The Middle Bridge over Antietam Creek from the bluffs on the eastern bank. *Library of Congress.*

General Sykes comes to a similar conclusion. After paying a high compliment to the behavior of Dryer's men he says, "had there been an available force for their support, there is no doubt he could have crowned the Sharpsburg crest."

General Porter has been severely and unjustly blamed for his inaction at Antietam. All the operations at the middle bridge were ordered by McClellan. He ordered Pleasonton across the stream; he ordered a part of Porter's infantry to Pleasonton's support. Being present he was responsible for the action or want of action of Porter.

Chapter 21

The Burnside Bridge

We approach the concluding scenes of the day, the end of a disjointed battle. While Pleasonton's batteries and a few regulars of Porter's Corps were engaged in advance of the middle bridge, Burnside's Ninth Corps was engaged at the lower bridge and on the high ground between it and Sharpsburg, but there was no cooperation in the movement. It is necessary to repeat the plan of battle. In his preliminary report of the battle, made October 15, 1862, McClellan says:

"The design was to make the main attack upon the enemy's left—at least to create a diversion in favor of the main attack, with the hope of something more by assailing the enemy's right—and, as soon as one or both of the flank movements were fully successful, to attack their center with any reserve I might then have on hand."

In his elaborate report, dated August 4, 1863, but not made public until some months later, he says:

"My plan for the impending general engagement was to attack the enemy's left with the corps of Hooker and Mansfield, supported by Sumner's and, if necessary, by Franklin's, and, as soon as matters looked favorably there, to move the corps of Burnside against the enemy's extreme right, upon the ridge running to the south and rear of Sharpsburg, and, having carried their position, to press along the crest toward our right, and, whenever either of these flank movements should be successful, to advance our center with all the forces then disposable."

Burnside's understanding was that, when the attack by Hooker, Sumner, and Franklin should be progressing favorably, he "was to create a diversion in favor of the main attack, with the hope of something more." General

Cox, to whom Burnside communicated his understanding of the part the Ninth Corps was to take in the action, says:

> It would also appear that Hooker's movement was at first intended to be made by his corps alone, taken up by Sumner's two corps (2nd and 12th) as soon as he was ready to attack and shared in by Franklin if he reached the field in time, thus making a simultaneous oblique attack from our right by the whole army except for Porter's corps, which was in reserve, and the Ninth Corps, which was to create the "diversion" on our left and prevent the enemy from stripping his right to reinforce his left. It is hardly disputable that this would have been a better plan than the one actually carried out. Certainly the assumption that the Ninth Corps could cross the Antietam alone at the only place on the field where the Confederates had their line immediately upon the stream which must be crossed under fire by two narrow heads of column, and could then turn to the right along the high ground occupied by the hostile army before that army had been broken or seriously shaken elsewhere, is one which would hardly be made until time dimmed the remembrance of the actual positions of Lee's divisions upon the field.

Colonel William F. Biddle, in a highly laudatory article on McClellan, says that the movement planned and persistently ordered across the bridge as a "forlorn hope."

McClellan visited Burnside's position on the 16th and, after pointing out to him the proper dispositions to be made during the day and night, informed him that he would probably be required to attack the enemy's right on the following morning.

The Confederate artillery opened fire early on the morning of the 17th and was replied to by all of Burnside's guns in position and others on his right and Durell's Pennsylvania battery of Sturgis' Division, supported by the 21st Massachusetts, was advanced to the crown of the bluff overlooking the Antietam, and took position on the left of Weed's Battery and the enemy's guns were soon silenced. The fire of Benjamin, Durell and others was then directed to the right, at the Confederates engaged with Hooker and Mansfield, around the Dunker Church and, though the distance was from 3,200 to 3,600 yards, it was quite accurate and very effective. To meet what Sturgis reports as a heavy concentration on the right and center Clark's Battery (E, 4th U. S.), was sent forward to a position on Durell's left. The batteries of McMullin, Muhlenberg, and Cook were advanced to positions on Benjamin's left and somewhat to the front and to Benjamin's Battery was added two guns of Simmonds'. Willcox was brought up and held in reserve.

VOL. 3: THE MIDDLE BRIDGE TO HILL'S COUNTERATTACK

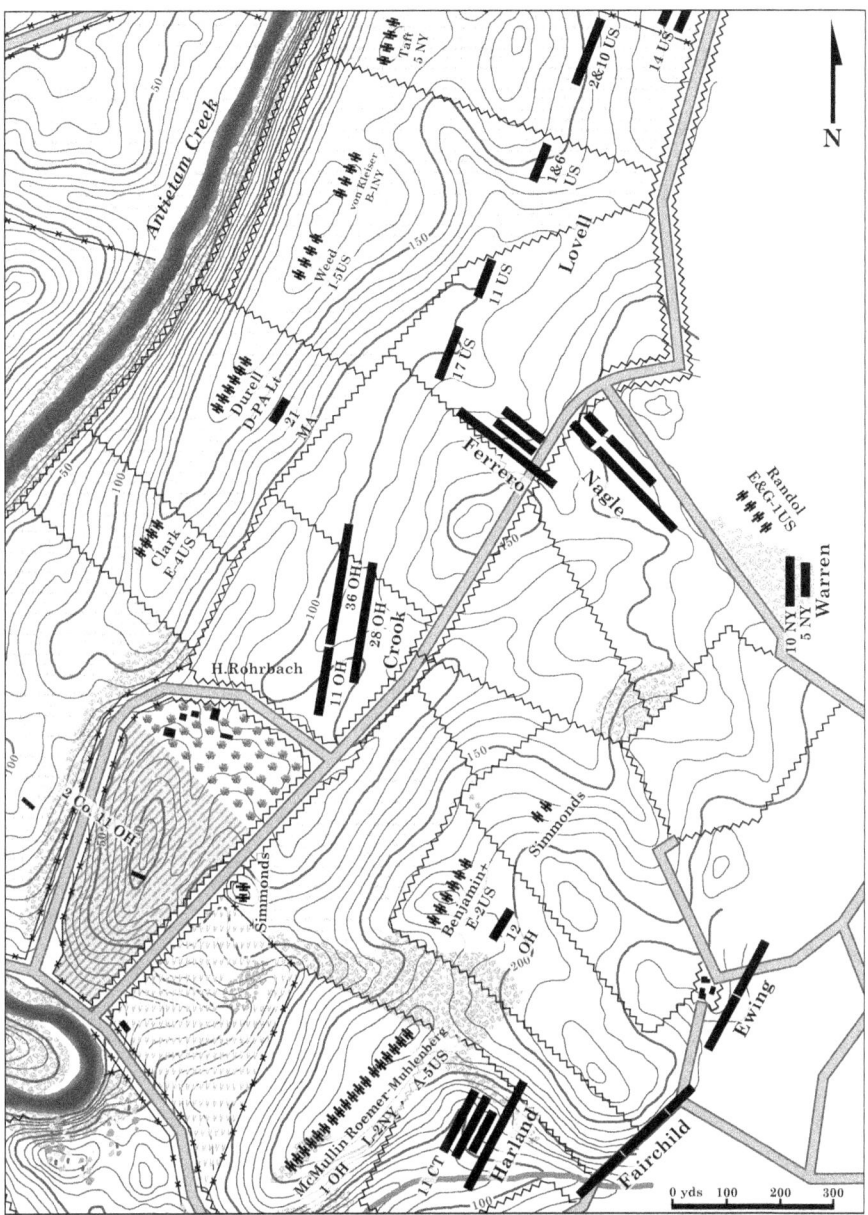

Ninth Corps artillery positions, at bottom, during the morning but several hours after dawn. Fifth Corps and Artillery Reserve batteries line the banks of the Antietam at top.

While this artillery fire was going on and some of the troops being shelled out of the exposed positions to which, owing to McClellan's fault, they had been conducted in darkness the night before, Burnside received the following from McClellan:

HEADQUARTERS ARMY OF THE POTOMAC,
September 16, 1862.
Major-General BURNSIDE,
Commanding Ninth Corps, & c.:

GENERAL: The general commanding has learned that, although your corps was ordered to be in a designated position at 12 m. to-day, at or near sunset only one division and four batteries had reached the ground intended for your troops.

The general has also been advised that there was a delay of some four hours in the movement of your command yesterday. I am instructed to call upon you for explanations of these failures on your part to comply with the orders given you, and to add, in view of the important military operations now at hand, the commanding general cannot lightly regard such marked departure from the tenor of his instructions. I am, general, very respectfully, your obedient servant,

Lieutenant-Colonel, Aide-de-Camp, and Actg. Asst. Adjt. Gen.[2]

This was not, on McClellan's part, a very judicious or auspicious opening of the day on the left, and probably had no bearing upon subsequent events, but we note it to show the state of mind at army headquarters. Burnside did not permit it to affect his determination to do all that the situation and the country required of him, and replied:

HEADQUARTERS, September 17, 1862.
Brig. Gen. S. WILLIAMS, Assistant Adjutant- General:

GENERAL: Your dispatch of yesterday this moment received. General Burnside directs me to say that immediately upon the receipt of the order of the general commanding, which was after 12 o'clock, he ordered his corps to be in readiness to march, and instead of having

---

[2] Pasted by Carman into the manuscript. U. S. War Department, *War of the Rebellion: A Compilation of the Official Records of the Union and Confederate Armies*, Series I, vol. 19, part II, p. 308. Hereafter cited as *OR*. All references are to Series I unless otherwise noted.

Top of the ridge where Clark's Battery E, 4th United States was positioned in the early morning. Looking south. *Author's collection.*

Captain Duane post the division in detail, and at the suggestion of Captain Duane, he sent three aides to ascertain the position of each of the three divisions, that they might post them. These aides returned shortly before 3 o'clock, and they immediately proceeded to post the three columns. The general then went on an eminence above these positions to get a good view of them, and whilst there, during the progress of the movement of his corps, an aide from General McClellan came to him and said that General McClellan was not sure that the proper position had been indicated, and advising him not to hasten the movement until the aide had communicated with the general commanding. He (General Burnside) at once went to General McClellan's headquarters to inform him that he had seen large bodies of the enemy moving off to the right. Not finding the general commanding, General Burnside returned to his command and the movement was resumed and continued as rapidly as possible. General Burnside directs me to say that he is sorry to have received so severe a rebuke from the general commanding, and particularly sorry that the general commanding feels that his instructions have not been obeyed; but nothing can occur to prevent the general from continuing his hearty cooperation to the best of his ability in any movement the general commanding may direct.

I have the honor to be, general, very respectfully, your obedient servant,

LEWIS RICHMOND,
Assistant Adjutant- General.[3]

About 7 o'clock, Burnside received an order to make his dispositions to carry the stone bridge over the Antietam but to await further orders before making the attack. In accordance with these instructions Cox was directed to advance the whole corps to the ridge nearest the stream and hold it, keeping the troops under cover as much as possible.

Early in the morning Rodman's Division was northeast of the stone bridge; Harland's Brigade lying east of the road that ran past the Rohrbach house to Porterstown, its left opposite the Rohrbach orchard. Fairchild's Brigade, on the left of Harland's, was in the northeast part of a cornfield that ran down the road skirting the Antietam. It had been put in position in the darkness and when morning came, found itself exposed to the fire of Eubank's Battery across the Antietam, by which it suffered many casualties before it could change position, which was almost immediately done, the

---

[3] *OR*, vol. 19, part II, p. 314.

VOL. 3: THE MIDDLE BRIDGE TO HILL'S COUNTERATTACK

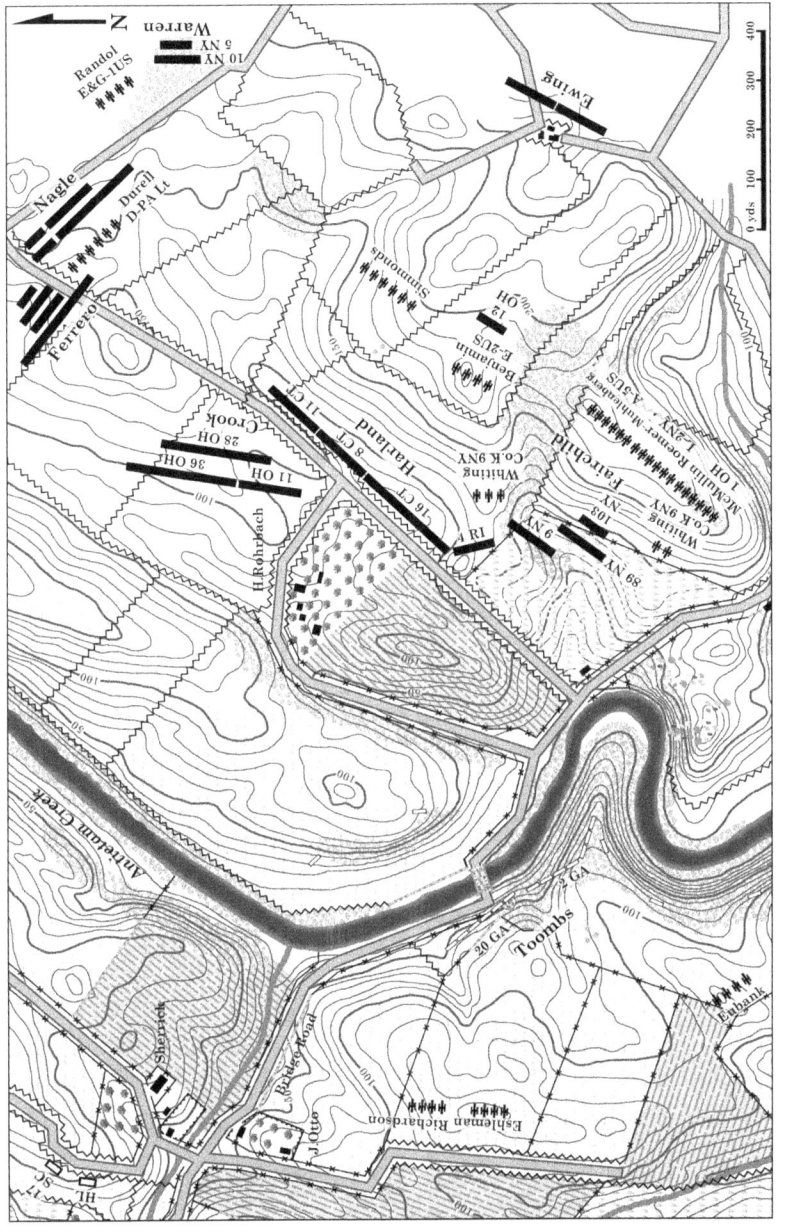

The Union lines at the Lower Bridge at dawn. Eubank's Battery had an almost perfect enfilade against Fairchild's brigade, forcing it to fall back at first light to the position shown here.

brigade moving up the ridge in the rear and under cover of the woods. Harland followed later. Sturgis' Division was on the right of Rodman and on both sides of the road that led from Rohrbach's to Porterstown, with Crook's Ohio Brigade on its right front, a short distance northeast of Rohrbach's. Willcox's Division was in rear of Sturgis, as a reserve, and Ewing's Ohio brigade was with Rodman. Burnside had directed that, in case of an attack on the bridge, Crook should make it; as a compliment to Cox's Kanawha division for its brilliant conduct at South Mountain. Crook threw forward two companies as skirmishers before whom some Confederate skirmishers, who had been sent across the bridge, retired, and all awaited orders to go forward.

Meanwhile, Burnside and Cox were watching the contest on the right. From the high ground occupied by them they saw the struggle between the East Woods and West Woods, and around the Dunker Church, and cheered every well aimed shot that Benjamin sent in that direction, and they saw the advance of French's Division to the Sunken Road, and at this time Colonel Sackett, of McClellan's staff, rode up and handed Burnside this order:

> HEADQUARTERS ARMY OF THE POTOMAC,
> September 17, 1862—10 a.m.
> Major-General BURNSIDE:
>
> GENERAL: General Franklin's command is within one mile and a half of here. General McClellan desires you to open your attack. As soon as you shall have uncovered the upper Stone bridge you will be supported, and, if necessary, on your own line of attack. So far all is going well.
>
> Respectfully, GEO. D. RUGGLES,
> Colonel, &c.

In his official report, made October 15, 1862, McClellan says: "Burnside's corps...was entrusted with the difficult task of carrying the bridge over the Antietam, near Rohrbach's farm, and assaulting the enemy's right, the order having been communicated to him at 10 o'clock a.m." Burnside says: "At 10 o'clock I received an order from the general commanding to make the attack." Cox says the order was received at the time French was engaged at the Sunken Road, and: "The manner in which we had waited, the free discussion of what was occurring under our eyes and our relation to it, the public receipt of the order by Burnside in the usual and business-like form, all forbid the supposition that this was the reiteration of a former order." Immediately upon receipt of the order

Brigadier General Jacob D. Cox
Engraving made when Major General
Library of Congress

Burnside directed Colonel Kingsbury, with the 11th Connecticut, to move forward as skirmishers and drive the enemy from the head of the bridge, and instructed Cox to detail Crook's Brigade, supported by Sturgis' Division, to make the assault and, after the bridge was carried, to deploy to the right and left and take the heights above it. Rodman was ordered to cross at a ford below and join the column to be thrown over the ridge.

Directly opposite the east end of the bridge is a bluff rising at an angle of over 35 degrees to a height of 110 feet, wooded on the top and on the east, but open on its western slope. About 300 yards below the bridge another hill, plowed at the time, rises at an angle of 35 degrees to a height of 110 feet above the Antietam. At a point on the road 260 yards below the bridge a farm road—Rohrbach's—runs northerly through the ravine separating these two hills from, to the Rohrbach farm house, thence to the Porterstown road. East and south of the second hill and 375 yards below the bridge was a cornfield of some 30 to 35 acres, on a sloping hill side, the southwest corner of which came down to the stream where the road leaves it to go southeast over a high ridge and on to Rohrersville. In this cornfield is a ravine from which the ground ascends southerly 180 to 190 feet above the stream, and on this elevation were placed the batteries of Benjamin, McMullin, C.P. Muhlenberg, Roemer and Cook, commanding a view of the field and overlooking the bridge, 900 yards distant. From the southwest corner of the cornfield, which came down to the road where the Antietam begins to make a graceful sweep to the west, to the bridge is 375 yards. The road turns square to the left to pass the bridge, which is 175 feet in length and but 12 feet wide. Cox gives an excellent description of the bridge and its surroundings:

> The bridge itself is a stone structure of three arches, with stone parapet above, this parapet to some extent masking the approach to the bridge at either end. The valley in which the stream runs is quite narrow, the steep slopes on the right bank approaching quite to the water's edge. On this slope the roadway is scarped, running both ways from the bridge end, and passing to the higher lands above by ascending through ravines above and below, the other ravine being some 600 yards above the bridge, the turn about half that distance below. On the hill side immediately above the bridge was a stone fence, running parallel to the stream; the turns of the roadway were covered by rifle pits and breastworks made of rails and stone, all of which defenses, as well as the woods which covered the slope, were filled with the enemy's infantry and sharpshooters. Besides the infantry defenses, batteries were placed to enfilade the bridge and all its approaches. The crest of the first hill above the bridge is curved toward the stream at the extremes, forming a sort of natural tete-du-pont. The next ridge

The Lower Bridge a few days after the battle. This is the view and area fought over at various times by several Union regiments as they attempted to storm the bridge by following the road. *Library of Congress.*

beyond somewhat higher, though with less regularity, the depression between the two being but slight, and the distance varying in places from 300 to 700 yards.

McClellan, after stating in his report that Burnside had been given a "difficult task," says:

> The valley of the Antietam at and near the bridge is narrow, with high banks. On the right of the stream the bank is wooded, and commands the approaches both to the bridge and the ford. The steep slopes of the bank were lined with rifle-pits and breastworks of rails and stones. These, together with the woods, were filled with the enemy's infantry, while their batteries completely commanded and enfiladed the bridge and ford and their approaches.

The bridge was defended by about 400 men of Toombs Brigade, supported on the right by a regiment of 110 men of Drayton's Brigade and a company of Jenkins' Brigade. The 20th Georgia, Colonel John B. Cummings, rested its left about 40 yards above the bridge with skirmishers on the left, some 200 yards overlooking the Antietam, and, in a good position, among some trees on the immediate bank of the stream, was a company of the 20th Georgia. On the right of this regiment, about two-thirds way up the bluff and nearly opposite the head of the bridge, was a quarry from which the bridge could be raked its entire length. Twenty-five to 30 men were in this quarry. On the right of the 20th was the 2nd Georgia, Lieutenant Colonel William R. Holmes, prolonging the line down the stream about 300 yards below the bridge, where it curves sharply to the west, opposite the point where the Rohrersville road leaves it and ascends a sharp ridge. Thus the greater part of the line was placed below the bridge. This disposition was adopted because the road to the bridge on the opposite side of the stream ran from below up the bank, near the water, for over 300 yards. Colonel H. L. Benning, 17th Georgia, had immediate command of these two regiments. The line was on the crest of the bluff, well sheltered and hidden by the trees, and strengthened by rail fences, fallen trees, and everything that could give protection. Farther to the right was the 50th Georgia, Lieutenant Colonel F. Kearse, of Drayton's Brigade, about 100 men, which held a line on the right of the 2nd Georgia. It was deployed in a very open order to guard a blind plantation road leading to a ford in the bend of the Antietam between the right of the 2nd Georgia and Snavely's Ford. Between the 2nd and 50th Georgia was half a company of Jenkins' South Carolina brigade, and on the right of the 50th, was the other half of this company, overlooking and observing Snavely's Ford. Toombs was in general command of the whole line. On a ridge about 500 yards in

Confederate position along the west bank of Antietam Creek. Looking south along the slope of the hill. *Author's collection.*

rear was Richardson's Battery of the Washington Artillery but, finding that it was too far in rear to render service in defending the passage of the bridge, Toombs obtained Eubank's Battery of Colonel S. D. Lee's Battalion, which took position in his rear and about half way between the stream and Richardson. Until near noon Eshleman's Battery was on Richardson's right. The batteries on Cemetery hill had complete range of the bridge and the road to Sharpsburg and, after its passage, inflicted many casualties upon the troops that had crossed.

Toombs minimizes the strength of his position, but says: "Its chief strength lay in the fact that, from the nature of the ground on the other side, the enemy were compelled to approach mainly by the road which led up to the river for near 300 paces parallel with my line of battle and distant therefrom from 50 to 150 feet, thus exposing his flank to a destructive fire the most of that distance."

Cox says:

> I do not hesitate to affirm that the Confederate position was virtually impregnable to a direct attack over the bridge; for the column approaching it was not only exposed at point-blank range to the perfectly covered infantry of the enemy and two batteries which were assigned to the special duty of supporting Toombs, and which had the exact range of the little valley with their shrapnel, but if it should succeed in reaching the bridge its charge across it must be made under a fire plowing through its length, the head of the column melting away as it advanced, so that as every soldier knows, it could show no front strong enough to make an impression on the enemy's breastworks, even if it should reach the other side. As a desperate sort of diversion in favor of the right wing, it might be justifiable, but I believe that no officer or man who knew the actual situation at that bridge thinks a serious attack upon it was any part of McClellan's original plan. Yet, in his detailed official report, instead of speaking of it as the difficult task the original report had called it, he treats it as little different from a parade or march across, which might have been done in half an hour.

Cox had immediate command of the Ninth Corps during the battle. On the afternoon of the 16th, when expecting a battle, he remained with his division, desiring to lead it, and urged Burnside to assume the immediate command of the corps, to which Burnside objected "that as he had been announced as commander of the right wing of the army composed of two corps, his own and Hooker's, he was unwilling to waive his precedence or to assume that Hooker was detached for anything more than a temporary service," but that he would assist Cox in every way he could, till the crisis of the campaign should be over.

View from the Confederate position looking almost straight down to the damaged bridge. Notice the first line of trees in the background along the first road to the Henry Rohrbach house, and the plowed field behind it. *Library of Congress.*

Cox was an earnest and gallant soldier but new to the Army of the Potomac, and three of the divisions were strangers to him. He had conducted a very successful and brilliant campaign in the Kanawha Valley, West Virginia, in the summer of 1861, and had a well disciplined and good division, that, under his command, had done good and brilliant service at South Mountain, and, to anticipate, he handled the Ninth Corps well at Antietam.

It would have been better had he handled it alone. It has been well said that "Burnside became a mere receiver and transmitter of orders to the commander of the Ninth Corps, and on the other hand it may easily be believed that so good a soldier as Cox would have shown more activity and accomplished more, if he had felt himself really the commander of the corps. With Burnside close to him, he probably felt as if he were the mere tactical leader of the corps, not thinking for it, but simply seeing that it executed orders which came to him from or through Burnside." It can be stated upon unquestionable authority that had he felt that he was in responsible command he would not have depended upon reconnaissances made by McClellan's engineers and aides for knowledge of the crossings of the stream, but would have ascertained that matter in person, and that he would have had two divisions at Snavely's Ford, before 10 o'clock on the morning of the 17th, ready to cross when McClellan gave the order to attack. However, this was not to be; we take things as we find them, and continue the narrative.

It had been determined that Crook's Brigade should lead in the attack on the bridge and that Sturgis' Division should support it. It was thought that by advancing part of Sturgis' command to the plowed field below the bridge, it could cover the advance of Crook, who could make a straight dash down the hill directly opposite the bridge and carry it, and orders were given accordingly; Crook preceded by the 11th Connecticut, as skirmishers, to assault the bridge. The 11th Connecticut was then detached from its brigade, and went forward to the crest of the hill east of the Rohrbach road, where it was halted and a battery put in position near it, that shelled the opposite bank of the Antietam. When the artillery firing ceased the regiment went down the plowed hill, crossed the Rohrbach road near the stream, and, in skirmishing order, with a reserve, went over a wooded spur, and, under a severe fire, pushed for the bridge. The left of the line reached the creek opposite the end of the Rohrbach road, and the right gained the level ground at the foot of the hill opposite the bridge; Captain Griswold, on the left, endeavored to lead his men across the creek and was mortally wounded in the water; on the right Colonel Kingsbury was severely and then mortally wounded, while leading the reserve toward the bridge, and, after a short but gallant effort, in which it lost over one third of its men, the regiment fell back.

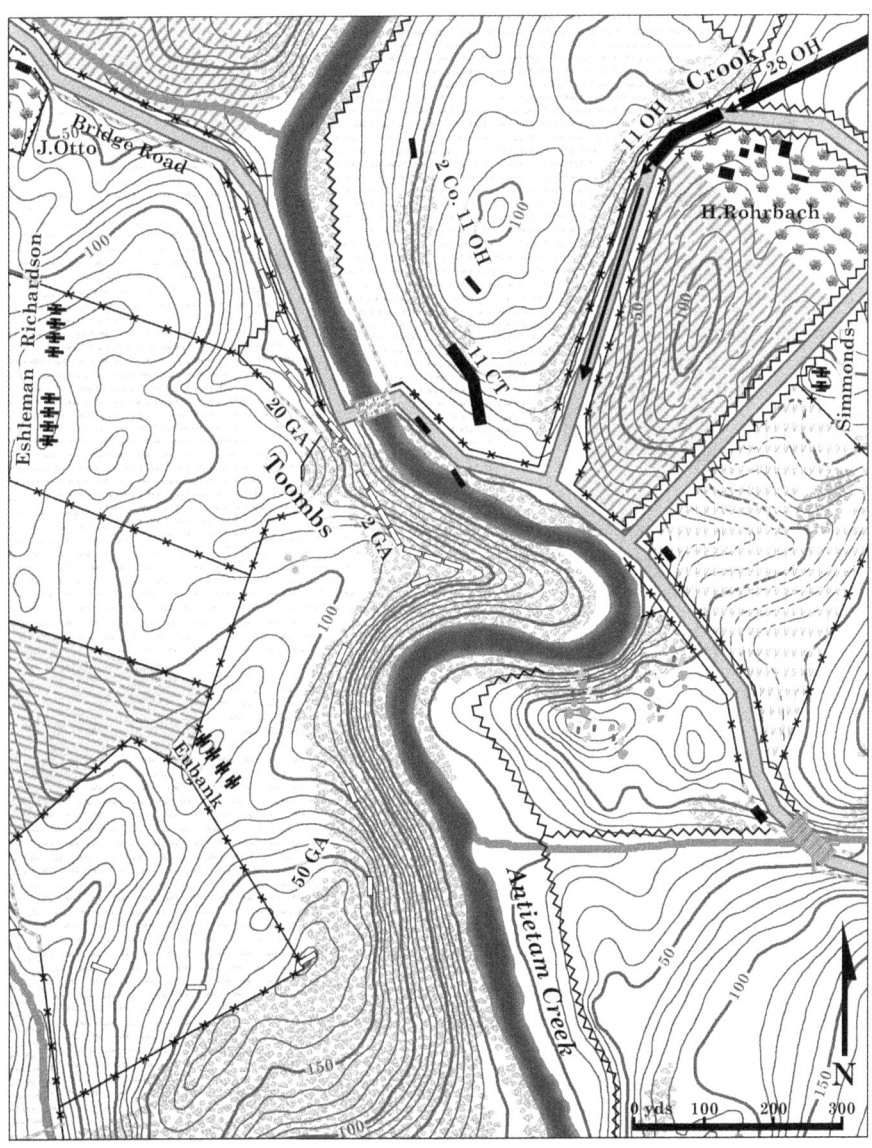

Crook's brigade advances to attack the Lower Bridge. The 11th Connecticut, detached from Harland's brigade, attacks alone before Crook arrives. Companies A and B under John D. Griswold attempt to ford the creek but are driven back, with Griswold mortally wounded.

The 11th Connecticut was soon followed by Crook, who seems to have misunderstood the orders under which he was acting, as he says they were "to cross the bridge over Antietam Creek after General Sturgis had taken the bridge," but upon his arrival in the vicinity he found that Sturgis had not arrived, so he sent the 11th Ohio ahead as skirmishers, in the direction of the bridge. Early in the morning, before the general advance had been ordered, two companies of the 11th Ohio, were sent forward as skirmishers on the wooded bluff, to watch the enemy closely and give notice of any movement made by them. They were fired upon as they made their appearance on the west side of the bluff, fell back under cover and returned the fire upon the Georgians beyond the creek. This was prior to the advance of the 11th Connecticut, and when that advance was made, the two companies were on the right of it, and still skirmishing.

Crook's Brigade consisted of the 11th, 28th and 36th Ohio, attached to it was a Kentucky Battery, commanded by Captain Seth J. Simmonds. One section of this battery had been detached to Benjamin, one remained with the brigade. When Crook received his orders he was a short distance northeast of Rohrbach's. He advanced, left the 36th Ohio in Rohrbach's orchard, and went down the road with the 11th and 28th, halting in the road about 200 yards from the house. Four companies of the 28th Ohio were sent over the wooded hill on the right, as skirmishers, and as they approached the open field looking down on the bridge, the fire from the opposite bank of the stream was so severe that they fell back and rejoined the regiment on the Rohrbach road. Five companies of the 28th were now ordered to place in position, on the crest of the wooded hill overlooking the bridge, two guns of Simmonds' Battery, and Crook, ordering the 11th Ohio to advance on the bridge, led the other five companies of the 28th, by the right flank over the wooded hill to co-operate with the 11th in a charge on the bridge, but lost direction and, instead of coming out at the bridge, went down the hill and came to within 50 yards of the creek, at a point where there was a bend in the stream and a ford about 350 yards above the creek, where seeking shelter under a low sandy ridge and fence, he engaged the Confederate skirmishers opposite and remained until the bridge had been carried by Sturgis' Division. When Crook led the five companies of the 28th to the right, the 11th Ohio was formed in line on the left of the road, on the side of the plowed hill, and advanced, but, under conflicting orders, it became broken, the right wing moving across the road to the wooded hill, where the two companies had remained as skirmishers, while the left wing moved straight down the open hill to its base, about 100 yards from the creek, where it came under severe fire of infantry and artillery. Lieutenant Colonel Coleman, commanding the regiment, was mortally wounded, the ranks were thrown into confusion, and Major Lyman J. Jackson, finding

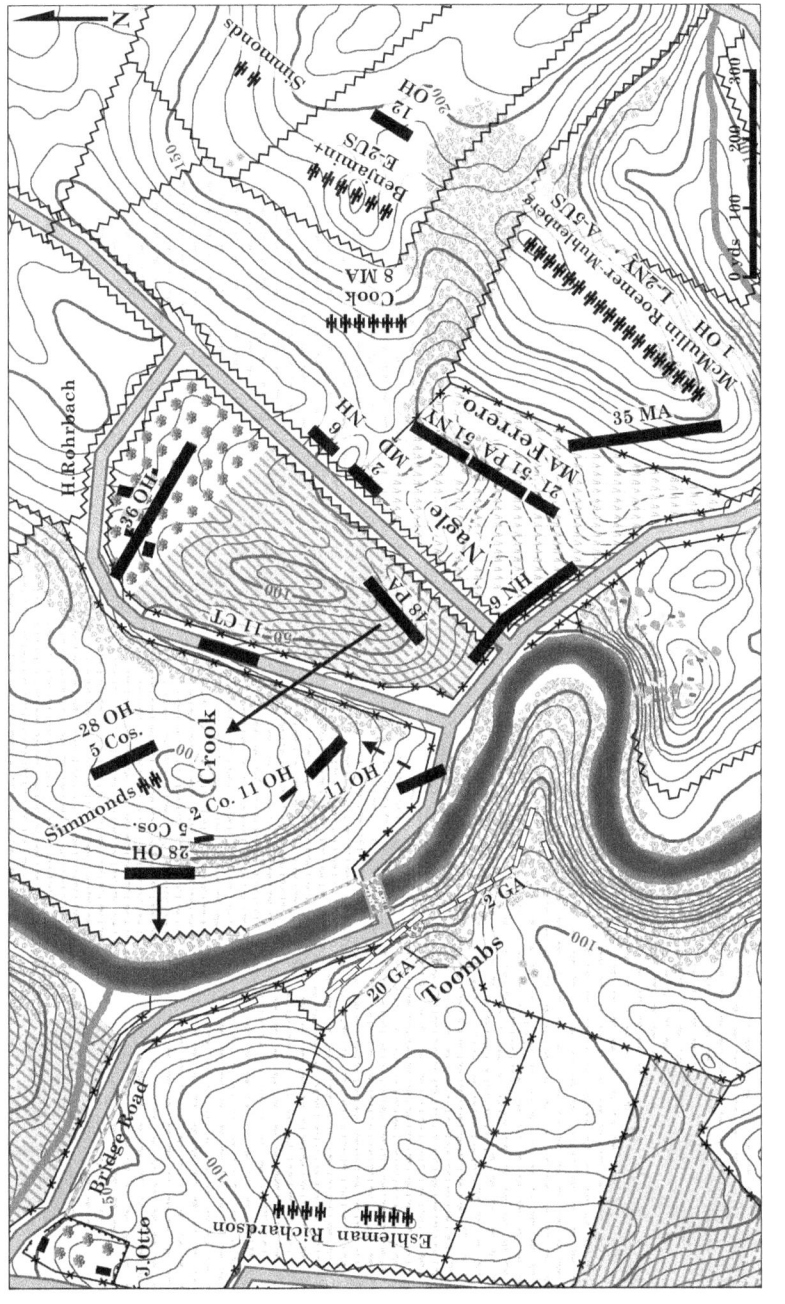

Crook's brigade attacks, but the advance becomes disjointed. Both the 11th and 28th Ohio split into wings, the 11th unintentionally. Crook is unable to concentrate his brigade at the bridge and the attack stalls.

himself in a useless and very exposed position, moved with a part of the regiment to the right, recrossed the field and the Rohrbach road, under cover of the fire of some of the 11th Connecticut, who had held on to the fences bordering the stream, and halted at a point of the hill opposite the bridge, where he reunited his command, formed under cover, and kept up fire until he was ordered to retire and join the 36th Ohio in the Rohrbach orchard. Crook handled his command badly, his loss was trifling, and he reported to Cox that he had his hands full and could not approach closer to the bridge.

Crook's movement having failed, Sturgis was ordered to take the bridge. Intending to act as a support to Crook and take advantage of any success gained by him, he had moved his division to the left and front, in such position that it could make a quick dash up the road, skirting the stream, to the bridge. Nagle's Brigade lay nearest the bridge. The 2nd Maryland, Lieutenant Colonel J. E. Duryea, had marched down a stock lane from Rohrbach's and halted, with its right at the southwest corner of the cornfield, 375 yard below the bridge; the 6th New Hampshire, Colonel S. S. Griffin, was at the side of the stock lane, in rear of the 2nd Maryland, and under cover of the plowed hill immediately west. The 48th Pennsylvania, Lieutenant [Colonel] Joshua K. Sigfried, marched down through the corn to a small log building, in the southwest corner, near the 2nd Maryland; and the 9th New Hampshire, Colonel Enoch A. Fellows, went down through the corn to the fence bordering the road and opened fire upon the enemy's skirmishers across the stream. Ferrero's Brigade followed Nagle's and took position in the cornfield, three regiments about 200 yards from its western edge, the 35th Massachusetts on their left and rear, on a hill side overlooking them. Some of the batteries were engaged when Crook was making his movement, but now all the guns that could be brought to bear opened a furious fire upon the west head of the bridge and the wooded heights below it, and further preparations were made to carry the bridge.

Rodman's Division, supported by Ewing's Brigade, had been directed to cross at the ford below the bridge. General Cox says:

> Burnside's view of the matter was that the front attack at the bridge was so difficult that the passage by the ford below must be an important factor in the task; for if Rodman's Division should succeed in getting across there, at the bend of the Antietam, he would come up in rear of Toombs, and either the whole of D. R. Jones' Division would have to advance to meet Rodman, or Toombs must abandon the bridge...and Rodman was ordered to push rapidly for the bridge...We were constantly hoping to hear something of Rodman's advance by the ford, and would gladly have waited for some more certain knowledge of his progress, but at this time McClellan's sense of

The Lower Bridge from the Rohrbach road. Union regiments took shelter behind the trees and fence that lined the road and engaged the Confederates across the bridge. Their position can be clearly seen. *Library of Congress.*

the necessity of relieving the right was such that he was sending reiterated orders to push the assault. Not only were these forwarded to me, but to give additional weight to my instructions Burnside sent direct to Sturgis urgent messages to carry the bridge at all hazards.

Nagle had taken position before the failure of Crook's attack; soon after its cessation Sturgis ordered him forward, up the road to the bridge. The movement was initiated by the 48th Pennsylvania, which had left its place near the log building in the cornfield, moved to the right over the slope of the plowed field, crossed the Rohrbach road and formed line on the wooded knoll in front of the bridge, near where the 11th Ohio had been engaged, and from which they were now retiring, and where five companies of the 28th Ohio were getting two of Simmonds' guns in position. Here the regiment opened fire upon the Confederates beyond the stream.

To lessen the long stretch of the road along which it was necessary to move, under flank fire of the enemy, within easy pistol shot, the 2nd Maryland was counter-marched up the lane, about 200 yards to where the 6th New Hampshire had halted, and, under cover of the plowed hill, the two regiments, about 150 men each, were formed for the charge. It required but a few moments, when, side by side, with bayonets fixed, they went down the hill for its southwest corner. The Rohrbach road was fenced with stout chestnut posts and rails, and was quite high. The officers ran ahead, soon removed a short panel and as the head of the 2nd Maryland came to the opening it met with such a withering fire that the leading files began to shrink and elbow out of the ranks, but the vehement commands and the example of the officers steadied the ranks, the line straightened up and charged up the road toward the bridge under a severe front and flank fire. About midway from where they had struck the road and the bridge the road bends slightly to the right; upon reaching this point the head of the column came under the fire of the Georgians posted in the quarry, just south of the head of the bridge, and those on the brow of the bluff, behind rail barricades and trees, not over 100 yards distant, and fully one third of the Maryland men went down, but the regiment still went on and had reached to within 250 feet of the bridge when the right wing was so shattered that the survivors fell back and sought such cover as the fences, logs and trees afforded. The left wing essayed a farther advance, but it, too, was checked and sought cover. The 6th New Hampshire severely suffered before it cleared the opening in the fence, but it was close on the heels of the 2nd Maryland, and met the same fate; it was badly shattered, sought cover and opened fire across the stream, in which it was joined by the Maryland men. The 9th New Hampshire followed the charging regiments as far as the Rohrbach road, where it halted; its left about 100 yards from the road

VOL. 3: THE MIDDLE BRIDGE TO HILL'S COUNTERATTACK

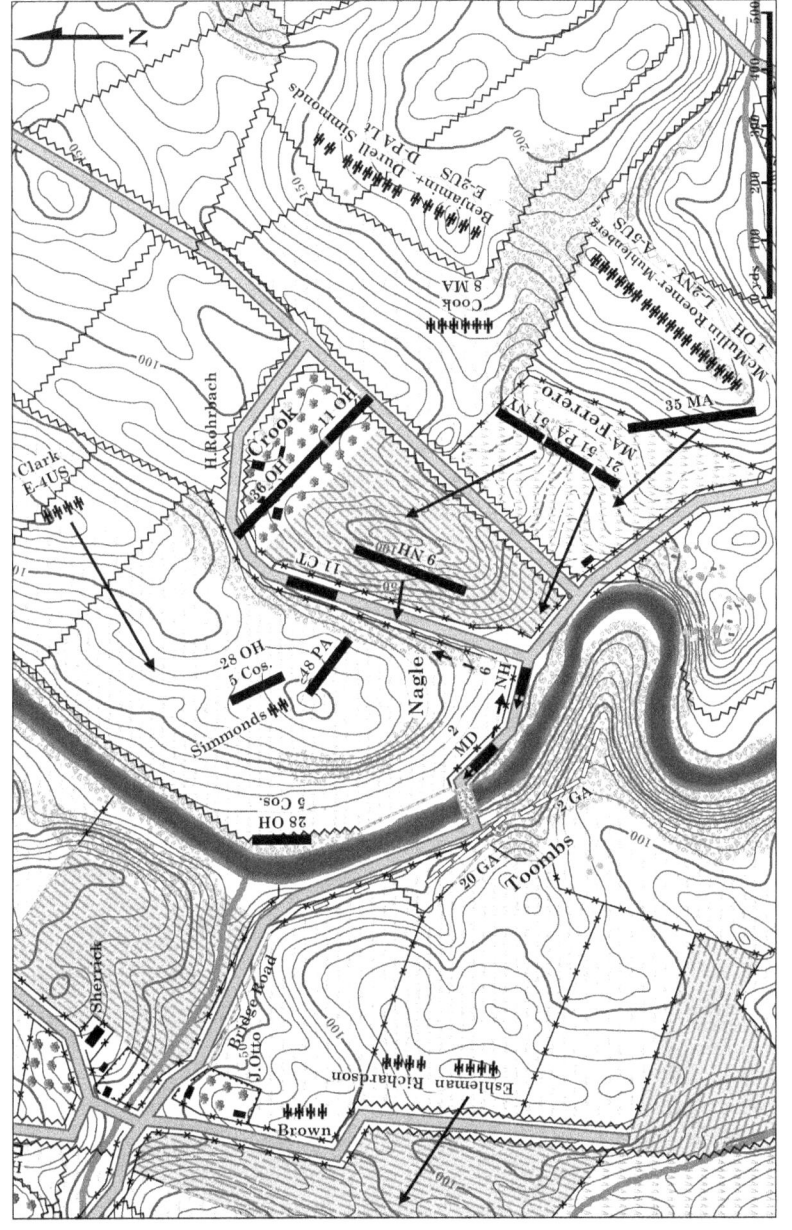

Nagle's brigade moves into action, but the 2nd Maryland and 6th New Hampshire are unable to force the bridge by moving along the road. Ferrero's brigade advances in support.

which ran to the bridge, the right extending up the road in which it had halted, and all well covered from the fire beyond the creek, which was answered by crawling up the hillside and delivering an accurate and constant fire.

Cox now ordered Sturgis to take two regiments from Ferrero's Brigade, which had not been engaged, and make a column by moving them by the flank, side by side, so that when they passed the bridge they could turn to right and left, forming line as they advanced on the run. As the effort along the main road had been so disastrous it was determined that these two regiments should charge from the hill opposite the bridge where Crook had made his futile attempt. This charge was to be supported by artillery on the right, and on the left by infantry lying along the road below the bridge— 2nd Maryland, 6th and 9th New Hampshire, and 21st Massachusetts—the 35th Massachusetts to follow the two charging regiments. Under Cox's instructions Ferrero selected the 51st Pennsylvania, Colonel John F. Hartranft, and the 51st New York, Lieutenant Colonel Robert B. Potter. The two regiments piled their knapsacks in the cornfield, filled their canteens from the spring near the road, marched out of the corn, went over the lower plowed hill, crossed the Rohrbach road, and ascended the eastern slope of the wooded knoll that looked down upon the entrance to the bridge, and formed behind the 48th Pennsylvania, at a point where a dip in the ground concealed them from view, the 51st Pennsylvania on the right. The two regiments had about 335 officers and men each.

Meanwhile Simmonds' two guns had been placed in position, supported by five companies of the 28th Ohio, and opened fire upon the heights above the far end of the bridge; Clark's Battery (E, 4th U. S.) of six guns, was brought down the north side of the hill and opened fire at the same time, and a battery in rear of Clark, probably Taft's, added its fire. The 21st Massachusetts, Colonel William S. Clark, about 150 men, moved from the cornfield, took position behind the fence at the foot of the plowed hill and engaged the enemy's skirmishers beyond the stream. When everything was ready a heavy skirmishing fire was opened all along the bank of the stream, the guns were active with canister and shell, and the two regiments, led by Hartranft, sprang from cover, passed over the 48th Pennsylvania, and, side by side, went down the hill by the flank, straight for the bridge, a little over 300 yards distant, and were met by such a severe fire that the progress of the columns was checked. When going down the hill, the company commanders, at least some of them, of the 51st Pennsylvania, came to the conclusion that it would be impossible for the two regiments to charge in a body across such an exceedingly narrow structure as they saw before them, and changed their course to the right and, before Hartranft could stop them, gained a stone fence running north from the bridge abutment, and parallel to the creek, when, under good cover, they opened fire across the

VOL. 3: THE MIDDLE BRIDGE TO HILL'S COUNTERATTACK

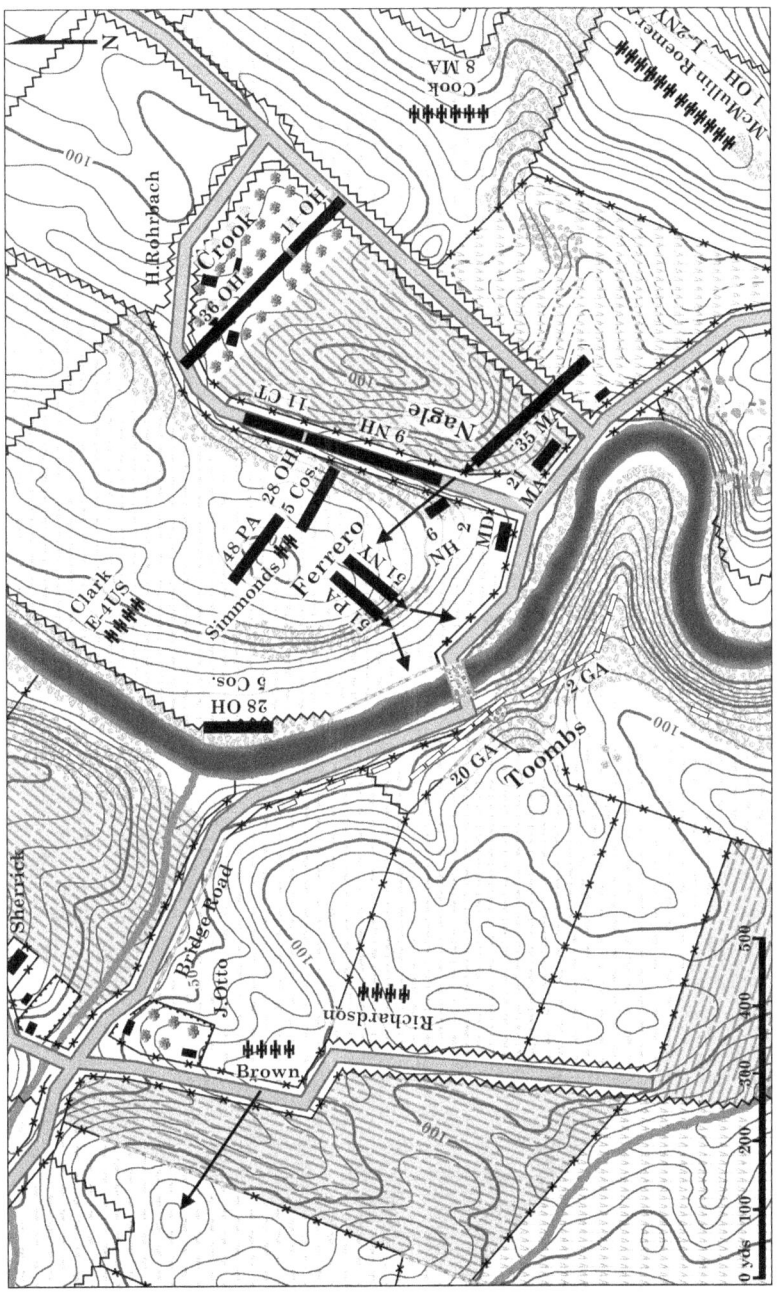

After amassing direct artillery support and fire from the nearby infantry regiments, the 51st Pennsylvania and 51st New York charge the bridge. Enemy fire forces them to take cover along the fences and walls on either side of it.

stream. Potter, at the head of the 51st New York, perceiving this movement and fearing that his exposed flank would lose very heavily, under the concentrated fire of the enemy, brought his regiment forward into line and then obliqued to the left, down to the road, on the edge of the stream below the bridge, where a rail fence offered some cover, and joined the 51st Pennsylvania in a rapid fire across the stream, principally upon the quarry near the far end of the bridge. When Colonel Clark of the 21st Massachusetts saw this condition of affairs he double quicked his regiment along the road and formed on the left of the 51st New York, where he was joined by a company of the 35th Massachusetts.

After firing in this position a few minutes and perceiving a slackening in the Confederate fire, and that some of them were leaving, Potter became satisfied that a rush would carry the bridge, and suggested to Hartranft that it be made, but the latter replied that his men had received so heavy a fire that it would be very difficult to get them to leave cover, upon which Potter asked permission to lead his own regiment over, which was granted. Potter communicated his order to his nearest company commander on the right and, rushing toward the bridge, waved his sword for the regiment to follow, and it started on the run. When it reached within a few feet of the bridge, the 51st Pennsylvania, which had seen the enemy in its front retiring by two's and three's, and spurred by the action of the New York men, ran by the left flank through a gateway in the fence, close to the bridge, and the regiments, side by side, their colors close together, crossed the bridge amid the most enthusiastic cheering from every part of the field from which they could be seen. Upon clearing the bridge the two regiments turned to the right and halted in the road leading to Sharpsburg. Toombs' men fell back, some were taken prisoners, and a few sharpshooters were found in the trees, who could not make their escape.

The 21st Massachusetts did not cross the bridge at this time, as it was out of ammunition, but the 35th Massachusetts, was close upon the heels of the of the two charging regiments. It had followed them from the cornfield, after a brief interval, and skirting the base of the plowed hill, passing along the rear of the 21st Massachusetts, crossed the Rohrbach road, made a short halt on the wooded hill, then went out of the woods by the flank, but seeing the forces below engaged along the banks of the stream, it was ordered in line to join in the firing, but the movement was scarcely completed when the charge for the bridge was seen, upon which it came at once into column and rushed across the bridge, close upon the heels of the two 51sts, the third regiment to cross, and turning to the right, passed the two regiments and formed in the road, on their right, about 1 p.m. Nagle's Brigade quickly followed; the 48th Pennsylvania, which had been on the bluff and over which the 51st Pennsylvania moved in its charge, went down the hill close behind the 35th Massachusetts, crossed the bridge, turned to

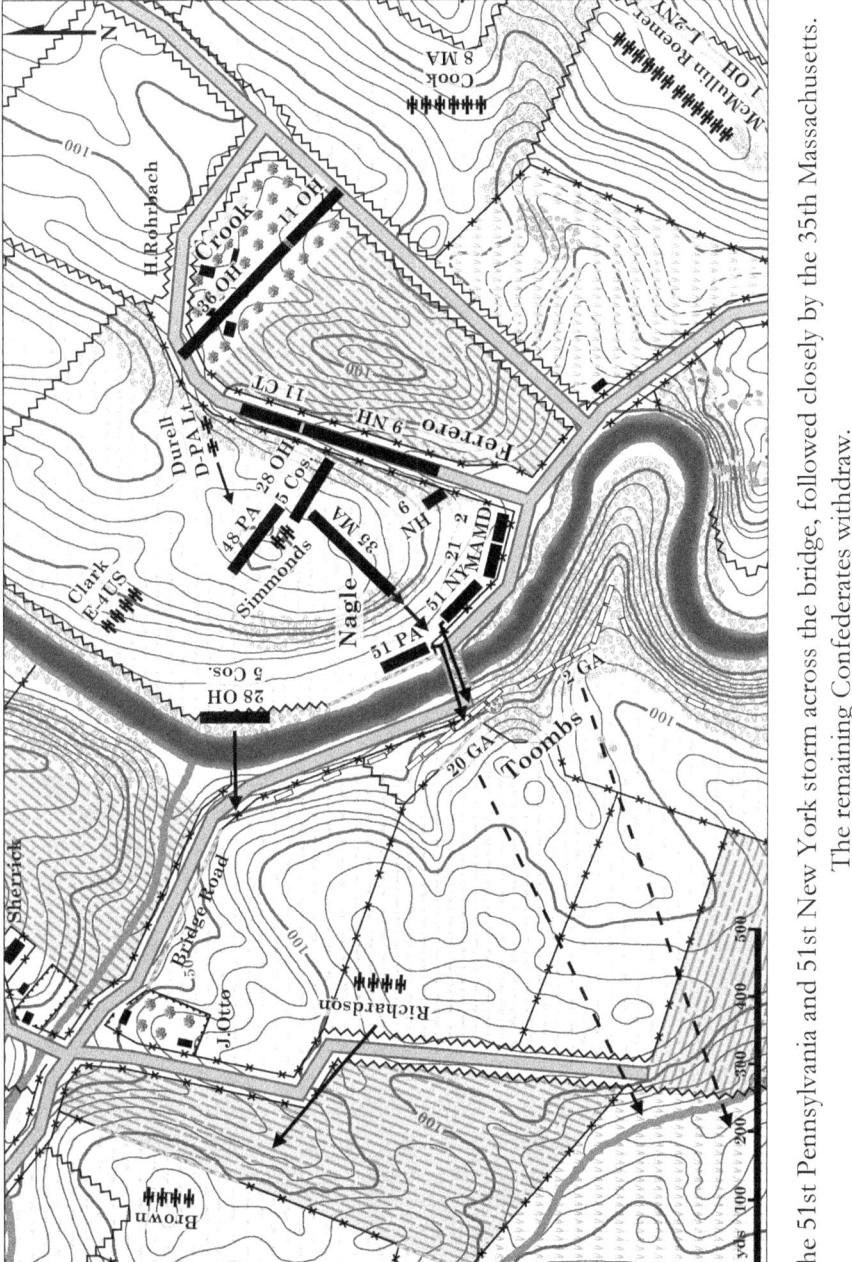

The 51st Pennsylvania and 51st New York storm across the bridge, followed closely by the 35th Massachusetts. The remaining Confederates withdraw.

the left, ascended the heights by a very rough farm road and threw out skirmishers to the front and left, those on the left going down the stream until they met the advancing skirmishers of Rodman's Division, which had crossed the Antietam at Snavely's Ford. The 6th and 9th New Hampshire followed the 48th Pennsylvania across and up the road on the left, came under heavy artillery fire and formed line under cover of the ridge beyond, upon which skirmishers were deployed, who became warmly engaged with those of the enemy about 350 yards distant, covered by a stone fence. Eubank's Confederate Battery had been driven from the field by the furious fire of the Union artillery about 10 a.m. Richardson's Battery remained until Toombs fell back, when it went down the Otto lane and then through Sharpsburg, but Brown's Battery, about 900 yards to the front and right of where Nagle's men had halted, poured in a rapid fire of shell and shrapnel. At the same time the Confederate guns on Cemetery hill threw their shell and shrapnel into the ranks of the men lying in the road near the bridge, killing and wounding many; among those killed was Lieutenant Colonel Thomas S. Bell, 51st Pennsylvania. About the time the bridge was carried Crook crossed his five companies of the 28th Ohio at the ford 350 yards above and covered the Sharpsburg road, where, later, he was joined by the rest of his brigade, which crossed at the bridge. Captain H. F. Duval's company of the 36th Ohio was sent to the right of the road, on the high ground overlooking Sherrick's to dislodge some skirmishers, who were giving much annoyance.

Very soon after crossing the bridge, and while Nagle's Brigade was going up the road on the left and taking position, the 35th Massachusetts was ordered to ascend the heights on the right. About 75 yards above the bridge is a ravine beyond is a very bold hill overlooking the road and stream. The regiment was ordered up this hill. It started in line of battle, the left in the ravine, climbing with difficulty high rail fences and the steep ground, soon swung into column and moving by the right flank as it neared the top. When it reached the bare brow of the hill Brown's Battery opened fire upon it, killing and wounding several, and it fell back under the brow of the hill and lay down in a grass field. Soon after the 21st Massachusetts came up and formed on its left. The 51st Pennsylvania and 51st New York remained for a time in the road near the bridge.

Sturgis' artillery followed his infantry across the bridge. We left Durell's Battery early in the morning engaged on the bluff overlooking the Antietam, from which position it went back to near where Benjamin was using his long range guns, and two guns were advanced to assist Simmonds and Clark in silencing the enemy at the head of the bridge, but did not get in action before the bridge was carried, when they went down the hill, crossed the bridge and up the road to the right and began to ascend the ravine, by which the left of the 35th Massachusetts had gone up the bluff.

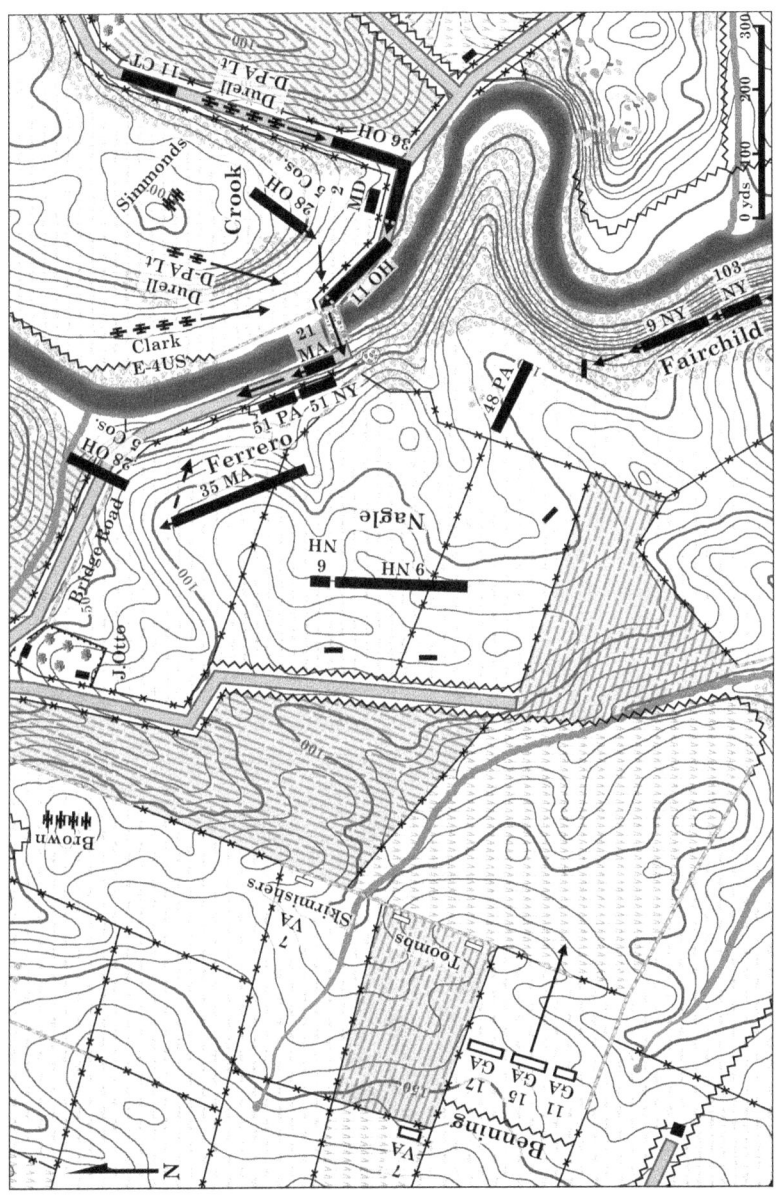

The Union regiments move forward to develop the enemy position. Contact is re-established with Rodman's division coming from the south. The 35th Massachusetts is forced back by Brown's Battery.

No favorable position could be found for the guns and they returned to the bridge, then up the road to the left and joined the other four guns which had crossed the bridge and taken a position on a ridge 450 yards nearly west of the bridge and overlooking a deep valley beyond which about 900 yards from the battery the ground rises from 40 to 60 feet higher, and along which runs the road from Sharpsburg to the mouth of the Antietam and Harper's Ferry. At first the two guns of the battery were on the right of Clark's, these were brought to the left and the battery united, its left about 25 yards from the northeast corner of a 40 acre cornfield, through which ran a deep ravine south to the Antietam at Snavely's Ford. When the battery went into position it became hotly engaged with Brown's Battery on the right and front. Clark's Battery while going into position on the right of Durell's four guns, two of Durell's being on his right, was greeted with a rapid fire of spherical case from Brown's guns. Lieutenant W. L. Baker was killed, Captain Clark severely wounded and compelled to leave the field, and the command devolved upon Sergeant C. F. Merkel, who fought the battery the rest of the day with skill and courage.

In the several efforts to carry the bridge, the Union loss was about 500; that of the Confederates in defending it about 120, and they held it until the colors of the 51st Pennsylvania and 51st New York were upon it, when most of the Georgians retreated, but the commander of the 2nd Georgia, Lieutenant Colonel Holmes, appealing to some of his men to follow him, ran down to the bank of the stream, and with a cry of defiance shook his sword in the faces of the Union men and fell pierced by many bullets. Thus fell, says Colonel Benning: "a good officer, and as gallant a man, I think, as my eyes ever beheld." Benning pays this tribute to his men: "during the long and terrible fire not a man, except a wounded one, fell out and went to the rear—not a man."

Scant justice has been done the brave men who fought at the Burnside bridge. It is true that there was not such a holocaust of dead as on other parts of the field, but the fighting was brilliant. Allan, the historian of the Army of Northern Virginia, writes:

> There was no part of the bloody field of Sharpsburg which witnessed more gallant deeds both of attack and defense than did the Burnside bridge...A fierce contest was waged for its possession...The 500 Federal soldiers who lay bleeding or dead along the eastern approach to the bridge were witnesses to the courage of the assaults. On the Confederate side of the stream Toombs' two small regiments held their ground, and threw back assault after assault with a coolness and tenacity unsurpassed in history.

Looking across the bridge toward the Confederate position on the heights above. This is what the 51st Pennsylvania and 51st New York would have seen as they stormed across the bridge. *Author's collection.*

There has been much unjust criticism at the delay in taking the bridge. The events narrated followed each other in quick succession and were as energetically pushed as were the movements on any other part of the field. General Cox says:

> The successive efforts had been made as closely following each other as possible. Each had been a fierce combat; in which the men, with wonderful courage, had not easily accepted defeat, and even when not able to cross the bridge had made use of the walls at the end, the fences, and every tree and stone as cover, while they strove to reach with their fire their well-protected and nearly concealed opponents. The lulls in the fighting had been short, and only to prepare new efforts. Nearly three hours had been spent in a bitter and bloody contest across the narrow stream. The severity of the work was attested by our losses.

Confederate reports confirm Cox's statements and show the condition of affairs on that side. Colonel Benning, who was in immediate command of the 2nd and 20th Georgia, after giving their position, without supports and the general line of battle nearly or quite three quarters of a mile in rear, says:

> In this forlorn condition were the two regiments when the fight opened in earnest. At this time the enemy's infantry, aided by the fire of many pieces of artillery, opened on our whole line as far up as the bridge. It was bold and persevering. The enemy came to the creek. The fire not only from their infantry, but from the artillery, was incessant, the artillery being so placed that it could fire over the heads of the infantry. It was met by a rapid, well directed, and unflinching fire from our men, under which the enemy, after a vain struggle broke and fell back. This attack was followed by two similar ones from apparently fresh bodies of troops, and with like results, the last of the two extending above the bridge to the upper part of our line. At length, toward 12 o'clock, the enemy made preparations for a still more formidable attack. A battery was placed in position from which it could command at almost an enfilade the whole face of the hill occupied by our troops. Soon it opened fire, and the infantry, in much heavier force than at any time before, extending far above as well as below the bridge, again advanced to the attack. The combined fire of the infantry and artillery was terrific. It was, however, withstood by our men until their ammunition was quite exhausted, and until the enemy had gotten upon the bridge and were above and below fording the creek. I then gave the order to fall back.

Looking toward the Lower Bridge from the slope to the east. The 51st Pennsylvania fought behind this wall before storming the bridge. The lightly wooded slope occupied by the Confederates is easily visible. *Library of Congress*.

The position to which the Georgians retired was a stone fence about 900 yards in rear, some of them went farther to the south and skirmished with the advance of Rodman's Division, which had crossed at Snavely's Ford.

There is no doubt that an earlier appearance of Rodman on this part of the field would have rendered unnecessary much of the great loss sustained in the successive attacks on the bridge. His delay is partly attributable to the want of knowledge of the fords. On the 16th McClellan's engineer officers made reconnaissances for fords and gathered information regarding them, and Burnside was informed by them that there was a ford less than a half mile below the bridge, and when Rodman's Division was led to its bivouac that night Fairchild's Brigade was supposed to be opposite this ford. Cox says all the orders for the movement of troops were based on the reports of the engineer officers. Burnside reports that in the morning, after the preliminary movements were made and before the general advance was ordered, "Rodman's Division, with Scammon's Brigade in support was opposite the ford, some three-quarters of a mile below the bridge." Cox reports that it was "about one-third of a mile below the bridge." In reality the nearest ford below the bridge, the one referred to by the engineer officers—was two-thirds of a mile, and was impracticable, not properly situated, being at the foot of a steep bluff, rising more than 160 feet, over which it would have been almost impossible to deploy infantry against a skirmish line; and the passage of the ford would have consumed much time. It was not until after Rodman had been ordered to advance, about 10 o'clock, from the heights to which he had retired early in the morning, and had marched some distance that he became aware of the fact that the only ford by which he could cross was a mile distant—as the crow flies from his starting point—and that he would be required to march two miles over very rough ground to reach it. This was Snavely's Ford 680 yards below the ford indicated in the orders of the day. It does seem probable that had one or two of the regiments of Pleasonton's cavalry been used on this flank, some good results would have followed, not only in finding and crossing the ford, but protecting Rodman's flank from its surprise and disaster later in the day.

Rodman's Division consisted of two brigades commanded by Colonels Harrison S. Fairchild and Edward Harland. Fairchild had the 9th New York (Hawkins' Zouaves), 89th and six companies of the 103rd New York. To this brigade was attached a battery of naval howitzers, under command of Captain J. R. Whiting, 9th New York. Harland had the 8th, 11th and 16th Connecticut, and 4th Rhode Island. Battery A, 5th U. S. Artillery, Lieutenant Charles P. Muhlenberg, was attached to the division, but did not accompany it to the left, nor did the 11th Connecticut. The division was followed by the 12th, 23rd and 30th Ohio of Scammon's Brigade. Scammon being in command of the Kanawha division, his brigade was

Deep Ford, the one initially described by the engineer officers, from the north bank. The water level is higher than it was in 1862. *Author's collection.*

commanded by Colonel Hugh Ewing, 30th Ohio. The entire force numbered about 3,200 officers and men.

Rodman moved from his position on the high ridge at 10.30 a.m., crossed the Rohrersville road about 1000 yards below the bridge, marched some 500 yards after crossing the road, and halted opposite the great bend in the Antietam, where the course of the stream changes from due south to west. Whiting's five guns were put in position to shell the wooded bluff opposite the ford by which it was proposed to cross, and shelled the road and woods on the opposite side of the creek, driving the enemy from their positions. This fire of Whiting's enfiladed the line of Georgians, at and below the bridge, and the annoyance it caused them is referred to in some of their reports. Meanwhile skirmishers had gone down to the creek and Rodman had come to the conclusion that this ford was not one that could be crossed and directed Colonel Harland to make further reconnaissance. Harland says: "I then sent out two companies of skirmishers from the 8th Connecticut Volunteers to discover, if possible, a ford by which the creek could be crossed." These two companies were under command of Captain C. L. Upham. The bank of the stream was quite heavily wooded, with dense undergrowth, but Upham soon reported that he had found a practicable ford, and the column, Fairchild's Brigade in advance, marched down to it. Whiting's Battery supported by the 8th Connecticut, was put in position on a hill just below the ford to cover the crossing. Much time had been lost and it was nearly 1 o'clock. Cox says the winding of the stream made Rodman's march much longer than was anticipated, and that, in fact, he only approached the rear of Toombs' position from that direction about the time when the last and successful charge upon the bridge was made, between noon and 1 o'clock.

From Snavely's Ford to the bridge, in a direct line, a little east of north, it is 1,275 yards. When the head of column halted on the hill overlooking the ford, at an elevation of 100 feet, it had an extensive view of a stretch of country toward the front and right, and above the bushes and over the trees, could be seen the smoke of the contest at the ridge and the charge of the 51st Pennsylvania and 51st New York, and while the contest was in progress Fairchild's Brigade, the 9th New York leading, marched by the left flank, down an old trail or wood road and entered the stream; which is about 75 feet wide, with a swift and strong current, the water hip deep. At the far side was a meadow, partly plowed, beyond which the ground rose gradually to a stone fence, running parallel to the stream and about 165 yards from it, and on the right the high, steep wooded bluff, the eastern part of which commanded the ford 680 yards above Snavely's.

When partly across the ford the 9th New York received the fire of Confederate skirmishers—the company from Jenkins' Brigade and some of the 50th Georgia—who were behind the stone fence, by which some men

Snavely's Ford from downstream. *The Ohio Antietam Battlefield Commission.*

were wounded, but, without replying to it, the column moved on, reached the opposite bank, and, filing to the right came under shelter of the wooded bluff. The regiment then faced to the left and began the ascent of the bluff, which was very steep, rocky and covered with a tangled undergrowth. Rodman was with the regiment, which broke into detachments right and left, to avoid impassable places, also to drive therefrom any of the enemy, who might be secreted in the woods, and in this manner, overcoming many difficulties, reached the summit of the bluff, 185 feet above the Antietam, closely followed by 103rd and 89th New York, and the entire brigade, marching by the right flank, near the bank of the stream, met the advancing skirmishers of the 48th Pennsylvania, and made a junction with the troops who had forced the bridge. Under a very severe artillery fire from the enemy's guns in the direction of Sharpsburg the brigade halted in a depression of the ground in rear of Durell's and Clark's batteries.

Harland followed Fairchild and while the latter was making his difficult way up the bluff, on the right, the 4th Rhode Island crossed the creek under fire of the enemy behind the stone fence, filed to the left on open ground, then one company to the front and one to the left as skirmishers, and advancing drove the enemy from the stone fence and formed behind it, and almost immediately received a musketry fire from the left, which was almost immediately silenced by Whiting's guns across the creek. The 16th Connecticut followed the 4th Rhode Island and moved to support its left. Two companies were sent to the left, beyond the Snavely buildings and were deployed behind the stone and rail fences of the road leading to Myers' Ford, and at the foot of a bluff, upon which was a large cornfield, in which Munford had his cavalry skirmishers, who advancing to the brow of the bluff, opened fire, and Eshleman's Louisiana battery, about 600 yards to the right and front dropped shrapnel among them. Some casualties resulted and the skirmishers were ordered back to the regiment, which moved to the right along the rear of the 4th Rhode Island, which, as soon as the 16th Connecticut had passed, moved to the right and formed under cover. The 8th Connecticut now came up and the brigade marched up the ravine and to the right, the two Connecticut regiments forming in Fairchild's rear, and the 4th Rhode Island farther to the left in the woods near the creek. Ewing's Ohio brigade followed Harland, came under fire of Eshleman's guns and, marching under cover, halted some distance below the bridge, thus forming the extreme left of the line, and it was 2 o'clock.

After the infantry had crossed the ford, Whiting went over with his five guns, under a fire of shrapnel from Eshleman's Battery but found it impracticable to follow the infantry. His guns were brass navy howitzers, 12-pounders, two rifled and three smooth bore, each gun hauled by two horses and the trail guided by a man on each side with a rope fastened to it, going down hill the men had to hold the gun back with a rope. There were

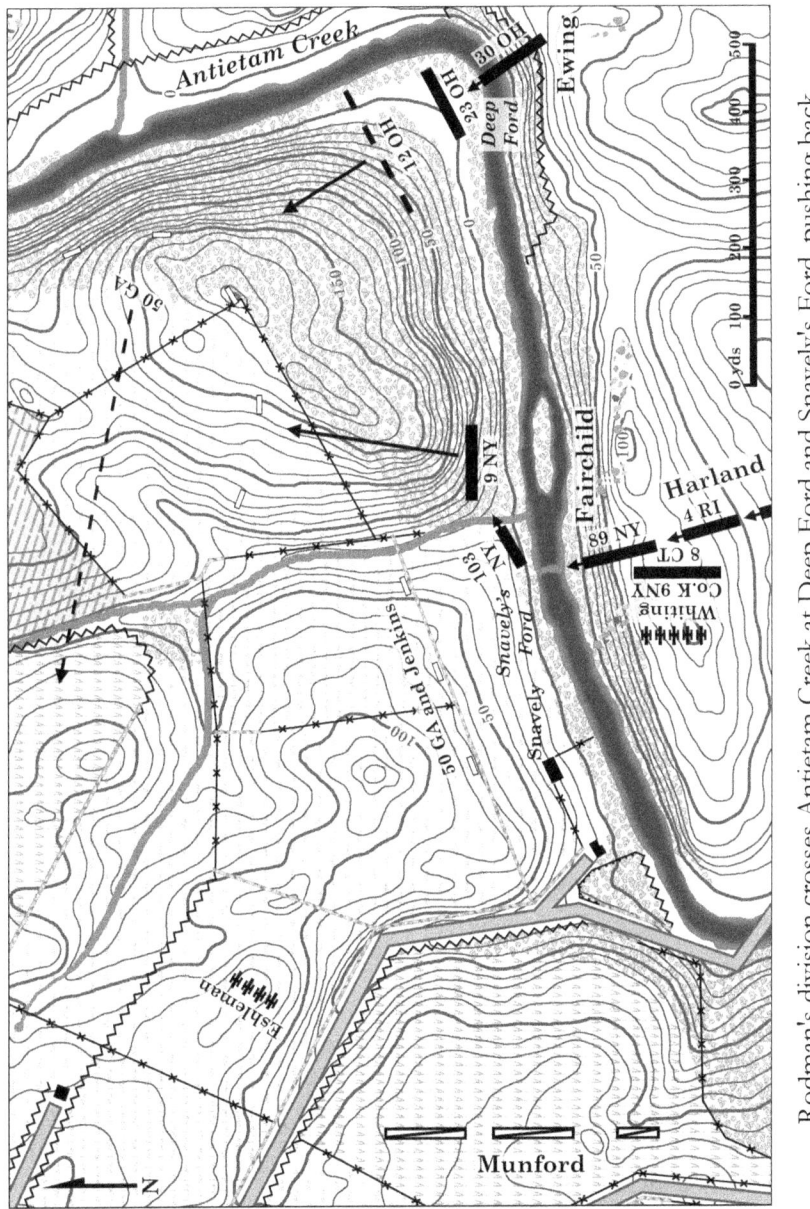

Rodman's division crosses Antietam Creek at Deep Ford and Snavely's Ford, pushing back Confederate skirmishers opposing them.

no limbers, the ammunition being carried in an army wagon, together with the rifles of the men, who, when not acting as artillery, served as infantry. After crossing the stream Whiting found the ground too rough for the movement of his guns, he could not supply them with ammunition and was ordered to recross the stream and rejoin the command by way of the bridge. He followed the bank of the stream, under the bluff, to the right, and crossed at the ford 680 yards above Snavely's. When nearing the bridge Burnside was met, who ordered Whiting to leave his guns behind, under guard, get the rifles from the wagons, cross the bridge and report to Cox, all of which was done, but it was late in the day.

Three divisions of the Ninth Corps had now been thrown across the Antietam and formed in one curved line; the left resting on the stream, at its bend below the bridge, the right on the Sharpsburg road, close to the stream, 300 yards north of the bridge. Sturgis' Division, supported by Crook's Brigade, was on the right; Rodman's Division, supported by Ewing's Brigade on the left. It would have been well if they had been in condition to go forward; both Burnside and Cox say they were not: "The ammunition of Sturgis and Crook's men had been nearly exhausted, and it was imperative that they should be freshly supplied before entering into another engagement. Sturgis also reported his men so exhausted by their efforts as to be unfit for an immediate advance." On this Cox, who had accompanied the troops across the bridge, sent to Burnside the request that Willcox's Division be sent over, with an ammunition train, and that Sturgis' Division be replaced by the fresh troops, remaining, however, on the west side of the stream as support to the others. "This was done as rapidly as was possible," says Cox, "when everything had to pass down the steep hill road and through so narrow defile as the bridge." Meanwhile McClellan, abandoning effort on every other part of the field and holding Pleasonton in check, was sending Burnside pressing orders to advance, but offered him no assisting hand, although in his order of 9:10 a.m. he gave him the positive assurance that when he should have uncovered the middle bridge he would be supported, and, if necessary, on his own line of attack. Pleasonton had crossed the middle bridge, there was no obstacle to the prompt support of Burnside, the way was open, and when Pleasonton suggested lending a helping hand it was determined not to do so.

Willcox's Division, which had now been joined the three regiments detached the night before for service on Elk Ridge and was about three-fourths of a mile from the bridge, went up the road, over the bridge and along the Sharpsburg road to near where it leaves the creek and turns northwest. The division had two brigades commanded by Colonel B. C. Christ and Thomas Welsh, of the 50th and 45th Pennsylvania respectively. In Christ's Brigade were 28th Massachusetts, 17th Michigan, 79th New York, and 50th Pennsylvania. Welsh had the 8th Michigan, 46th New York,

Brigadier General Orlando B. Willcox
Photographed after promotion to Major General
Library of Congress

45th and 100th Pennsylvania. Captain Asa McCook's 8th Massachusetts battery accompanied the division; Benjamin's Battery remaining east of the Antietam. The head of the division crossed the bridge about 2 o'clock. Crook's Brigade was in support. After Willcox had crossed the bridge, the 51st Pennsylvania and 51st New York, which had remained in the road near the bridge, ascended the high ground and took position on the left of the 21st and 35th Massachusetts, the line being in rear of Rodman's right.

The road from the bridge to Sharpsburg runs along an open hollow or ravine, which winds along to the village, overlooked by the heights to the right and left. Once on the heights, the country is rolling and with many field fences, some of which were of stone. The Confederate skirmishers were posted behind these fences as well as haystacks, which also, with orchards and cornfields, served to conceal their lines. Batteries of field guns commanded the road and hollow down to the Antietam and the whole plateau above was swept by cross fire of artillery. Such was the character of the ground over which Willcox was obliged to pass, but we must now get a more extended view of the field over which the entire Ninth Corps is to move and the Confederate dispositions to hold it.

If the reader consults the map he will see that that portion of the field of battle south of Sharpsburg and west of the Antietam is included by the Boonsboro and Harper's Ferry roads, running at nearly right angles to each other and the southeast quarter of the village lies in the angle. Cemetery hill lies east of the village and descends sharply east and south, on the south to a broad ravine, or hollow, through which runs a spring-branch from the village to the Antietam, which it reaches about 375 yards above the bridge. The road to the bridge runs over the southwest slope of the hill, then crosses the spring-branch and follows it on the west side until it reaches the Antietam, which it follows and overlooks to the bridge. From the hollow south of Cemetery hill the ground again rises to a ridge running southwest gradually widening to a plateau along which runs, south, the road from Sharpsburg to Harper's Ferry. From the hollow through which runs the branch and the road to the bridge are ravines running southwest, gradually narrowing and terminating before reaching the Harper's Ferry road. These ravines are deep near the hollow with rounded beds and capable of concealing an entire army corps. The plateau along which runs the road to Harper's Ferry is 40 to 70 feet higher than the ridge upon and behind which the Ninth Corps deployed, completely commands it, and is favorable to the movement of artillery. From this road to the Antietam, where the bridge crosses, is 1,360 yards, and it is 940 yards from the road to where the batteries of Durell and Clark took position. The intervening ground was open, with plowed ground, grass fields and cornfields.

The defense of this part of the field was entrusted to General D. R. Jones's Division of six brigades—Toombs', Drayton's, Garnett's, Jenkins',

The stone house and mill along the bridge road as seen by the 45th Pennsylvania as it charged the Confederates occupying them. *History of the Forty-fifth Regiment Pennsylvania Veteran Volunteer Infantry.*

G. T. Anderson's and Kemper's—the Washington Artillery Battalion of four batteries—Squires', Miller's, Richardson's and Eshleman's—Frobel's Battalion of Hood's Division, three batteries—Garden's and Bachman's of South Carolina and Reilly's of North Carolina—Eubank's Battery of S. D. Lee's Battalion, and Brown's Battery (Wise Artillery) of D. R. Jones's Division, in all 9 batteries aggregating 40 guns.

The position selected for Jones' Division and the artillery was Cemetery hill and the ridge running southwest to the Harper's Ferry road, the right of the division and the entire army—Kemper's brigade—being about 175 yards from the Harper's Ferry road. There were some changes of position made earlier in the day, but at 3 o'clock when the Ninth Corps was about to advance Jones' had on Cemetery hill, 4 guns of Moody's Battery, 4 guns of Squires', 6 guns of Garden's and the brigades of Garnett and Jenkins. Moody's guns and 2 of Squires' with Garnett's Brigade were engaged with the Union advance from the middle bridge, while 2 of Squires' guns and all of Garden's were firing at the troops that had crossed the Burnside bridge; and in advance, on the southeast slope of the hill were the 17th South Carolina and Holcombe Legion, of Evans' Brigade, with a detachment, under Captain Twiggs, of G. T. Anderson's Brigade. Across the Burnside bridge road and the spring-branch, on the crest of the ridge running southwest and a short distance to the right of the southwest corner of Avey's orchard were Brown's 4 guns and 2 of Reilly's, and about 100 yards in rear of a stone and rail fence that ran on the crest of the ridge were the brigades of Drayton and Kemper, in a deep ravine, and now on the point of ascending to the fence above them. The number of men at this time with the two brigades was about 560. The 15th South Carolina, Colonel W. D. DeSaussure, of Drayton's Brigade, was deployed as skirmishers, covering the ravine and road to the bridge. In front of this position, about 750 yards southeast, near the middle of a 40 acre cornfield, were the 15th Georgia, Colonel W. T. Millican, and 17th Georgia, Captain J. A. McGregor, of Toombs' Brigade, and five companies of the 11th Georgia, Major F. W. Little, of G. T. Anderson's Brigade, all under command of Colonel H. L. Benning. What was left of the 500 men who had defended the bridge joined Benning a few minutes later. About 450 yards in rear of Benning, deployed along a rail fence bounding a small cornfield on the east, and about 230 yards from the Harper's Ferry road, was the 7th Virginia, 113 men, Captain Philip S. Ashby, and 340 yards, farther to the right, behind a stone fence on the Harper's Ferry road, was the 24th Virginia, 150 men, Colonel W. R. Perry. About 375 yards in front of the 24th Virginia was Captain B. F. Eshleman's Battery of 4 guns. Richardson's Battery which had been driven back at 1 p.m. and retreated through Sharpsburg, when Toombs abandoned the bridge, had one gun disabled, but his section of howitzers was put in position on the west of the Harper's Ferry road a short distance south of

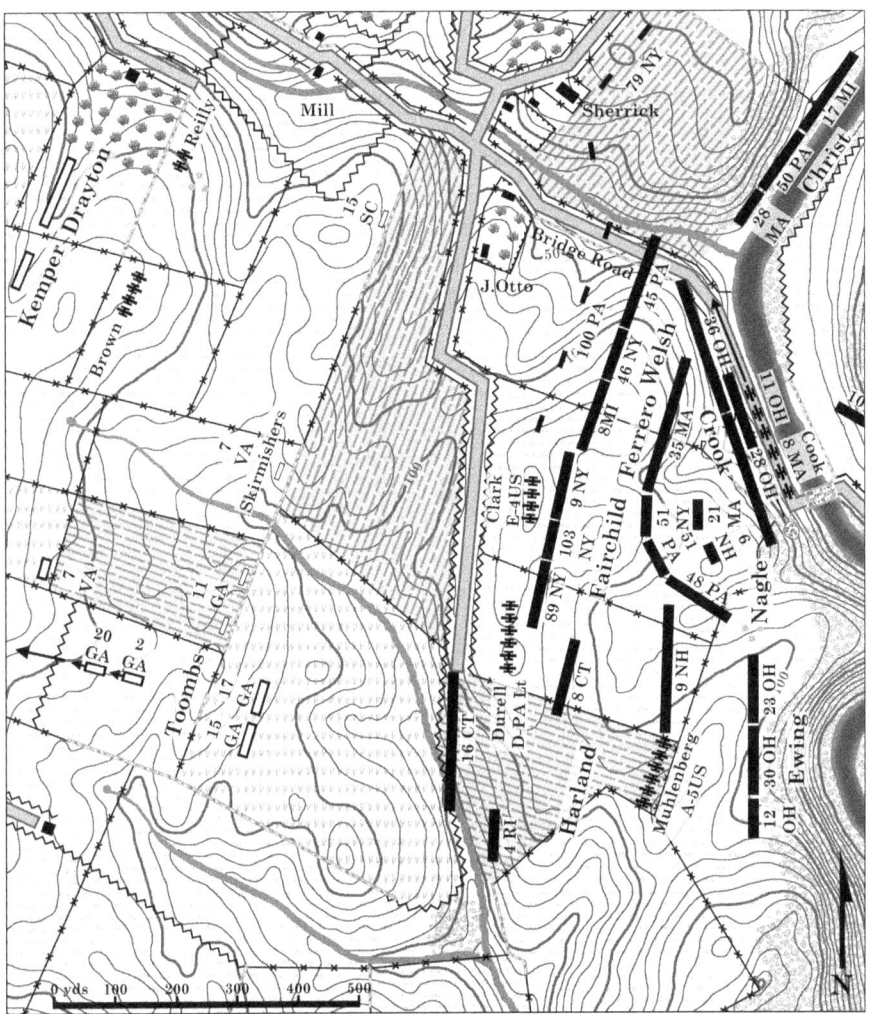

The Ninth Corps formed and ready to advance during the afternoon. The 2nd and 20th Georgia fall back to replenish their ammunition. The location of the 7th Virginia skirmishers is approximate.

Sharpsburg, where, a little later, Richardson, having received ammunition and repaired his disabled gun, joined his howitzer section and reported to Toombs. To the right and rear of the line was Munford's Cavalry Brigade, Munford having his headquarters at the Blackford house, where, at this hour, he greeted A. P. Hill, whose advance was coming upon the field. D. R. Jones had for the defense of his line, the extreme right of the army, about 2,785 infantry, 430 artillery, with 28 guns, and the cavalry of Munford, but Garnett's Brigade, of 260 men and 6 guns, had their hands full with the Union troops moving from the middle bridge upon the eastern slope of Cemetery Hill. During the engagement about to open, and about at its opening, A. P. Hill came upon the field with 3,300 infantry and four batteries of artillery; and batteries, sections of batteries and single guns which had been in action earlier in the day, on the left and in the center and had been disabled or expended ammunition, were hastened to the threatened point, and thrown into position under the supervision of General Lee. About mid-day General Lee had sent this message to General Pendleton, commanding the Reserve Artillery at Shepherdstown Ford:

> If you have fifteen or twenty guns, suitable for our purpose, which you can spare, the general desires you to send them, with a sufficiency of ammunition. You must not take them from the fords if essential to their safety. Send up the stragglers. Take any cavalry about there and send up at the point of the sword. We want ammunition, guns, provisions.

Pendleton could not collect the stragglers, he sent up but little ammunition, and it was not until the engagement had closed that one battery arrived at Sharpsburg. Not a battery, not an infantry soldier, save as stragglers, did Lee take from his left or center to strengthen his right, he depended upon D. R. Jones and A. P. Hill, to whom he gave general directions, and upon such disabled batteries and single guns as could be gathered, and to the movement of these he gave personal attention.

We now return to the deployment of Willcox's Division and the General advance on Sharpsburg. Willcox's head of column had crossed the bridge at 2 o'clock and, upon arriving where the road leaves the creek and goes to Sharpsburg, deployed his command. Christ's Brigade filed across the hollow on the right, under artillery fire, and formed under a high bluff, on a narrow strip of low level ground bordering the Antietam, and Captain Duval's company of the 36th Ohio, which had been skirmishing in advance, on the right of the road, fell back and rejoined its regiment. After the formation of the corps line, but before the general advance was ordered, Christ's Brigade scaled the steep bluff and drew up on the crest of the high ground, the 79th New York, Lieutenant Colonel Morrison, deployed in double skirmish line,

Major General Ambrose P. Hill
Library of Congress

the 50th Pennsylvania, 28th Massachusetts, and 17th Michigan in line of battle, in order named from left to right. Here it was subjected to a severe fire from Garden's and Squires' guns in front, and suffered from a wicked enfilading fire from Brown's and Reilly's guns on the left, and the men, lying down, sought such shelter as the ground afforded, which, on the left, was very slight. Welsh formed on the heights to the left of the road, deploying the 100th Pennsylvania as skirmishers and forming the other three regiments in line, 45th Pennsylvania on the right, 46th New York, in center, and 8th Michigan on the left. In going forward to position the left of the line passed over the 35th Massachusetts of Sturgis' Division and when halted, waiting for the order to advance, the left regiment was about 100 feet on the immediate right of the 9th New York, the right regiment of Rodman's Division, and also about 160 feet in its rear. These movements were made under fire from the moment Christ began to cross the hollow or a man appeared at the crest of the high ground on either side of the road.

The disposition of the corps line being completed about 3 p.m., in accordance with instructions received from McClellan, Cox was now directed by Burnside, who had crossed the bridge to assist Cox and hasten matters, to move forward with the whole command, except Sturgis' Division, which was held in reserve, in the order in which they were formed and attack Sharpsburg and the heights on the left.

Meanwhile the Confederates kept up an incessant fire of artillery and, having the exact range of the valley and the ravines, their shells came in very fast, causing much annoyance and numerous casualties, notwithstanding the men were kept lying on the ground near the crests of the hills while the changes in the line and the partially new formation, after the arrival of Willcox's Division, were being made.

In the formation as made Willcox's Division was on the right, Christ's Brigade north and Welsh's Brigade south of the road leading to Sharpsburg, with Crook's Brigade in support to Willcox. Rodman's Division was on the left, Fairchild's Brigade joining Willcox, and Harland's Brigade having the left, with Ewing's Brigade as a support or reserve. Sturgis' Division was to hold the crest of the hill above the bridge. It was determined that Willcox, supported by Crook, should move directly upon Sharpsburg, and that Rodman, supported by Ewing, should follow the movement of Willcox, first dislodging the enemy in their immediate front, and then inclining to the right, so as to bring the left wing in echelon on the left of Willcox.

The order to advance was given by Cox at 3:15 p.m., and responded to in the most cheerful and gallant manner, officers and men moving with the greatest enthusiasm and, on the right and in the center, carrying everything before them.

The move was made as nearly simultaneous as such movements are generally made and we follow it from right to left, first accompanying

The scene that greeted Christ's brigade as they ascended the slope above Antietam Creek and reached the crest. The Sherrick farm lies in a hollow to the left, and Cemetery Hill is directly ahead. *Author's collection.*

Willcox in his successful advance to the edge of the town and the expulsion of the Confederates from Cemetery hill, and then returning to the advance of Fairchild's Brigade of Rodman's Division.

We left Christ's Brigade on the high ground east of the road, with the 79th New York deployed in double line as skirmishers. When the order was given to advance this regiment went forward and in its movement came upon the left of Poland's 2nd and 10th United States, and with its assistance drove back McMaster's small command (17th South Carolina, Holcombe Legion and Twiggs' detachment) to the small apple orchard on the southern slope of Cemetery hill and to the stone house and mill on the road to Sharpsburg, and when within 300 yards of the Confederate guns on Cemetery hill found that the brigade had failed to follow, but had halted, and that Poland's orders would not permit the further advance of the 2nd and 10th United States, upon which the regiment was halted and, lying down, continued its fire upon Moody's two guns and their infantry support. The brigade had halted because of the very severe enfilading fire of the artillery on the left, in addition to the artillery fire on Cemetery hill and that of Garnett's and Jenkins' infantry. Welsh had not yet come up on the left and for a few minutes, until he did come up, Christ was exposed to a fire of round shot, shell and canister by which he suffered severely.

Welsh had a greater distance to move and over much more difficult ground. His brigade preceded by the 100th Pennsylvania as skirmishers and supported by Crook's Ohio brigade, went forward, the 45th Pennsylvania on the right, 46th New York in the center, and 8th Michigan on its left. The 45th Pennsylvania and 46th New York, swept over the hill in their front, down into the ravine and then up the hill to the Otto buildings and apple orchard, the 45th Pennsylvania passing either side of the barn. On the left, the 8th Michigan, in starting, became involved with the 9th New York, a few files going with it, but, swinging to the right with its brigade the entire line after a short, sharp encounter, assisted by Crook, drove part of the 15th South Carolina of Drayton's Brigade, deployed as skirmishers, from a stone fence, beyond the ravine, and 130 yards from the Otto barn, and then descended into the ravine. Here the troops were somewhat crowded and the 45th Pennsylvania moved by the right flank out of the ravine, crossed the stone fence from which the 15th South Carolina skirmishers had been driven and the entire brigade became engaged with these and Jenkins' Brigade, which had taken position in the orchard on the slope of Cemetery hill, and with McMaster's command, which, driven back by Welsh and Poland had rallied in the orchard and occupied the stone house and stone mill on the road.

Meanwhile a section of Cook's Massachusetts battery under Lieutenant J. H. Coffin, was brought forward. The battery had crossed the Antietam with Willcox, four guns were halted in the road near the bridge, and two under

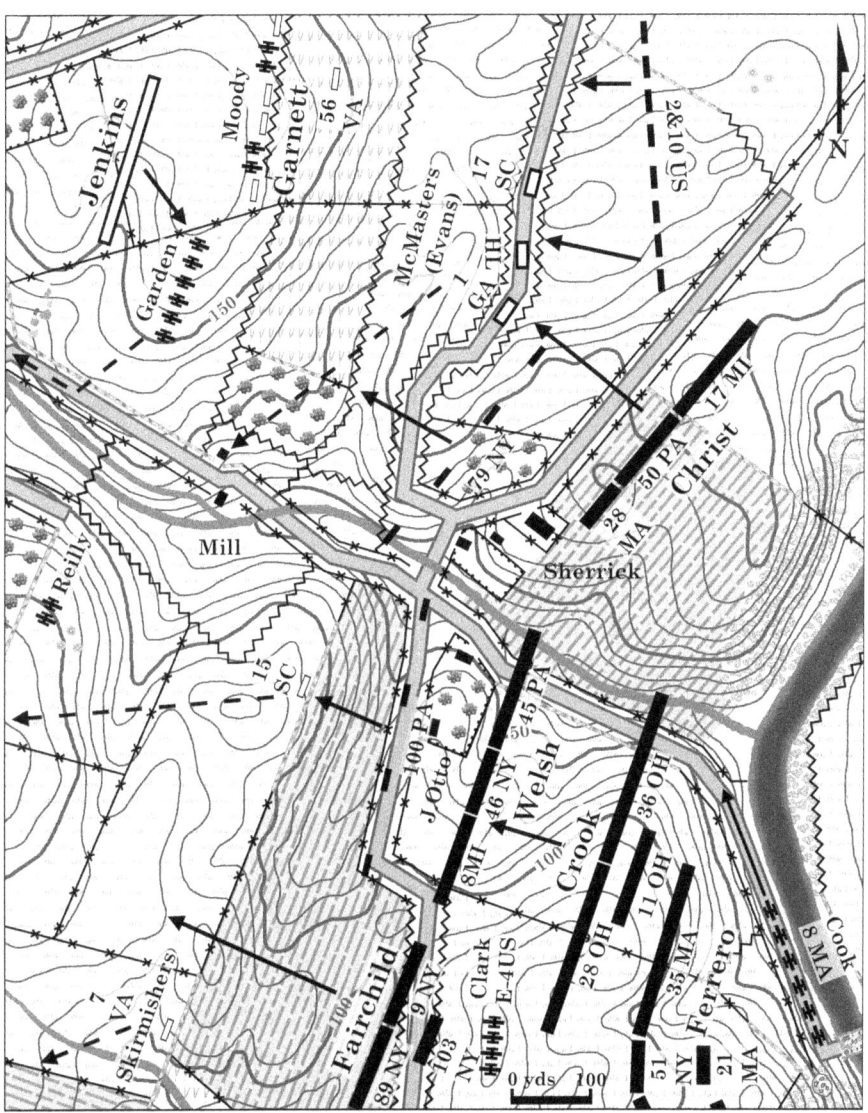

The Ninth Corps begins its advance. Willcox's division moves along the bridge road toward Sharpsburg. The two brigades push back McMaster's small command and the 15th South Carolina.
Many of the subsequent maps follow the flow of Carman's text, so are not necessarily in chronological order.

Coffin, went forward up the road, Coffin says: "200 yards in advance of the column." He went from the road, to the left, up the Otto lane and taking position in the orchard, near the barn, opened with shell upon the artillery on Cemetery hill and upon Jenkins' Brigade and McMaster, in the orchard. As we have said in the preceding chapter, Squires' two rifled guns, after shelling Willcox's advance from the bridge, had been withdrawn, because [they were] out of ammunition, and Jenkins' Brigade, which was supporting them, then advanced "some 400 yards in an apple orchard, under a heavy fire of artillery and small arms." Colonel Joseph Walker, commanding the brigade, threw out the 1st, 5th and 6th South Carolina and engaged Christ on his left, and the Palmetto Sharpshooters and 2nd South Carolina Rifles in front and to the right to meet Welsh and "from this position," says Walker, "we continued to pour a destructive fire into the ranks of the enemy, a short range."

Garden's South Carolina battery of 12-pounders, which had been placed east of the road, just north of the stone house, in full view of the long range guns beyond the Antietam, came under their accurate and destructive fire that they could not return, but opened upon Willcox's infantry as it crossed the bridge and during its advance up the road, over the hill, and while ascending the elevation on which the battery was posted. Garden's ammunition had now run out; Lieutenant S. M. Pringle had been mortally wounded, several men wounded and many horses killed, one of his guns dismounted, the carriage being entirely destroyed, another rendered useless by the bursting of a shell, and the remaining guns were run down the hill by hand to a ravine in the rear, the disabled guns were then hauled off, the horses attached, and the entire battery entering the road, one gun without wheels, but dragging the ground, went through Sharpsburg, barely escaping the men of Welsh's Brigade, who had now reached Avey's orchard, almost in its rear, and some of whom were running forward to the street down which it retired.

Meanwhile Welsh had pressed forward; the 45th Pennsylvania obliqued across the road and, with the assistance of Christ, who had now advanced to the Sherrick's lane, on his right and rear, on high ground, and the forward movement of the rest of the brigade on the left, forced Jenkins' Brigade back and the 45th, supported by a part of the 100th Pennsylvania, after a sharp and severe fire from the stone mill and house, by which it lost several men, carried them and took a number of prisoners, among them Captain Twiggs, who had been wounded. Meanwhile Fairchild had driven back Kemper and Drayton, and as Jenkins was over the hill and out of sight, Welsh moved his entire brigade forward and to the left, into Avey's orchard where he joined a part of Fairchild, and prepared to engage Jenkins, who was now seen on his right and enfilading him, and to advance into the town. Skirmishers were then thrown forward to the first street and some of

Garden's Battery position on the southern edge of Cemetery Hill. Across the wooded hollow in the center is the hill where Fairchild's brigade drove Kemper and Drayton's from the stone wall. *Author's collection.*

them went beyond, one of whom was killed in the street running north from Avey's house.

Jenkins' Brigade fell back over the hill about 300 yards to the edge of the town and changed front to the right, parallel and close to the Burnside bridge road, his right looking down the first street of the town, and the entire brigade overlooking the low ground beyond which was Avey's orchard. Walker gives reasons for falling back to this position: "Perceiving that the enemy had advanced three heavy columns some 400 yards in rear of the brigade and to the right across a ravine leading up from the creek, and was steadily driving back the brigades of Generals Kemper and Drayton, I moved the brigade into line parallel with the turnpike [bridge road] and ravine and near to the latter, and opened a destructive enfilade fire upon the enemy." This position the brigade maintained; its day's losses were 26 killed and 184 wounded. Among the killed were two captains of the Palmetto Sharpshooters; five officers were seriously wounded, two of whom were commanding regiments.

Jenkins' Brigade having been driven out of range, Coffin now directed the fire of his two guns on the right section of Moody's Battery and at the same time Christ, who had been severely engaged with Jenkins and also suffering from the fire of Moody's section and its supporting infantry, charged it with the 17th Michigan (this being the regiment immediately in front), supported by the 50th Pennsylvania and 28th Massachusetts, but when within 100 yards of the guns, which were then retiring, and covered by a hill which prevented the advance from shooting either the horses or their riders, the guns escaped, and the charging party was ordered back, an order very reluctantly obeyed the 17th Michigan, who saw that Cemetery hill had been abandoned, but Christ "did not deem it prudent to advance after the artillery had retired, for the reason that the woods were lined with sharpshooters" and he could only have exposed his command without gaining anything, so the charging party was withdrawn and remained with the brigade, until the entire command was ordered to fall back.

As stated in the preceding chapter the pressure of the regular infantry on the Boonsboro and Sharpsburg road, the advance of Willcox's Division and Fairchild's Brigade from the south and in rear forced Garnett and S. D. Lee to abandon Cemetery hill. Both claim that they could have held ground against the advance of the regular infantry, but that the movement to their right and rear endangered their escape. S. D. Lee made an effort to check this Union movement and to support Jenkins' Brigade.

Just before he withdrew Moody's Battery, Lee requested Captain T. H. Carter to take position with his battery about 130 yards in Moody's rear and, facing Cox's advance, open fire upon it. Carter had been engaged earlier in the afternoon at the Sunken Road, and just before receiving Lee's request had, with three rifled guns of his own battery and the assistance of

The farthest advance of Willcox's Division. When Harland and Fairchild gave way to the left, the division was enfiladed by the increasing numbers of Confederate artillery arriving and deploying along the Harper's Ferry Road. Cox ordered the division to withdraw.

two rifled guns of Brooks' South Carolina battery, under Lieutenant William Elliott, opened fire "upon an imposing force of Yankees" which had "advanced in fine style" upon the right of D. R. Jones' Division. Carter moved to the position designated by Lee, on the hill about 100 yards south of the Sharpsburg road and 300 yards east of the Lutheran Church, and overlooking Jenkins' Brigade, but before he could get his guns in position, there was such a heavy reverse artillery fire poured upon him from the long-range guns beyond the Antietam, that he found the position untenable, and Lee advised him to withdraw. A little later, Colonel Walker, having sent for artillery to assist his brigade, Boyce's South Carolina battery then on Cemetery ridge, north of the road, was ordered to report to him. Boyce crossed the road, east of the church, as ordered, but could find no one there to give him information as to who gave him the orders or what was required. Boyce says: "This was late in the afternoon, and the battle soon ended."

In its early advance, Willcox's Division was closely supported by Crook's Brigade which moved on the left of the road. It assisted in driving the skirmishers of the 15th South Carolina from the stone fences behind Otto's and, when Welsh moved forward, the 28th and 36th Ohio charged across the ravine, under a heavy fire of artillery from the front and left, from which Colonel Melvin Clarke of the 36th was killed, in the ravine, parts of the two regiments went beyond the stone fence but were soon recalled to it, and the 11th Ohio was halted in Otto's lane, south of the barn, to command the ravine leading to the left, where A. P. Hill's attack was now developing. We have now accompanied Willcox and Crook to their extreme advance, have seen the artillery and Garnett's Brigade abandon Cemetery hill, Jenkins' Brigade driven back to the edge of the town and now return to Fairchild's Brigade, that advanced on Willcox's left, and of which we have had an occasional glimpse, as its movements assisted Welsh and stopped the enfilading artillery fire that temporarily checked Christ.

Fairchild's Brigade was composed of the 9th New York (Hawkins' Zouaves), Lieutenant Colonel Edgar A. Kimball; 89th New York, Major Edward Jardine, of the 9th, and 103rd New York, Major Benjamin Ringold. It was a well drilled, disciplined brigade and had seen much and varied service in North Carolina and elsewhere, and carried into the battle about 940 officers and men. In coming upon the field it took position immediately in rear of the advanced high ridge upon which were the batteries of Clark and Durell, its right about 200 yards south of the Otto house and about 100 feet from the left of Willcox's Division, its left opposite the northeast corner of the 40 acre cornfield. The 9th New York was on the right, its left in rear and very close to Clark's Battery and, with it, under a merciless fire of shot and shell, killing and wounding a number of

The Otto house. *Scott Felsen.*

men, and of which Lieutenant M. J. Graham, of the 9th, says that Clark's Battery,

> did not appear to do so much in the way of firing, as it seemed to me that every time they would get fairly at work, the rebels would concentrate such a fire on them as to silence them, and the men would be obliged to lie down in such shelter as they could get, until the weight of the enemy's fire was directed to another part of the line. Their 'park' was on a lower level, and almost in line with, and in rear of the battery, and it caught a good deal of the fire that missed the battery. The practice of the rebel artillerymen was something wonderful in its accuracy; they dropped shot and shell right into our line repeatedly. They kept the air fairly filled with missiles of every variety...The shrapnel or canister was very much in evidence...I watched solid shot—round shot—strike with what sounded like an innocent thud in front of the guns, bounding over battery and park, fly through the tree tops, cutting some of them off so suddenly that they seemed to me they lingered for an instant undecided which way to fall. These round shot did not appear to be in a hurry. They came along slowly and deliberately, apparently, and there appeared no horror in them until they hit something.

Clark's Battery and the 9th New York were not alone the recipients of this artillery fire, it was received on the left by Durell's Battery also, and the other regiments of the brigade, the 103rd New York being in the center of the line, between Clark and Durell, though a little retired, under the crest of the ridge, and the 89th in rear of Durell's Battery, which was on the ridge a few yards to the right of the 40 acre cornfield. The fire poured upon this line came from six guns of Brown's and Reilly's batteries, on the heights between it and Sharpsburg and from Richardson's Battery beyond the Harper's Ferry road, which, earlier in the day, occupied the position now held by Clark's Battery.

All this time, while the firing was increasing in severity and its range more accurate, the field officers were walking up and down the rear of the line, waiting impatiently for the order to advance. At length General Rodman came up, and, after surveying the Confederate position for a moment, sent forward a company of each regiment as skirmishers, these had scarcely gone forward and engaged the skirmishers of the 7th Virginia, behind a stone fence, when Willcox was seen to move on the right, and Rodman ordered Fairchild to advance; the regimental commanders received and repeated the order, the men sprang to their feet and under the heavy artillery fire went on to and down the ridge; the 9th New York being the battalion of direction, the objective point Brown's and Reilly's six guns and

Clark's Battery E, 4th United States on the hill overlooking the Otto 40-acre cornfield. *Author's collection.*

the bold elevation upon which they were in position, the distance being about 800 yards from Clark's Battery. It descended the slope and went over the fences of Otto's lane. The 89th on the left passing to the right of the cornfield, while the 9th on the right, becoming slightly involved with the 8th Michigan of Welsh's Brigade which had advanced at Manly at the same time, but this was promptly rectified, the Michigan men swinging to the right, and the entire brigade, went down into a plowed ravine under fire of artillery and skirmishers of the 7th Virginia, and, after advancing about 200 yards, Fairchild ordered a charge and, with a wild hurrah, the men started on a double quick, ascended out of the ravine and went over the stone and rail fences that extended along the west edge of the 40 acre cornfield down to the Burnside bridge road at Otto's, captured the skirmishers of the 7th Virginia at the fence and drove the regiment to the left and back to the Harper's Ferry road, receiving its fire but not returning it. As they climbed the fence shell fell fast along the whole line from the batteries in front and from McIntosh's Battery that had come upon the field and taken position at the Blackford house about 1,500 yards to the left. One shell killed 8 men of the 9th New York and round shot carried away men's heads and crashed through their bodies, reminding one of the officers, at the moment, of Lannes' description of the battle of Austerlitz: "I could hear the bones crack in my division like glass in a hailstorm." A few yards beyond the fence and in a depression the brigade was halted to rest and dress the line, although dressing was not necessary, for the moment the line halted every man was in his place, but it had been much shortened, and its dead and wounded marked the steps of its advance. Full one fourth of the brigade had fallen. No enemy save the 7th Virginia was yet to be seen and another elevation was before it. With but a moment to draw breath it again went forward under the fire of the merciless guns, now using both shell and canister, making great gaps in the line, and descended into a slight vale, halted a minute or two to draw breath and gather strength for the final struggle with a foe whom they had not yet seen, but who were known to be at the crest of the hill, in support to the six guns, that were yet exploding shrapnel into the ranks.

This hill is a broad spur of the plateau along which runs the Harper's Ferry road, and terminates at the spring-branch which runs from the town through a ravine to the Antietam. From this spring-branch there was a stone fence running southwest on this hill or spur, bounding Avey's orchard on the east, for a distance of 300 yards to its highest point, which is over 80 feet higher than the spring-branch, when a stout post and rail fence continues in the same southwest direction. This elevation is some 70 feet higher than the depression where Fairchild had now halted to draw breath. Kemper's and Drayton's brigades had been lying in a ravine beyond this spur, and 100 yards from the fence, well sheltered from artillery fire.

Looking from Clark's Battery E, 4th United States toward Drayton and Kemper's Brigades on the opposite slope. The Otto 40-acre cornfield is to the left. The 9th New York monument is barely visible to the right of the center tree. *Author's collection.*

Brown's Battery was still engaging Clark's Battery, which, by its fire, was covering Fairchild's advance, when, knowing that Fairchild was advancing, Kemper and Drayton ordered their men up the hill to the fences. Kemper was on the right, his left, the 11th Virginia, Major Adam Clement, rested at the point where the stone and rail fences united; and on its right was the 1st Virginia, Colonel W. H. Palmer, and on the right of the 1st, was the 17th Virginia, Colonel M. D. Corse. The three regiments had an aggregate of about 210 officers and men. Drayton's Brigade, formed on Kemper's left, the right of the 51st Georgia at the point where the stone and rail fences united, its left the 15th South Carolina, Colonel W. D. DeSaussure, extending down the hill in skirmishing order, and principally employed in opposing the advance of Welsh. On the immediate left of the 51st Georgia was the 3rd South Carolina Battalion. of 17 men. The brigade numbered about 380 men; the aggregate of the two brigades about 590 officers and men. They came into position under a severe fire from Clark's guns and from those of Benjamin beyond the Antietam, by which Captain J. T. Burke and Lieutenant F. B. Littleton of the 17th Virginia were killed. Fairchild was now reported advancing up the hill; Captain J. S. Brown of the battery was wounded, and his four guns, moving to the right, across the field, gained the Harper's Ferry road and went through Sharpsburg. Reilly's two guns went through a gateway of the fence and through the town, and the Union artillery soon ceased firing. Kemper's men rested their rifles on the lower rails of the fence and Drayton's on top of the stone wall. The hill shut out the view but the commands of the Union officers, the clanking of equipment, and the steady tramp of the approaching line was easily distinguishable.

Fairchild made but a brief halt, and in beautiful line, as well dressed as on parade, the brigade began the ascent of the hill, at a quick step, but the line had been much shortened and did not now number over 700 men, nearly a third had fallen. Not a shot had been fired, but the muskets were loaded and bayonets fixed, and the orders were that not a shot was to be fired until orders were given to do so, then to deliver a volley and charge with the bayonet. Brown's and Reilly's guns were now getting out of the way, but the line was enfiladed by Richardson's Battery on the left, and Clark's friendly guns were firing over it at the enemy on the hill top. Clark's fire soon ceased and as the brigade appeared at the crest of the hill, and the clear sky showed behind the heads and shoulders of the men, there was a crash of musketry from Kemper and Drayton that sent down scores of men in every regiment, and was particularly destructive to the 9th New York, that had come up in front of the stone fence, behind which and about 50 yards distant was the right of Drayton's Brigade. The entire color guard of that regiment went down and the colors lay on the ground. "one or two of the men staggered to their feet and reached for the colors, but were shot down

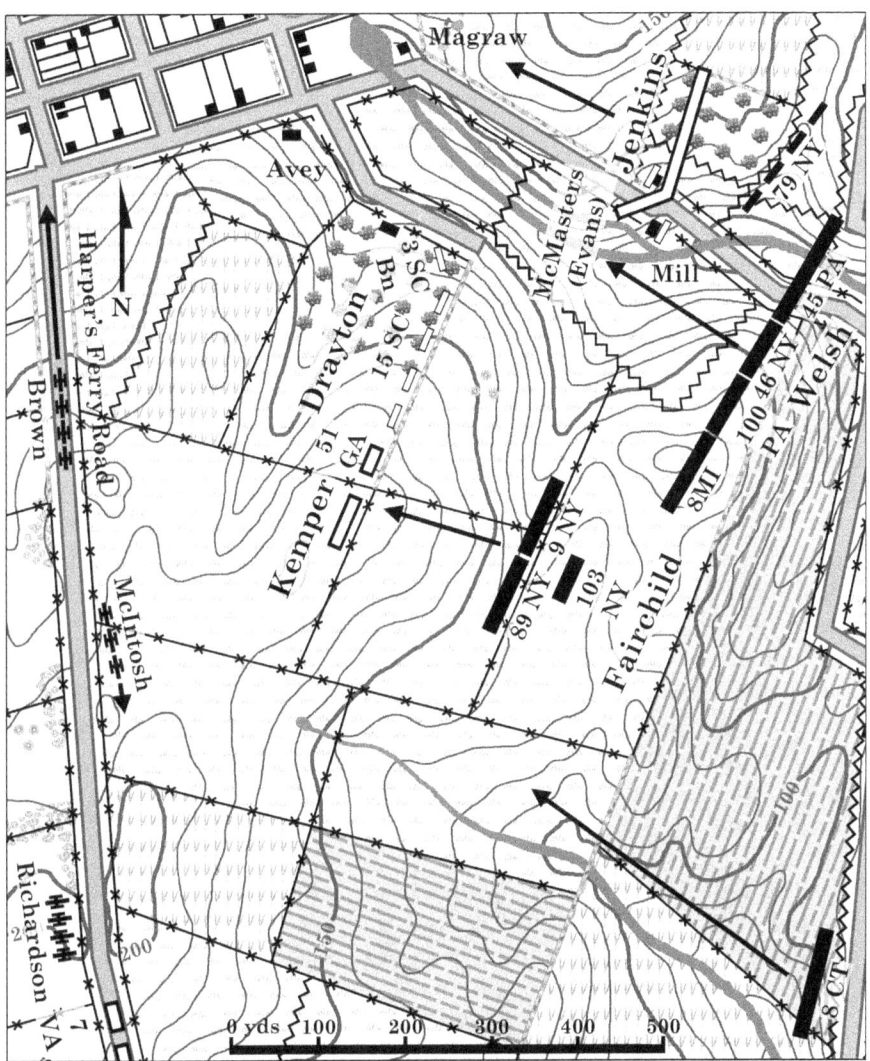

Fairchild's brigade charges Kemper and Drayton at the stone wall. Welsh's brigade pushes up the bridge road, pushes back Jenkin's Brigade, and captures the stone house and mill.

at once. Then there was what seemed a spontaneous rush for them by a dozen or more from several companies, who were shot down in succession as each one raised his flag. The flags were up and down, up and down, several times in a minutes. Lieutenant Sebastian Meyers was hit just as he picked up one of them."

The men had now lain down and opened fire. At last Captain Adolphus Le Baire seized one of the colors, and, swinging it around his head, shouted to his company, to get up and follow him; Captain Lawrence Leahy seized the other color; the entire regiment rose to its feet, and, officers in front, charged to the stone fence, across which there was short struggle, in which bayonets were used, and Drayton's men were routed, some of them captured, and the rest pursued through Avey's orchard, where Welsh came up, on the right. Some of Drayton's men escaped by the ravine to the Harper's Ferry road. Some of the 9th New York with others of Welsh's Brigade pushed clear into Sharpsburg, one was killed in the street, a number were captured. There were still about 100 men left in the regiment and these Kimball rallied on the colors at the fence, and with difficulty recalled those who had gone down the ravine. The 103rd New York, in the center, in its advance and from the first volley, lost over one half of its men, and did not reach the fence in the final charge, but halted within 50 feet of it, when it was seen that the enemy had retreated. On the left the 89th New York had a severe engagement with the right of Kemper's line, which it overlapped. Colonel Corse, commanding the 17th Virginia (9 officers and 46 men), the extreme right, says he, "engaged the enemy at a distance of 50 or 60 yards," and that his regiment, "came directly opposite the colors of the regiment to which it was opposed, consequently being overlapped by them, as far as I could judge, at least 100 yards." The historian of that regiment says:

> The first thing we saw appear was the gilt eagle that surmounts the pole, then the top of the flag, next the flutter of the stars and stripes itself, slowly mounting, up it rose, then their hats came in sight, still rising the faces emerged, next a range of curious eyes appeared, then such a hurrah as only the Yankee troops could give, broke the stillness, and they surged against us. 'Keep cool men, don't fire yet,' shouted Colonel Corse, and such was their perfect discipline that not a gun replied, but when the bayonets flashed against the hill-top, the 46 muskets exploded at once, and sent a leaden shower full in the breasts of the attacking force, not over 60 yards distant. It staggered them, it was a murderous fire, and many fell, some of them struck for the rear, but the majority sent us a stunning volley, and but for the fence, there would have been hardly a man left alive. The rails, the posts, were shattered by the balls, but still it was a deadly one, fully one half of the

Drayton's view of Fairchild's advance. The poignant description in the 17th Virginia's regimental history of the Union flags and hats cresting the slope occurred here. *Author's collection.*

17th lay in their tracks, the balance that is left, load and fire again, and for about ten minutes the unequal struggle is kept up...the combatants not over 30 yards apart...Our colonel falls wounded, every officer except five [2] of the 17th is shot down, of the 46 muskets 35 [24][4] are dead, dying or struck down.

The 89th New York rushed to the fence and 10 of the Virginians are captured, and then escaped. Colonel Corse was taken prisoner, but, soon after, was rescued by Toombs' Brigade. All of Kemper's Brigade had now been routed.

As a regiment, the 89th, with its colors, remained at the fence, but many men went over and down into the hollow and up to a rock ledge on the other side, some pushed forward up the hill to the edge of the town and not much over 300 yards from the town square. The entire regiment would have gone forward, but some Confederates were rallying with the apparent intention of turning its left upon which Major Jackson charged with the bayonet and drove them to the Harper's Ferry road, and then fell back under orders and rejoined the brigade which was ordered to withdraw to the ravine near Otto's, about 400 yards in the rear. The men went back with curses on their lips for those who had mismanaged affairs on this part of the field and Kimball reports, "with tears in their eyes at the necessity which compelled them to leave the field they had so dearly won."

From the time of its advance to the rout of the Confederates from the fences the brigade occupied about 30 minutes and lost nearly half its men. Including the few men lost early in the morning and before the charge 87 were killed, 321 wounded and 47 missing, an aggregate of 455, or 48 4/10 per cent of the 940 carried into action. The 9th New York had 373 in action, as officially reported, 45 were killed, 174 wounded, 14 missing, an aggregate of 235, or 63 per cent; the historian of the regiment says it had 54 killed (including mortally wounded), 158 wounded, and 28 missing, an aggregate of 240, or 64 1/3 per cent. The 103rd New York lost 117 or 58 1/2 per cent, and the 89th New York 103, or 28 per cent.

The Confederate loss was not so heavy, the fences were a great protection, the total loss of Drayton and Kemper was 102 killed and wounded and 20 missing, the greatest loss was that of the 17th Virginia 8 killed, 23 wounded and 10 missing, an aggregate of 41, or over 74 1/2 per cent; in killed and wounded alone, 56 1/3 per cent.

D. R. Jones, the Confederate division commander reports that

> The enemy advanced in enormous masses to the assault of the heights. Sweeping up to the crest, they were mowed down by Brown's Battery,

---

[4] Carman added the modifications to the casualties.

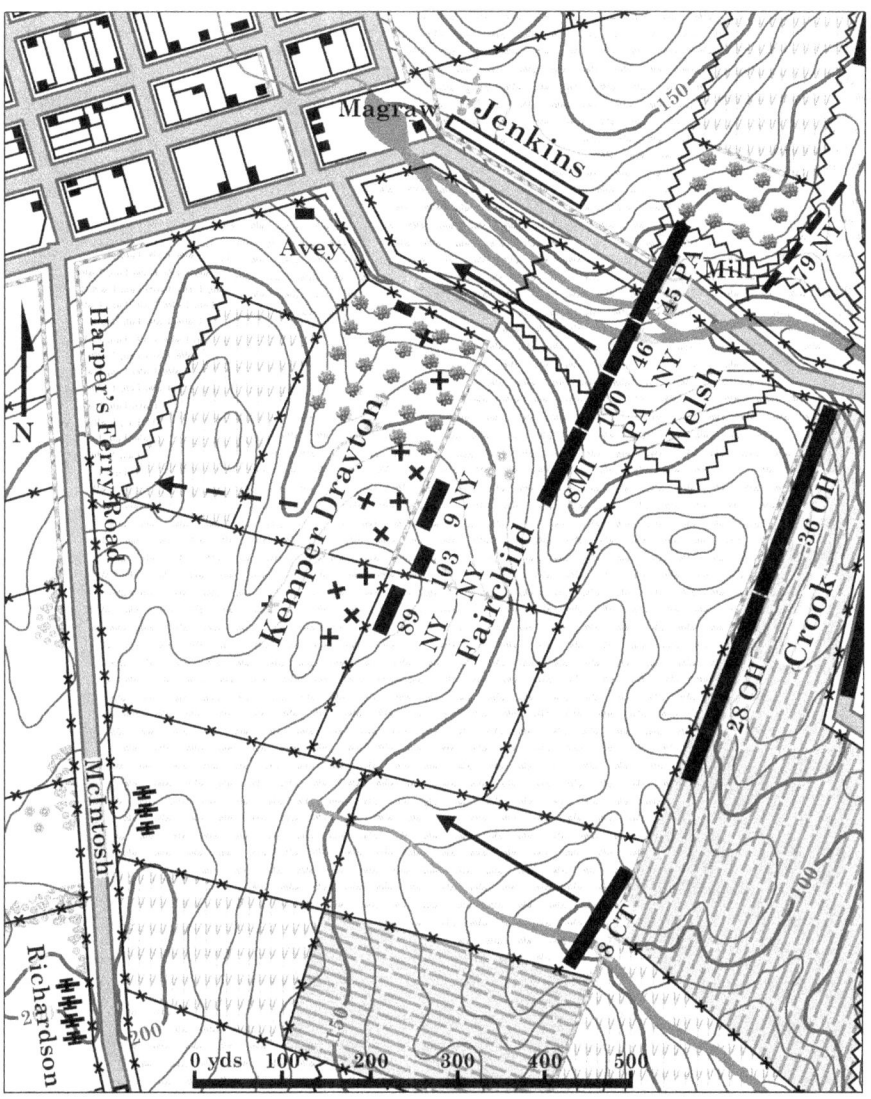

Kemper and Drayton are forced back from the stone wall. Individual groups of men pursue them into the ravine below and beyond. The 8th Connecticut moves up the low ground to their left.

the heroic commander of which had been wounded but a few moments before. They over came the tough resistance offered by the feeble forces opposed to them and gained the heights...Kemper and Drayton were driven back through the town. The 15th South Carolina, Colonel DeSaussaure, fell back very slowly and in order, forming the nucleus on which the brigade rallied.

All was now confusion in the town; artillery was dashing to the rear, through the rough and narrow streets, stragglers from the left, in squads, men of Garland's and Colquitt's brigades, who had been driven from Cemetery ridge by the 4th United States Infantry, men of Kemper and Drayton, and Garnett who were retreating from Cemetery hill, filled the streets, broken in organization; Jones, Kemper, Drayton, Garnett and other officers endeavoring to rally them. Earlier in the afternoon General Lee had been near Reel's directing affairs on the left and at the Sunken Road. When the advance of the Ninth Corps became serious he rode to the high ground near his headquarters, where he met A. P. Hill and gave him instructions, and ordered every gun that had wheels and horses to the south of the town; now that his right was broken, he directed that every man that could be gathered should be sent out on the Harper's Ferry road, to unite with Toombs, who had been ordered to join Kemper's right, and he rode into town and gave his personal assistance in stopping stragglers and rallying the broken commands. Drayton's men were rallied on the colors of the 15th South Carolina, in the road, just out of town, a few men of Kemper's Brigade were rallied on their colors, which were conspicuously displayed in the road, and Toombs was seen coming down the road, as the 8th Connecticut mad its appearance on the high ground from which Kemper had been driven but a little nearer the road and farther south.

When the order was given Rodman's Division to advance, Harland's Brigade was on the left of Fairchild, the 8th Connecticut, on its right, a little to the left and rear of Fairchild, overlooking the northeast corner of the 40 acre cornfield, the 16th Connecticut in the cornfield, into which it had entered at the northeast corner, and the 4th Rhode Island approaching to move on the left of the 16th Connecticut. When making dispositions for the advance, Major Thomas W. Lion of the staff, who had carried instructions to the left of the line, rode up to Harland and reported and reported that he and officers of Scammon's Brigade had seen Confederate infantry (Gregg's Brigade) forming on the left, which fact Harland reported to Rodman and then ordered his brigade forward. The 8th Connecticut wheeled slightly to the right, passed to the right of the cornfield, its right in rear of Fairchild's left, which preceded it a few minutes, but the 16th Connecticut, apparently, did not hear the order to advance, and Harland sent an aid to hasten them, and, when moving down the hill, suggested to

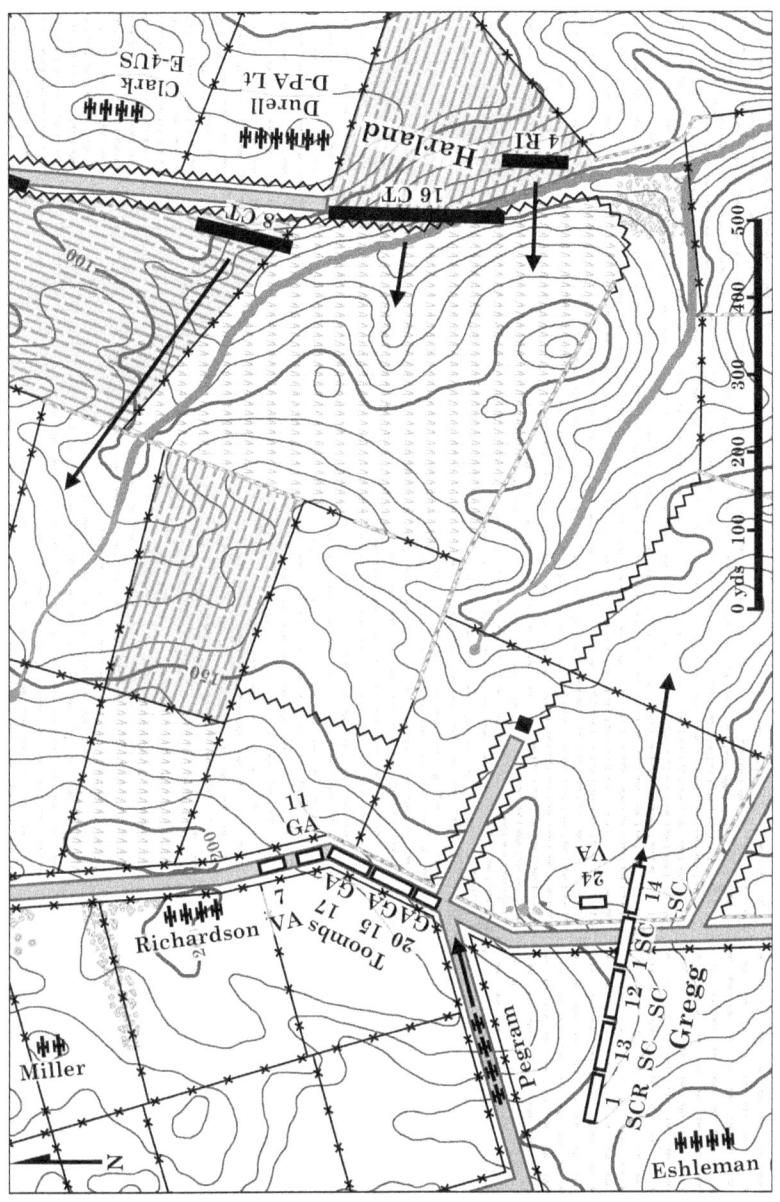

Gregg's Brigade crosses the Harper's Ferry Road and begins to deploy southwest of the 40-acre cornfield. Harland's brigade begins its belated advance, the delay caused in part by Gregg's appearance.

Rodman that the 8th Connecticut, when at the foot at the hill and under cover from the artillery fire pouring on it, should halt and wait for the 16th Connecticut and 4th Rhode Island to come up, but Rodman ordered the continued advance of the regiment, saying he would bring up the two regiments, so Harland kept on with the 8th Connecticut, and began firing at some skirmishers who appeared on his left. The two regiments not yet coming up Harland turned to see if they were advancing and saw instead some Confederate infantry—the 7th and 37th North Carolina—rapidly advancing on his left flank, upon which, Rodman having ridden ahead to Fairchild, ordering the 8th Connecticut to continue its advance, he put his spurs to his horse and rode back to hasten the advance of the 16th. The 8th Connecticut, under a scattering flank fire from the North Carolina skirmishers, moved on and soon came under the fire of McIntosh's South Carolina battery, but was somewhat protected, as it was moving under cover of the hill upon which the battery had just gone into position, though it suffered some casualties.

McIntosh's Battery was the advance of A. P. Hill's Division. After crossing the Potomac it preceded the infantry, came by the road from Blackford's Ford and, when nearing Blackford's house, near the Harper's Ferry road, left one howitzer and all its caissons and, with a Napoleon and two rifles, took position on the right of and near the Blackford house, and, after firing two or three shots at Fairchild's Brigade, moving to the left, was ordered by A. P. Hill to report to Kemper on the left of a cornfield and support the right of Jones' Division. The guns were limbered up and went at a gallop directly across the fields and came into the Harper's Ferry road at the northwest corner of what is known in the Confederate reports as the "narrow cornfield" and then moved up the road a few yards, in the direction of Sharpsburg, to a gate in the plank fence, where it waited in the road for Brown's Battery, leaving the field, to come out. Some of the men suggested that it was not a proper place for a battery, where another had been driven out, but McIntosh replied that he had been directed to go in there and fight and ordered the battery forward. It went through the gate as soon as Brown's guns had cleared it, and, obliquing to the right, took position 100 feet on the left of the narrow cornfield and 100 yards from the road, the guns not quite to the crest of the ridge. When taking this position there was seen about 300 yards to the left and front, Kemper's small brigade, huddled together behind a fence, firing upon Fairchild's Brigade, which was rapidly advancing, and about the time the guns began firing, less than three minutes after they were in position, Kemper's men were run over by Fairchild. In coming into position McIntosh came under fire of the Union artillery posted on the high ground from which Rodman had charged, to which he responded with vigor and while so engaged, himself working one of his guns, for the battery was short-handed, he saw the

McIntosh's Battery position looking east. Company K, 8th Connecticut advanced toward them in front, then veered to the left to avoid the flanking fire of the 7th and 37th North Carolina. *Author's collection.*

colors of the 8th Connecticut and occasionally the heads of the men as they approached under the hill, moving diagonally across his front from right to left, and opened fire upon them. McIntosh says the advancing columns "halted and lay down for some minutes when they began their advance again" and gradually came into view and as they approached to within 60 yards of his guns, as all his horses, but two, had been shot, he ordered the men to save themselves and abandoned the guns.

It was not the entire 8th Connecticut that McIntosh saw approaching him, it passed to his left, but the left company, under Captain C. L. Upham, that had been detached, while advancing, to take the battery, from which the gunners had apparently been driven, as, at the time, the battery was silent. But as Upham was crossing the field, ascending the hill and nearing the guns, apparently at the very moment McIntosh was abandoning them, his attention was called to troops approaching his left and rear through the narrow cornfield, upon which, without reaching the guns, he fell back. Upham says: "They came up company or division front and deployed on reaching the fence at the edge of the field, each division opening fire as soon as it came into line. We fell back to our regiment which changed front and engaged them." The Confederate force was the 7th and 37th North Carolina, whose skirmishers had been annoying the 8th Connecticut as it advanced.

When Upham rejoined his regiment it had gained the high ground to the left of where Fairchild fought. Fairchild had swung off to the right and down hill, in pursuit of Kemper and Drayton, and had then been ordered to fall back, but his dead and wounded marked the ground over which he had fought. Save those dead and wounded there was not a Union soldier in sight. The regiment was alone, over half a mile in advance of the position from which it had charged and with no support. It was 120 yards from the Harper's Ferry road and nearly parallel to it, and on its right front, in the road, were small remnants of Kemper's and Drayton's brigades that had retreated to a deep cut of the road, and, looking to the left was seen Toombs' Brigade, coming at a double quick down the road.

When Toombs fell back from the bridge to the stone fences he was joined by the 15th and 17th Georgia of his brigade and 5 companies of the 11th Georgia, under Major F. H. Little of George T. Anderson's Brigade. The 2nd and 20th Georgia were then ordered to the rear for ammunition, and the two fresh regiments into the 40-acre cornfield. Little's battalion was posted by Toombs behind a stone fence on the right of the two regiments, and Little reports that skirmishers were sent out and brisk firing began and that his skirmishers were driven in, the enemy's advancing to within 125 yards of him, a full line of battle drawn up in rear. He quietly awaited their advance, but the efforts of the Union officers to move them forward were unavailing. The skirmishers encountered by Little were those of the 48th

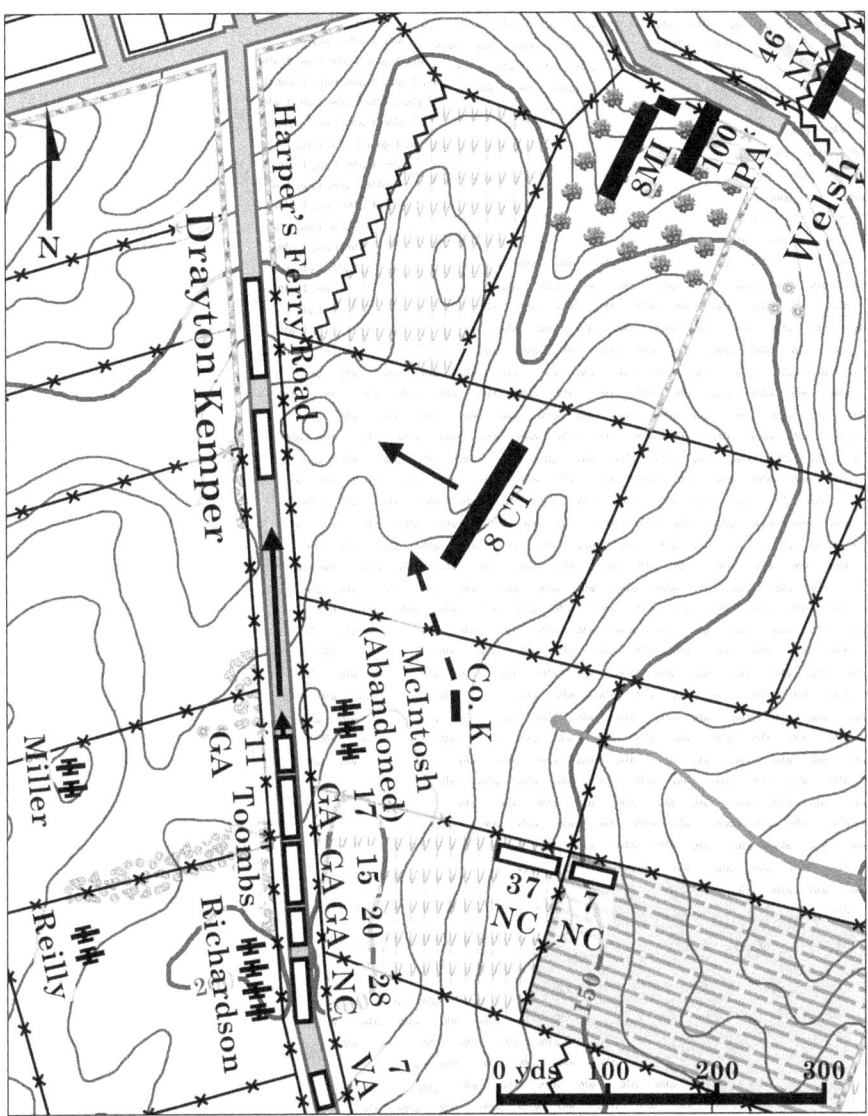

The 8th Connecticut moves forward alone, Fairchild's brigade to its right having withdrawn. Company K moves to capture McIntosh's Battery, but is driven off by the 7th and 37th North Carolina of Branch's Brigade. Toomb's Brigade marches north to intercept.

Pennsylvania and the movement seen by him of a full line of battle, were those of Nagle's Brigade taking position after crossing the bridge.

When A. P. Hill's Division was announced as approaching the field Toombs was directed, that as soon as Gregg's Brigade arrived and relieved him, to move his command to the right of his own division in the direction of Sharpsburg; before Gregg arrived he received an order to move immediately to meet the enemy, who had already begun his attack on Jones' Division. He quickly put his command in motion, and fell back to the Harper's Ferry road, where he was met by another order to hasten his march as the enemy had broken the line of Jones' Division and were nearly up to the road without a Confederate soldier in front. At this point Toombs was joined by the 20th Georgia, and the entire command went double-quick along the road, passed the 7th Virginia, which had fallen back before the advance of Fairchild, and in a short time the head of the line passed the "narrow cornfield," saw McIntosh's three abandoned guns, and the 8th Connecticut "standing composedly in line of battle," about 120 yards from the road, apparently waiting for support, on the very ground Toombs had been ordered to occupy. Colonel Benning reports that "neither in their front nor far to their right was a man of ours to be seen, but three abandoned guns of ours were conspicuous objects about midway between the road and the enemy's line." Little's battalion was in advance, followed by the 17th Georgia, Captain J. A. McGregor, 15th, Colonel William T. Millican, and a large part of the 20th in rear. All, however, made but a short line, and Benning, when he thought the rear had not quite cleared the cornfield, for he did not desire to see the enemy to see how short his line was, halted the head of his line opposite the right of the 8th Connecticut, and ordered it to begin firing: "the rest of the line as it came up joined in the fire. The fire soon became general. It was hot and rapid. The enemy returned it with vigor, and showed a determination to hold their position stubbornly."

Meanwhile General Rodman had fallen. He had gone forward with the 8th Connecticut, rode ahead to where Fairchild was engaged, saw the 8th Connecticut coming up and started to meet it, or to go for the rest of the brigade, when he was shot through the breast and fell from his horse. No one saw him fall, but two of Upham's men—Seth D. Bingham and T. H. Hawley— were falling back from the advance on McIntosh's guns, to rejoin their regiment, they heard his cry for help, went to him and took him to a sheltered position under the hill, from which he was moved across the Antietam to Roulette's house, where he died some days later.

While Toombs was engaging the 8th Connecticut, the 16th Connecticut and 4th Rhode Island were being engaged a half mile in the rear of the 8th, in the 40-acre cornfield, to which, in order to preserve the sequence of events, we now return. This 40-acre cornfield, covered at the time with

McIntosh's Battery looking toward the fight at the stone wall, and later, the 8th Connecticut. *Author's collection.*

dense corn, has running through it, from the northwest to the southeast corner a deep ravine. From its northeast corner the ground descends directly to the ravine, but in the southwest part of it there is a plateau, from which the ground descends quite abruptly 30 to 40 feet. The west edge of the field was bounded, the greater part of its extent, by a stone wall, broken in places by rail fences, and beyond this, between the high ground on which runs the Harper's Ferry road, there is quite a valley, lower by nearly 50 feet than the road. In the cornfield 130 yards from the stone fence on the west and parallel to it, is a stone ledge, upon which was an old board fence, partially thrown down and negligent, and its line was marked by trees. Seen through the dense corn and smoke of combat it had the appearance of a stone fence and is so called in the Confederate reports.

The 16th Connecticut, Colonel Francis Beach, 760 men, had entered the cornfield at its northeast corner and moved to the bottom of the ravine, where skirmishers under Captain Barber were thrown out up the hill to the edge of the plateau in the southwest part of the field. It did not advance with the 8th Connecticut and soon an order was received from Rodman to swing to the left to face Gregg's Brigade, of A. P. Hill's Division, then approaching.

A. P. Hill's Division had remained at Harper's Ferry until the morning of the 17th, when, at half-past six, he received orders from General Lee to march to Sharpsburg. Leaving Thomas' Brigade to complete the removal of the captured property he put his division in motion at half-past seven, marched up the Virginia side of the river, crossed at Blackford's Ford and, after an exhausting march of 17 miles, the head of his column arrived upon the field at 2:30 p.m. Hill reported in person to General Lee, by whom he was warmly greeted and who exclaimed: "General Hill I was never so glad to see you, you are badly needed, put your force in on the right as fast as they come up." Hill then rode to D. R. Jones, who gave him such information of the character of the ground as was necessary, and then rode to the Blackford house, where he met the advance of his division coming upon the field by the road leading from the ford. McIntosh's Battery had already taken position near the Blackford house, where it fired a few shots and was then sent forward to strengthen Jones' right. The infantry now came up and were rapidly thrown into position. Pender and Brockenbrough on the extreme right, looking to the road crossing the Antietam near its mouth, Branch, Gregg and Archer extending to the left to make continuation with D. R. Jones's Division. Hill says:

> Braxton's Battery...was placed upon a commanding point on Gregg's right; Crenshaw and Pegram on a hill to my left, which gave them a wide field of fire. My troops were not in a moment too soon. The enemy had already advanced in three lines, had broken through Jones'

The 16th Connecticut monument in the 40-acre cornfield. Looking toward Gregg's position at the southwest corner of the field. The uneven nature of the cornfield is clearly evident. *Author's collection.*

Division, captured McIntosh's Battery, and were in the full tide of success.

Hill's Division did not come upon the field in a body. As soon as one brigade crossed the river and climbed up its slippery bank, it was hurried forward, without waiting to allow the men to wring the water from their clothing and socks, or for the brigade immediately following, by which it came that the brigades arrived at the front, at varying intervals, not of many minutes, however, for they were small and promptly handled. It is impossible to say in what order the brigades arrived, but we first follow Gregg. The appearance of McIntosh's Battery had attracted the attention of the Union artillery and guns were trained in that direction, so, when Gregg's Brigade appeared, passing the Blackford house and nearing the Harper's Ferry road, it came under artillery fire from the guns beyond the Antietam and as well as those west of it, upon which it inclined to the right, went down under cover, then, changing direction to the left, crossed the Harper's Ferry road and formed line about 250 yards beyond it. The 14th South Carolina, Lieutenant Colonel W. D. Simpson, the leading regiment, was thrown out to the right, behind a stone fence, nearly at right angles to the brigade line, to protect that flank, and was so far beyond the Union left that it was not engaged. Gregg formed three regiments in line, the 1st South Carolina, Colonel D. H. Hamilton, on the right; the 12th South Carolina, Colonel Dixon Barnes, in the center, and the 13th South Carolina, Colonel E. O. Edwards, on the left. The first South Carolina Rifles, Lieutenant Colonel James M. Perrin, was held in reserve. The four regiments numbered about 750 men.

Pegram's Battery closely supported Gregg, and went into position a few yards east of the Harper's Ferry road and 355 yards a little north of west from the southwest corner of the 40 acre cornfield that Gregg was about to enter. It was on a very commanding position, giving a wide range of fire, that was immediately opened, principally upon the Union infantry, on the ridge beyond the cornfield. Braxton's Battery was put in position in rear of Gregg's right, 130 yards east of the Harper's Ferry road, 450 yards a little south of west of the cornfield, and 270 yards on Pegram's right. It followed Pegram in opening fire upon the Union infantry. We anticipate in saying that later, about 4.30 p.m., one gun of Pegram's Battery and 2 rifled guns of Braxton's were moved to the extreme right, on a hill, about 280 yards due north of Snavely's barn, giving them an enfilading fire and, as reported by Hill's chief of artillery, were worked "with beautiful precision and great effect, upon the infantry of the enemy until nightfall closed the engagement."

Gregg's skirmishers, who had been thrown to the front, were now withdrawn and Gregg ordered his three regiments to advance into the

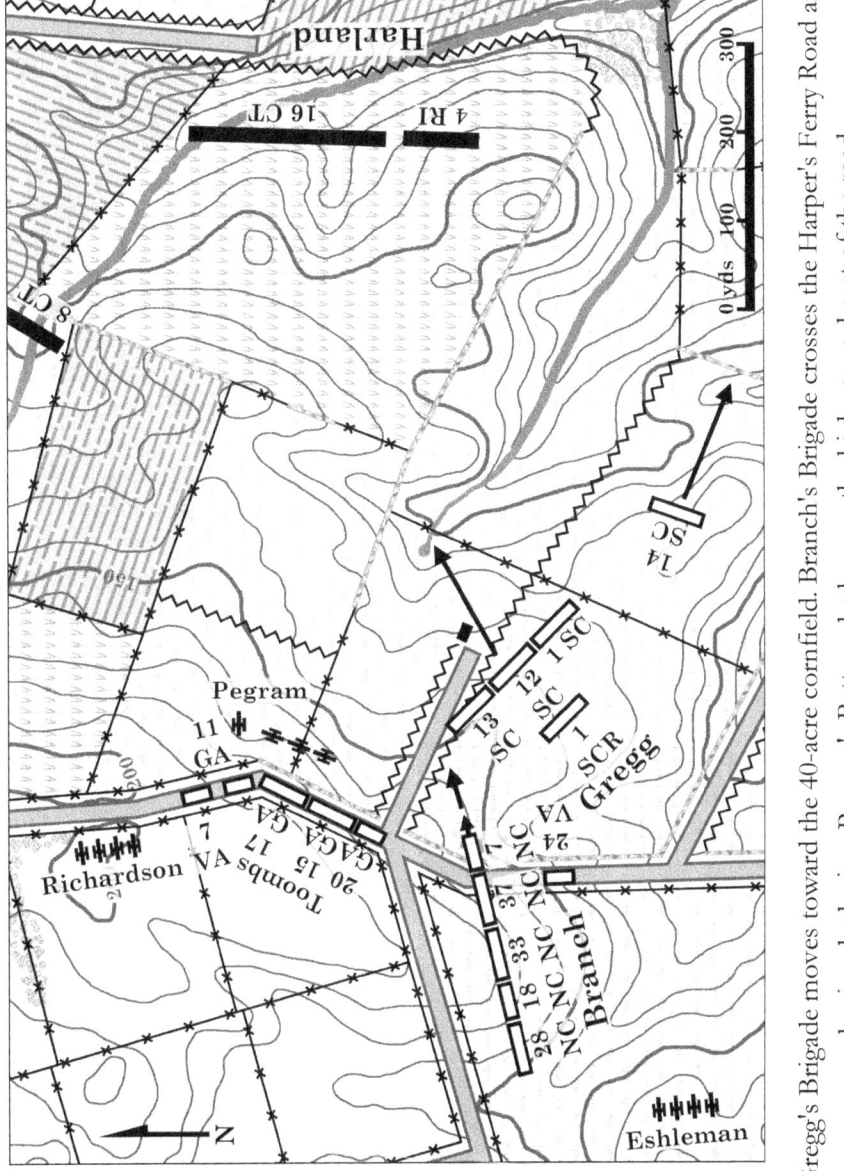

Gregg's Brigade moves toward the 40-acre cornfield. Branch's Brigade crosses the Harper's Ferry Road and begins deploying. Pegram's Battery deploys on the high ground east of the road.

cornfield that crowned a bold hill in his front and drive back the enemy, whom the skirmishers had reported as advancing through the corn. They advanced, went quickly over an intervening ravine and up the hill and struck the southwest corner of the cornfield; the 13th South Carolina under a misapprehension of orders, halted at the stone fence bordering the cornfield on the west, while the 1st and 12th went over the fence, both at the south and west sides of the field, moved northeast about 120 yards, driving back the skirmishers of the 16th Connecticut, and, reaching the highest part of the field, halted and opened fire upon the troops in the ravine at the foot of the hill and, also, upon those on the high, open ground beyond the corn, who were seen advancing, but the 12th South Carolina halted for a few minutes only on the left of the 1st, when, the Union skirmishers having fallen back to the old fence that ran through the corn, it charged down the hill upon the 16th Connecticut, which was then changing front beyond the low rock ledge and fence. The Connecticut skirmishers were driven from the fence, but the main body, though somewhat disordered, returned the fire with such spirit that the 12th South Carolina was checked and, coming under this fire in front and on both flanks, was, almost immediately after reaching the fence, compelled to fall back to prevent being flanked on the right, and the Union line again advanced to the fence. Barnes again charged with the 12th but was again repulsed by the combined fire of the 16th Connecticut and the 4th Rhode Island and, the movement of the Rhode Island regiment threatening his right, he fell back in some disorder carrying with him part of the left of the 1st South Carolina but quickly rallied in the southwest corner of the corn.

We left Harland riding back to this cornfield to hasten the advance of the 16th Connecticut. His horse was shot from under him before he had gone far, which delayed his arrival. He found that the regiment, by an order of Rodman, had changed front to the left and was heavily engaged and perceiving that the right of the 12th South Carolina was exposed ordered Colonel Beach to change the front of the 16th Connecticut to strike it; "which change was effected, though with some difficulty, owing to the fact that the regiment had been in service but three weeks, and the impossibility of seeing but a small portion of the line at once." It was this change of front of the 16th Connecticut and its attack, and the appearance of the 4th Rhode Island that caused the 12th South Carolina to fall back in some disorder, but, almost immediately after this, both the 16th Connecticut and 4th Rhode Island were flanked in turn, and driven from the field.

The 4th Rhode Island, Colonel W. H. P. Steere, 247 men, entered the cornfield by the right flank, under fire of the Confederate artillery in full view, and descending into the ravine came into line on the left of the 16th Connecticut, which was in some confusion, engaging the second advance of the 12th South Carolina, and crowding to the left, and rendering it almost

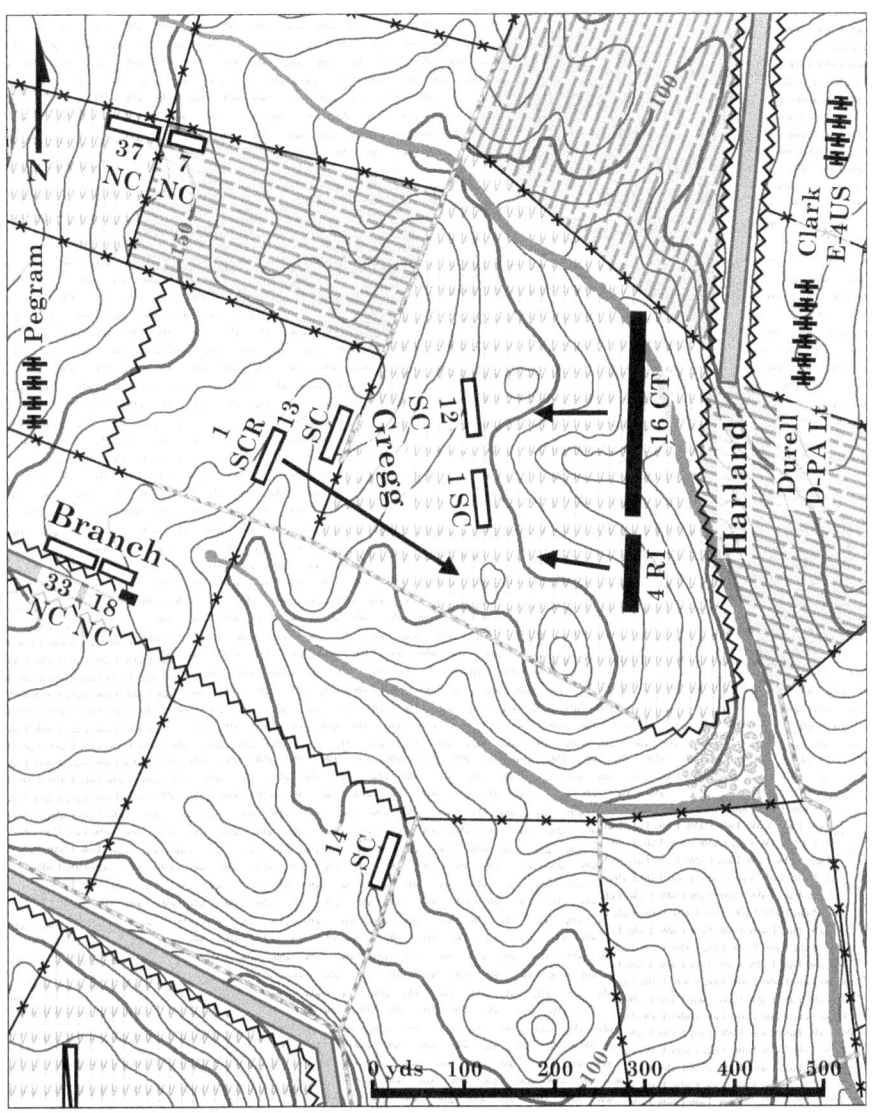

Harland's brigade pushes back the 1st and 12th South Carolina's initial advance and moves forward. The 1st South Carolina Rifles moves up and into position to flank Harland.

impossible to dress the line, which had become somewhat disordered in advancing through the corn, but its appearance assisted forcing back the 12th South Carolina and in compelling the 1st to move farther to the right, and throw back it three right companies, fearing a movement on that flank. In this position the 1st South Carolina opened fire on the 4th Rhode Island. At this moment the Rhode Island men mistook the colors of the 1st South Carolina for a Union flag, ceased firing, and Lieutenants George E. Curtis and George H. Watts volunteered to go forward, through the dense corn, and ascertain what was in front. Placing themselves on each side of the regimental colors, carried by Corporal Thomas B. Tanner, they went up the hill to within 20 feet of the enemy when they were fired upon and Tanner killed. Curtis seized the colors and ran back followed by Watts and the orders given to open fire and Steere sent Lieutenant Colonel Curtis to the 16th Connecticut, to see if it would support him in a charge up the hill, but the corn being very thick and high Curtis could find no one to whom to apply and returned to Steere to report that they must depend upon themselves, and Steere sent him to the rear for support. But before he could get back the crisis had come.

The 1st South Carolina, which was engaging the 4th Rhode Island, was running out of ammunition and about to fall back, when the 1st South Carolina Rifles, which had been held in reserve, was now sent forward by Gregg to sweep the field on the right and, ascending to the crest of the hill in its front and coming up on the right of the 1st South Carolina, saw the 4th Rhode Island which had turned the right of the 1st South Carolina, and was delivering a destructive fire on its flank. The Rifles advanced a short distance beyond the First, then forward to his right, so as to completely turn the left flank of the 4th Rhode Island and delivered a destructive fire before its presence seemed to be realized. The Rhode Island men attempted to return the fire, but so great was the disorder into which they and the 16th Connecticut had been thrown that, after a short, sharp fire, both were thrown into hopeless confusion, broke, and fell back, the Rifles capturing 11 prisoners, among them Captain Caleb T. Brown [Bowen], 4th Rhode Island, who had been wounded.

Colonel Harland, referring to the action of the 16th Connecticut, says:

> The right of the enemy's line, which was concealed in the edge of the cornfield, opened fire. Our men returned the fire and advanced, but were forced to fall back. Colonel Beach rallied them and returned to the attack, but they were again driven back, this time out of the cornfield beyond the fence. Here they were again rallied, but as it was impossible to see the enemy; and the men were under fire for the first time, they could not be held.

The 13th South Carolina's view of the 40-acre cornfield, and what the 1st South Carolina Rifles would have seen as it moved past them into the field. The 16th Connecticut's monument is visible in the middle of the field. *Author's collection.*

Lieutenant Colonel Curtis of the 4th Rhode Island reports that his regiment was outflanked and enfiladed:

> The regiment on our right now broke, a portion of them crowding on our line. Colonel Steere ordered the regiment to move out of the gully by the right flank, and I left him to carry the order to the left, of which wing I had charge, the Colonel taking the right...The regiment began the movement in an orderly manner, but, under the difficulty of keeping closed up in a cornfield, the misconception of the order on the left and the tremendous fire of the enemy...the regiment broke. Colonel Steere was severely wounded in the left thigh after I left him to report on the left the order to leave the cornfield.

An attempt was made to rally on Muhlenberg's Battery, which, some distance back from the cornfield, now opened with shell and canister upon the South Carolinians, in the southwest part of the cornfield, but before many could be collected the battery retired, when the efforts became unavailing. A few men rallied on the left of the 51st Pennsylvania and continued fighting until their ammunition was exhausted, when they recrossed the Antietam and rejoined their regiment and brigade. The loss of the 16th Connecticut was 42 killed, 143 wounded; that of the 4th Rhode Island 21 killed and 77 wounded.

As the 4th Rhode Island and 16th Connecticut were giving way, Ewing's Brigade—12th, 23rd and 30th Ohio—was charging toward the stone wall in front. This brigade was in support of the left of Rodman's Division, and when that division was ordered forward was lying down behind the ridge from which it advanced. Upon the report that the Confederates were massing on the left the brigade moved in that direction about a quarter of a mile and then directly back to the point from which it had started, and, without a halt, came into line to the left and charged; the 23rd Ohio, Major J. M. Comly and 30th Ohio, Lieutenant Colonel Theodore Jones, sweeping over the crest, between Clark's and Durell's batteries, then over the fence, down into the valley and up to the stone fences that ran along the west side of the cornfield and extended far to the north. The 23rd on the right, made its advance over open ground, 375 yards, under fire of artillery and musketry, and came to the fence on the right of the ravine, where it cuts the corner of the 40 acre cornfield, its left very near it, and its right extending up the hillside to higher ground. The 30th Ohio started over open ground, gained ground to the left and entered the corn as it went down hill, passed some men of the 16th Connecticut, who were still in the hollow, passed over their dead and wounded, and, under a severe fire that had been poured upon it from the moment it moved to the charge, which continued and increased as it advanced, reached the stone fence at the west edge of the

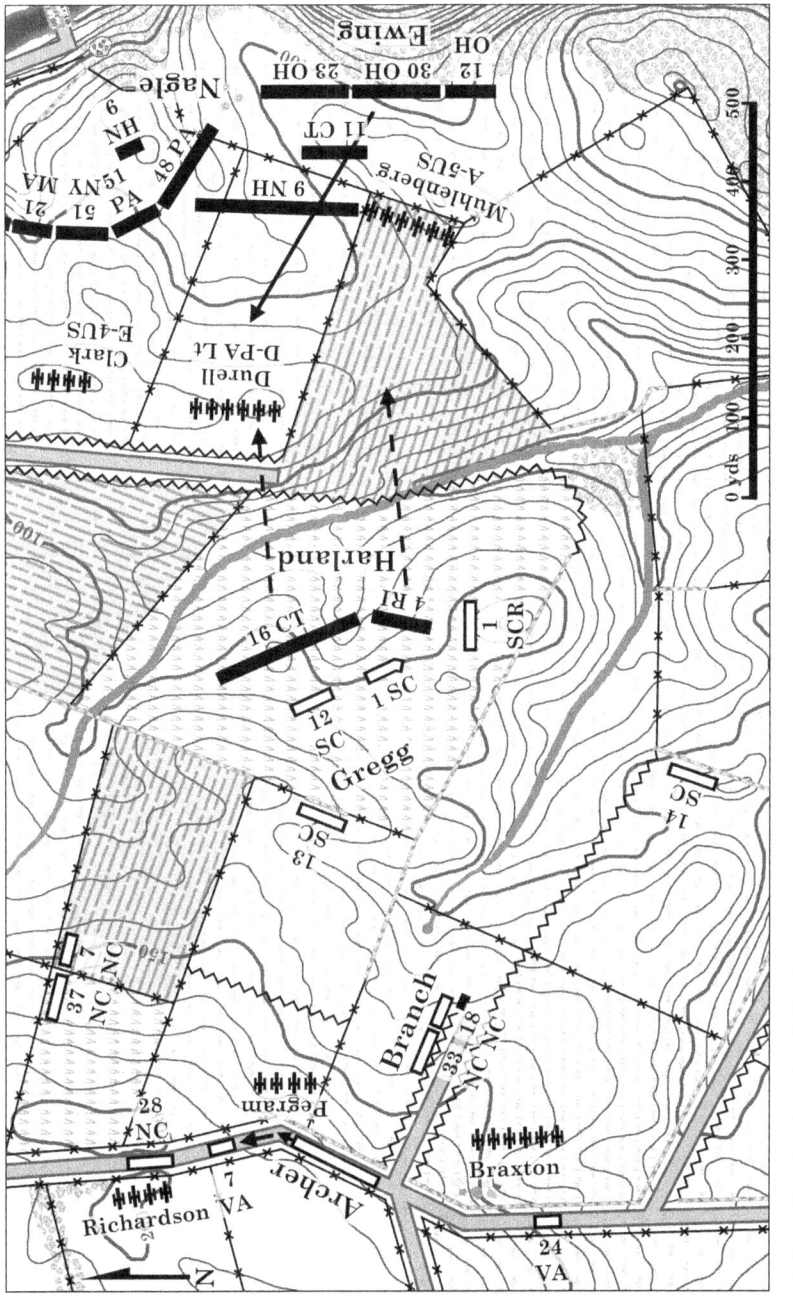

The 4th Rhode Island flanks Gregg, but is in turn flanked by the 1st South Carolina Rifles. Flanking fire rips down the 4th and the 16th Connecticut, and they both rout. Ewing's brigade moves forward to support.

corn. It was on a hillside sloping to the north, its left on the highest part of the hill and 240 yards from the southwest corner of the corn; its right at the base of the hill, close to the ravine, beyond which was the 23rd Ohio. Its entire front was covered by the stone fence.

Both regiments reached the fence about the same moment and saw, in the open field before them, the enemy, upon whom they opened fire, and leaving them here for a moment we return to the 8th Connecticut and the troops now encountered by the two Ohio regiments.

In Benning's desire to front the right of the 8th Connecticut he had carried his line so far that his rear had passed 100 yards beyond the narrow cornfield, but he was in an excellent, well sheltered position in the road, which, at this point, ran in a cut, much lower than the bank in front, and on the left were parts of Kemper's and Drayton's brigades. The entire line engaged the 8th Connecticut with some spirit, inflicting upon it much loss, and, in addition to this fire in its front, it was suffering from a fire upon its left flank and rear, which caused it to change the front of its left wing. This flank and rear fire came from the 7th and 37th North Carolina of Branch's Brigade.

When Branch's Brigade came upon the field by the road passing Blackford's, a battery opened upon it, upon which it turned sharply to the right, down hill, then resumed its first course and after the leading regiment, the 7th North Carolina, had fired two or three volleys at a regiment beyond the cornfield, crossed the Harper's Ferry road and marched east until the 8th Connecticut was seen, marching in line northwest, upon which skirmishers were sent out and the 7th North Carolina, Colonel Edward S. Haywood, and 37th North Carolina, Captain W. G. Morris, were detached and sent on the double quick to the left, north, the 7th on the right. The running skirmishers soon opened fire upon the moving 8th Connecticut, and the two regiments followed by the flank. The 37th, on the left, went through the lower part of the "narrow cornfield," and the 7th over open ground on its right, and both came into line, behind the fence on the northern edge of the cornfield and the fence continuing east from it. The fence was approached as Upham was advancing to seize McIntosh's guns and opened fire upon the left and rear of the 8th Connecticut, not quite 300 yards distant, which caused it to make a partial change of front. This fire and that of the enemy in the road was more than the Connecticut men could stand. Richardson's Battery from across the road now opened upon them and, after an engagement of less than 30 minutes, losing nearly one half its men (34 killed and 139 wounded) and with no hope of support, the regiment was ordered to retreat. Toombs and Benning say it retreated in confusion but officers of the 37th North Carolina testify that it "held ground quite stubbornly, fought splendidly, and went off very deliberately, firing back at the 37th and waving its flag." Officers of the regiment admit

The 7th and 37th North Carolina's view looking north toward the 8th Connecticut. *Author's collection.*

that some of the men retreated without halting to fire, but contend that a greater part of them stopped several times to fire at the enemy in the corn. While the 37th North Carolina was engaged a volley was poured into its right flank, also upon the flank of the 7th, from the fence of the 40 acre cornfield, by which some men of the latter were killed and wounded and some men of the 37th wounded, upon which the 7th immediately fell back, soon followed by the 37th. We shall see them later.

When the 8th Connecticut was seen leaving the field Toombs ordered pursuit, and his men, with those of Kemper and Drayton, a mere handful, climbing the bank and board fence, advanced to near where the regiment had stood, and Toombs ordered a charge over the hill, but Benning, who was a better soldier, thought otherwise. He says:

> We could not see what was below the crest of the hill, but I knew a very large force of the enemy must be somewhere below it, for I had from our last position seen three or four successive long lines of them march out from the bridge. I therefore suggested to General Toombs the propriety of halting the line, as its numbers were so small and it had no supports behind it, just before it reached the crest of the hill, and sending to the crest only the men armed with long-range guns. This suggestion he adopted.

As Toombs was about to leave the road Archer's Brigade came up on his right. This brigade, composed of the 1st Tennessee (Provisional Army), Colonel Peter Turney; 7th Tennessee, Major S. G. Sheppard; 14th Tennessee, Colonel William A. McComb; and 19th Georgia, Major James H. Neal, reached the field with less than 400 men, and turning to the left, marched right in front on the road to Sharpsburg, and formed line of battle, faced by the rear rank, in the road, the "narrow cornfield" of 150 yards width, extending along its immediate front; Toombs being in the road a few yards to the left and about to go forward. Skirmishers were immediately thrown into the cornfield and the brigade, scaling a board fence, went forward under a scattering fire, through the tall corn 225 yards to its eastern edge, overlooking open, plowed ground, but when the two left regiments—14th and 7th Tennessee—reached this advanced position, the others were found to have fallen back to the road, from which, meanwhile, Toombs had advanced. The 37th North Carolina, in falling back from the fences, under the enfilading fire received by it, had halted in the corn, and Archer's two right regiments, hearing the commands of the officers of that regiment to fall back, mistook these orders as for themselves, the corn was so dense that nothing could be seen, and fell back to the road. Archer, who was ill and very weak and had ridden in an ambulance, assuming command of his brigade, only, because he was on the soil of his native state, had not yet left

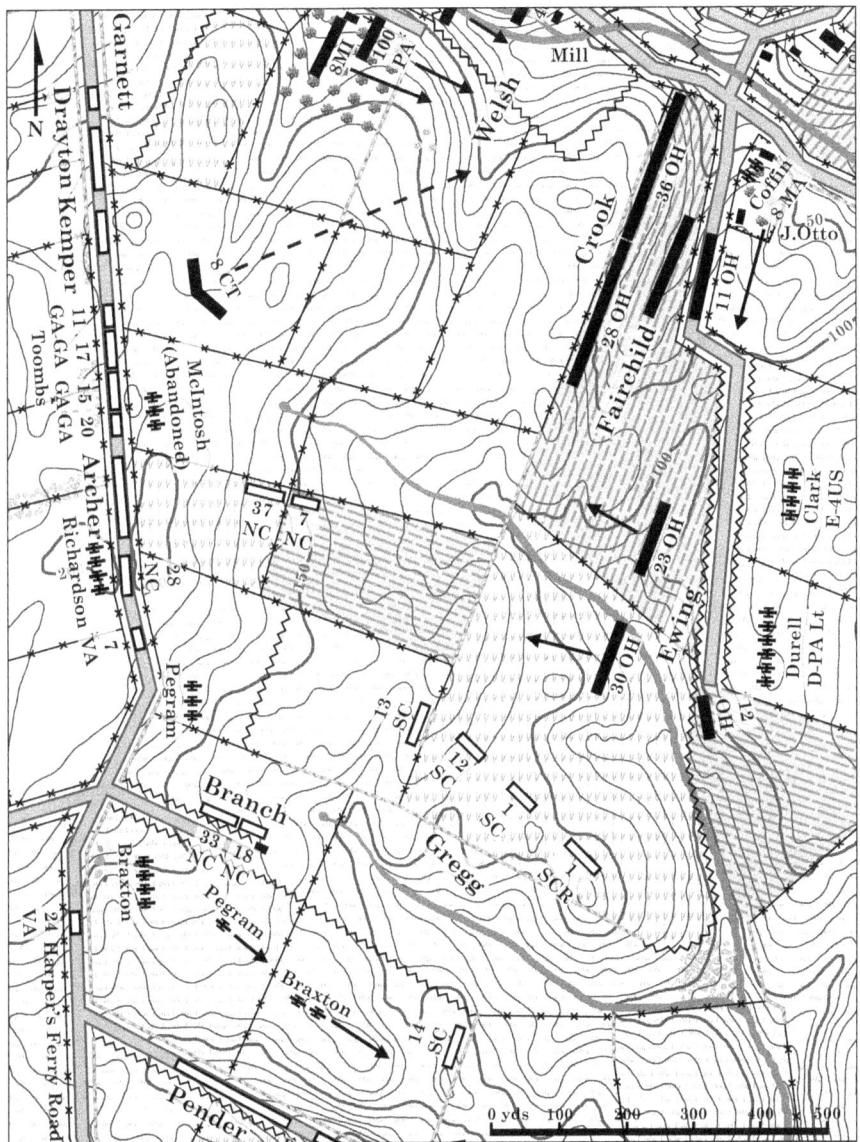

The 8th Connecticut is forced to withdraw after enduring fire from several directions. Ewing's brigade moves up to support Harland, although they have already left the field. The 12th Ohio halts to engage Gregg, while the other two regiments continue on. Coffin's section of the 8th Massachusetts Battery changes position.

the road. As quickly as possible he reformed line in the road and again the two regiments advanced through the corn to where the 14th and 7th Tennessee had halted, when the entire line, Toombs following on the left, charged over a plowed field 300 yards to the stone fence of the cornfield, behind which were the 23rd and 30th Ohio. Archer was met by a withering fire that caused him much loss; Colonel McComb was wounded and nearly one third of his brigade stricken down, but, with the assistance of Gregg on his right, Archer drove back the 23rd and 30th Ohio and halted at the fence.

It was the assistance given by Gregg that caused the retreat of the two Ohio regiments, without it, they could have held their position against the front attack of Archer and Toombs. When the two regiments reached the fence three of Gregg's regiments were in the southwest part of the cornfield and one behind the same fence, but on the other side and a few yards to the left of the 30th, but none of them were visible and but one, the 1st S.C Rifles, was firing and as this was so far to the left and supposed to be taken care of by the 12th Ohio, which it thought was moving on that flank, no attention was paid to it, and as the fence was reached fire was opened upon Archer. Major George H. Hildt of the 30th, reports: "Our men were at this time utterly exhausted from the effect of the double-quick step across the plowed field, and their fire was necessarily slow and desultory for several minutes. As soon, however, as our first volley had been given, and our colors rested at the wall, a withering fire was directed upon us from our left flank, and from which we suffered most severely." Its left company was on the crown of the elevated ground from which there was a rapid descent to the ravine on the right, beyond which was the 23rd Ohio on open ground.

Major Comly of the 23rd Ohio from the elevated position where he was standing saw what he took to be a Union line advancing on the left and toward the rear of the 30th and at the same time he saw that the 30th was still in position and that it was opening fire upon this supposed Union line and gave his men orders not to fire upon it, although it was rapidly approaching and within easy range. But, when a volley came down the flank and rear of the 30th, and enfiladed the 23rd, all doubt vanished and Ewing ordered Comly to change front perpendicularly to the rear, which was quickly done, and Lieutenant Colonel Jones was ordered to fall back with the 30th and form on the left of the 23rd. Jones, who was on the right of the 30th gave the order to move by the right flank and join the 23rd, which order was not heard, except by the four right companies, which moved in that direction, the remaining companies still holding position at the wall. Lieutenant Reese R. Furbay of Ewing's staff was sent with orders to these companies to fall back, but was killed before reaching them, and they remained a few minutes longer, until the enemy's fire upon their flank could not be borne, two color bearers had been killed, Archer's Brigade was at the

Ewing's line along the stone wall, and after they are pushed back, the Confederates facing the opposite direction. The stone wall and fence roughly followed the modern road. *Author's collection.*

fence, it was now discovered that the right of the regiment had gone, and the six companies fell back to the ravine, where they found a few men of the 16th Connecticut.

Archer's men gained the stone fence just as the Ohio men abandoned it; in fact Archer's left reached the fence abandoned by the right wing of the 30th before its left fell back and a few men charging over it, captured Lieutenant Colonel Jones, commanding the 30th. Archer soon came up and ordered his entire brigade, now reduced to less than 300 men, to charge into the cornfield, an order that was promptly responded to, but, when less than 100 yards in the corn, it was met by such a severe fire from the six companies of the 30th Ohio, and the few Connecticut men, who had rallied with them, in the ravine, that it was driven back with loss and lay down behind the stone fence.

There is a strong probability that some of the loss sustained by Archer's Brigade was inflicted by the 12th South Carolina, which, not perceiving through the dense corn that the Ohio men had fallen back, was still firing in that direction. When the firing came from the ravine the 12th South Carolina charged for the third time, and was met by a volley from the Ohio men, who immediately retreated through the corn and up the hill from which they had advanced, the 12th South Carolina following up to the north fence of the corn, and firing upon the retreating troops. In this last charge, Colonel Barnes of the 12th South Carolina was mortally wounded, and the command devolved on Major W. H. McCorkle, who remained at the fence until near sunset, when he fell back to the top of the hill, and then over the stone fence on the right of the 13th South Carolina, which had maintained its position during the entire engagement.

When the six companies of the 30th Ohio fell back out of the cornfield the other four companies and the 23rd Ohio were not in sight. This withdrawal had been hastened by the advance of Toombs' Brigade, charging on the left of Archer's, and fell back down the ravine leading to the Burnside bridge road, at Otto's spring, and the regiments when united bivouacked a little north and west of the bridge and about 100 yards from it.

We have said that the 23rd Ohio was hastened from its position by the advance of Toombs' Brigade. This is true only as to a part of Toombs. At Benning's suggestion Toombs halted his brigade just before reaching the crest of the hill from which the 8th Connecticut had been driven. Those men who were armed with long-range guns were advanced to the crest and opened fire on the retreating Connecticut men, and 2 guns of Richardson's Battery were ordered up and opened fire upon the retreating infantry and Coffin's section of artillery, which, after the retreat of Garnett and Moody's guns from Cemetery hill, had moved from Otto's orchard to a position south of it, where the guns were turned upon Archer's and Toombs'

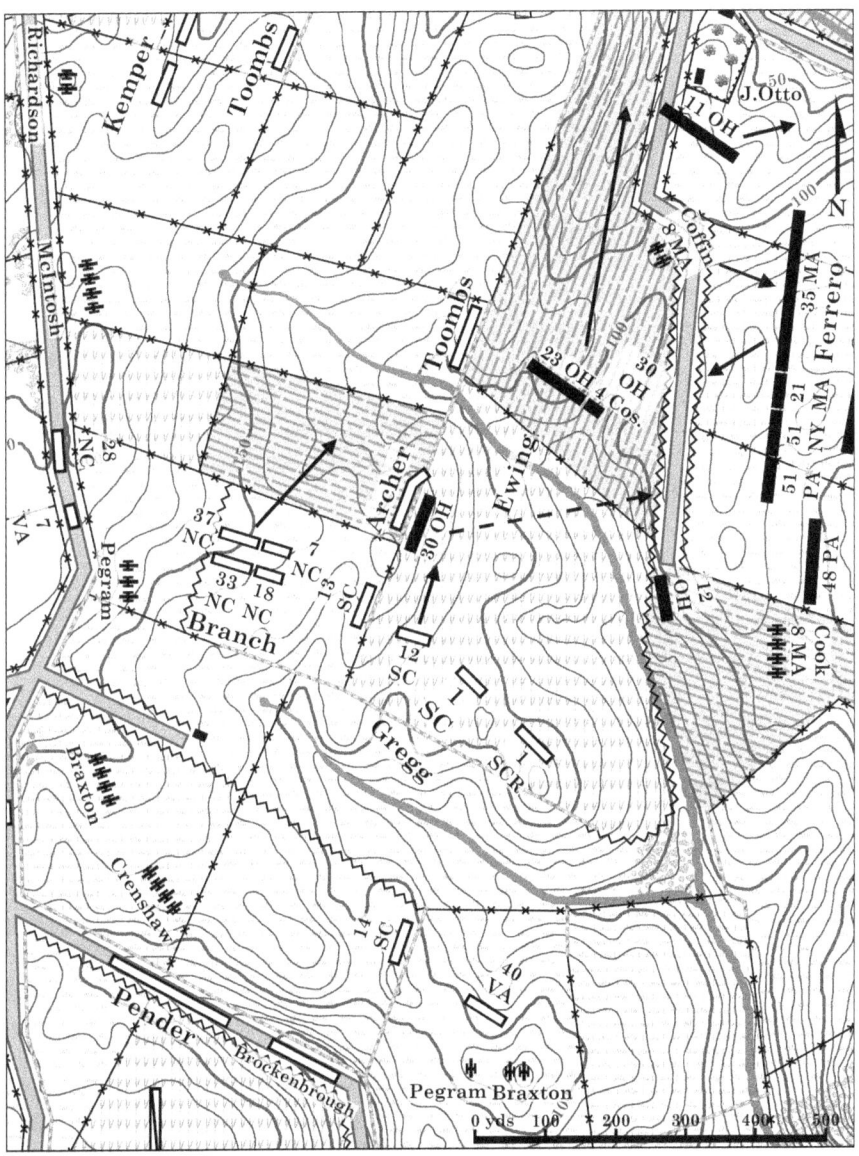

Ewing's brigade is forced back. The 23rd Ohio is overwhelmed by Archer and the 12th South Carolina. The 30th Ohio and four companies of the 23rd retreat out of the way. Ferrero's brigade moves forward to the crest of the hill to support.

infantry seen in the narrow cornfield and on the open ground north of it. Not deeming this position a good one Coffin moved farther to the left, "on a high eminence overlooking the enemy's infantry" and here he came under the fire of Richardson's guns about 650 yards distant.

Meanwhile Garnett had joined Drayton in the road. Having reached the rear of the town and hearing that Toombs had reinforced the right "and restored the fortunes of the day in that quarter," he gathered as many men as he could get to follow him, not over a small company, and joined Drayton in the road, just after Toombs advanced from it. Archer was now moving forward. Drayton and Kemper occupied the fence from which Fairchild had driven them, and Toombs' 15th and 20th Georgia charged forward to the fence and opened fire upon the retreating infantry—23rd and 30th Ohio—and Coffin's guns, and, with the assistance of Richardson's guns, compelled Coffin to fall back through the ranks of the 35th Massachusetts, which was moving to the front, to the position from which the 9th New York had charged. Coffin says his guns worked "with terrible effect" and fell back when "ammunition was exhausted."

Toombs desired "to pursue the enemy across the river" but had no artillery available and was about to content himself "to occupy the position at the bridge from which he had been driven." But the Union line, forming in his front, prevented this, perceiving which Toombs, leaving a small reserve with Colonel Benning, ordered the rest of his command down to the stone fence, following himself, and opened a hot fire with the 35th Massachusetts, on the hill about 300 yards opposite, during which Colonel Millican of the 15th Georgia was killed. Toombs reached the stone fence about the time Archer, on his right, was being driven out of the cornfield, and was soon followed by Branch's Brigade.

We have seen that when Branch's Brigade came upon the field the 7th and 37th North Carolina were pushed forward and engaged the left and rear of the 8th Connecticut and fell back under an enfilading fire on their right, probably from the 23rd Ohio, just before Archer charged. After these two regiments went forward, or about the time they were ordered forward, A. P. Hill came down the hill from the direction of Sharpsburg and seeing, nearly 200 yards beyond Toombs' right, an unsupported battery west of the road, nearly opposite the southwest corner of the cornfield, and not knowing, apparently, that the 7th and 37th were moving or about to move in that direction, for they were below the ridge out of view, ordered Colonel James H. Lane, 28th North Carolina, who was in rear of the brigade and had not crossed the Harper's Ferry road, to hasten up the road and support this battery, as Union skirmishers were reported moving on it through the corn. Lane quickly led his regiment up the road until he came to the corner of the cornfield, where he halted in the road and in front of the battery, but did not become engaged. The 7th and 37th were then engaged with the 8th

Looking across the valley from Toomb's and Branch's position (specifically the 37th North Carolina) toward the Otto lane and the 35th Massachusetts. *Author's collection.*

Connecticut though, himself in a deep cut in the road and they at the foot of a hill beyond and screened by the corn, Lane did not see them, at least he has no recollection of seeing them, but did see the advance of the 23rd and 30th Ohio and the movement of the 12th, and soon after Archer passed him and charged through the narrow cornfield. Though Lane did not see the two North Carolina regiments and had no recollection of seeing Archer's Brigade, Major W. J. Montgomery of the 28th, saw Archer pass and make his charge and from the high, open ground in front of the right of the regiment, saw the 7th and 37th North Carolina, advance from the position to which they had fallen back, cross the trail of Archer's Brigade over the plowed field and, swinging to the right go forward. In swinging to the right they came under the artillery fire that threw the left of the 7th into some confusion, but they charged up to the fence on Archer's left, the 7th coming in on the right of Toombs' men and at the northwest corner of the corn; Captain Morris, commanding the 37th, went over the fence on the right of the 7th, into the corn by the right flank, and fired at some retreating troops, met a warm fire, and immediately fell back as he saw the 33rd North Carolina come up and pass his left flank.

The 18th North Carolina, Lieutenant Colonel Thomas J. Purdie, and 33rd North Carolina, Lieutenant Colonel R. F. Hoke, that had immediately preceded the 28th, halted 200 yards east of the Harper's Ferry road as a reserve. Hoke, seeing the 7th and 37th going forward, the second time, followed without orders, passed closely in rear of Archer, at the fence, crossed the ravine and came into line on the left of Toombs, and the moment he passed the left of the 37th, that regiment came out of the corn, followed him and formed on his right. The 18th was halted by General Branch in a hollow in Archer's rear, and Branch rode forward to the high ground and fence where lay the 12th and 13th South Carolina of Gregg's Brigade, and had some conversation with Colonel Edwards and Major McCorkle. Raising his field glasses to get a better view of the Union line on the ridge beyond he was shot in the head and instantly killed.

Meanwhile Colonel Lane had been ordered to rejoin the brigade. He came up in Archer's rear as Branch was being carried off the field and was notified that, as senior officer, he was in command of the brigade. It was after sunset, and he found the 7th, 37th, and 33rd regiments posted behind the stone fence, and the 18th sheltered in a hollow in Archer's rear. He ordered the 28th to the left of the line, but the order was delivered to the 18th, which was posted to the left behind a rail fence, a portion of it being broken back to guard against a flank movement. The 28th was placed on the left of the 7th, in an opening caused by the withdrawal of Toombs' men, who were ordered to the left and bivouacked on Cemetery hill.

Meanwhile, the remainder of A. P. Hill's Division had come upon the field. Pender's Brigade followed Branch and was ordered by Hill to the

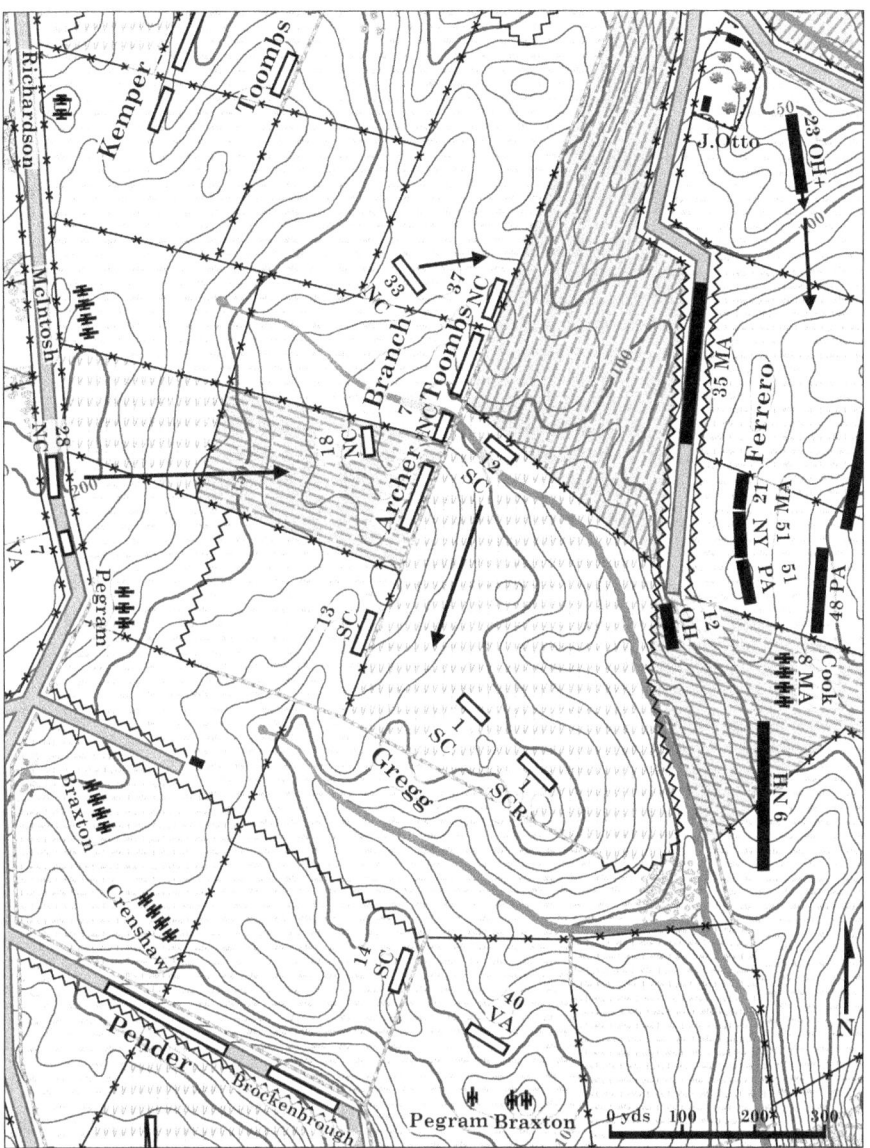

The Confederates move up to the stone wall and fences. Branch's Brigade fills gaps in the line where there is room. The 12th South Carolina falls back out of the line of fire.

extreme right "looking to a road which crossed the Antietam near its mouth." It was in an open field on Gregg's right, and not actively engaged. During the engagement it was moved from the right to the center, did not become engaged and, after sunset, bivouacked on Branch's left. Brockenbrough's Brigade was the last of the infantry to arrive; was thrown to the right, and the 40th Virginia sent to support the guns of Pegram and Braxton on the hill near Snavely's. It was not engaged and after dark was withdrawn and bivouacked south of the town near the stone mill. Crenshaw's was the last of Hill's batteries to reach the field and "took position on a hill in front of Captain McIntosh from which, disregarding the enemy's artillery, he directed his fire entirely at their infantry."

When McIntosh's guns were saved the men returned to them, bringing up the one gun which had been left behind, and opened fire, and batteries other than those of A. P. Hill's Division had arrived and were arriving and, by General Lee's orders, thrown in front (of Cox), along the high ground lying west of the Harper's Ferry road and south of Sharpsburg. Eshleman's Battery we have seen opposing the advance of Rodman's at Snavely's Ford, after which it received orders to hold the enemy in check until arrived, and Pender soon came to its support, and the battery "kept up a moderate shelling of the woods near the ford until night." It was on the right of the entire line of batteries and south of the road leading past the Blackford's house. Two guns of Miller's Battery had been withdrawn from the engagement at the Sunken Road because [they were] out of ammunition. Miller had replenished ammunition and "was returning to his former position, when he was directed by General Lee to an elevated and commanding position on the right and rear of the town, when General A. P. Hill had just begun his attack." He was about 170 yards west of the Harper's Ferry road and south of the narrow cornfield. Captain Richardson with his section of Napoleons and a 10-pounder Parrott gun of Squires' Battery, under Lieutenant J. M. Gailbraith, went to the right, near the guns under Miller, opened fire and continued in action until nightfall. Richardson's section of howitzers, at the same time, as we have seen, being assigned by Toombs a position near his brigade, and opening upon the men of the Ninth Corps and continuing the fire until they were out of range. At the time D. R. Jones' Division was giving way, Lieutenant J. A. Ramsay, with two rifled guns of Reilly's North Carolina battery came on the field from the artillery park near Lee's headquarters, and hurried into position on the right near Richardson and about 170 yards west of the narrow cornfield. He took position as Hill's men came up. Somewhat later Captain Squires, who had quit Cemetery hill, because [he was] out of ammunition for his section of rifled guns, having refilled his limber chests and reported to Toombs was, with his two guns, and a section each of the Maryland Light Artillery (Dements' Battery) and Reilly's Battery, sent to the right, but, as

Panoramic view of the southern end of the battlefield from Pegram's Battery position. It give a good view of how the ridge upon which lay the Harper's Ferry Road dominates the terrain. *Author's collection.*

the Union attack had been repelled, they were not brought into action, and about the same time, a gun each of Cutshaw's Battery and Chew's Battery of horse artillery dashed up. On the outskirts of the town and 450 yards west of the Harper's Ferry road, Bachman's four guns were placed on a commanding hill, and 600 yards in Bachman's rear and 450 yards southeast of Lee's headquarters two rifled guns of Read's Georgia battery were placed in position, by Lee's order, to bear upon the enemy across "some fields over on the right of the road." Bachman and Read were not engaged, being held in reserve. Some of these guns were in position when Cox advanced, others came up as Hill arrived and some came later, nearly all were engaged and the judicious posting of this artillery, aggregating, with Hill's batteries, 43 guns, made Lee's right very strong.

We return to the 12th Ohio. It had about 200 men and was commanded by Colonel C. B. White. By Ewing's order it was to go forward with the 23rd and 30th to the stone fence. Before moving, however, it was reported that the enemy were moving around the left and it was ordered to form line at right angles with the 30th, move down to the cornfield and engage the enemy's flanking column, then seen in the southwest corner of the cornfield. It reached the northeast corner of the cornfield but before it could close up on the left of the 30th, came under a heavy fire of shell and spherical case that threatened its destruction, and immediately Gregg's Brigade, about 375 yards distant, in the southwest corner of the corn, opened fire upon it. A Union battery in the rear now opened in reply to the Confederate battery, probably Pegram's, and the regiment was directly in the line of fire of the two batteries and on the high point of ground between them, receiving shots from both, and to add to its discomfiture a regiment of raw troops that had taken position on the left of the battery, apparently mistaking it for the enemy, or endeavoring to reach the enemy in the corn beyond, opened fire; fortunately the fire was wild and too high. The regiment was ordered to lie down to escape the rain of shot and shell that was sweeping across its position and Colonel White called on a volunteer to go back to the regiment and battery and explain the situation; Sergeant John M. Snook performed the service, and White undertook to move the regiment to the left, out of immediate range of the two batteries and less exposed to the fire of Gregg's infantry. The order was misunderstood by the companies on the left, and resulted in an oblique move to the southeast, towards the Antietam, which came near resulting in a break of the regiment—but it was rallied at a fence, where it was as fully exposed both to the fire of artillery and musketry, as in its first position, and, after some effort on the part of the officers, it advanced to the east edge of the cornfield, about the length of the regiment to the left of its original position. Here it remained exchanging fire with the 1st South Carolina Rifles, until, being relieved by a regiment of Sturgis' Division,

Colonel Carr B. White, commander of the 12th Ohio
Library of Congress

which was now taking position on the left of the corps line, it fell back to the brow of the hill in front of the bridge and rejoined its brigade.

When disaster came to Harland's two regiments in the cornfield, the extreme left of the Ninth Corps, Cox was in the center of his line, near Clark's Battery, watching the progress of affairs on the right. He saw Willcox's and Crook's successful advance, the brilliant charge of Fairchild's Brigade and the advance of the 8th Connecticut. He also saw the movement of the 7th and 37th North Carolina on the flank and rear of the 8th Connecticut, the advance of Toombs and Archer on the Harper's Ferry road; two regiments of Branch in near support to Gregg, and the movement of Pender towards his left. He saw also the Confederate batteries hastening into position on the high ridge near the Harper's Ferry road, and open fire, and concluded "that it would be impossible to continue the movement to the right, and sent instant orders to Willcox and Crook to retire the left of their line, and to Sturgis to come forward into the gap made in Rodman's. The troops on the right swung back in perfect order; Scammon's Brigade hung on at the stone wall with unflinching tenacity till Sturgis had formed on the curving hill in rear of them, and Rodman's had found refuge behind."

In his official report Cox says:

> The mass of the enemy on the left still continued to increase; new batteries were constantly being opened upon us, and it was manifest the corps would, without reinforcements, be unable to reach the village of Sharpsburg, since the movement could not be made to the right whilst the enemy exhibited such force in front of the extreme left, and the attack both to the right and left at once would necessarily separate the wings to such an extent as to imperil the whole movement unwarrantably. The attack already having had the effect of a most powerful diversion in favor of the center and right of the army, which by this means had been able to make decided and successful advances, and no support at the time for our exhausted corps, I ordered the troops withdrawn from the exposed ground in front to the cover of the curved hill above the bridge, which had been taken from the enemy earlier in the afternoon. This movement was effected shortly before dark, in perfect order and with admirable coolness and precision on the part of both officers and men.

Let us see how the movement was conducted. Sturgis' Division was ordered forward to fill the gap in the line caused by the advance of Rodman. This division, after being relieved by Willcox, had been placed behind the ridge from which Rodman advanced; Ferrero's Brigade on the right, Nagle's on the left. Just before and while advancing to the position

The Otto family 40-acre cornfield and the Confederate line beyond from the Otto lane and the location of the left flank of the 35th Massachusetts. Fire from this location enfiladed the regiment and caused significant casualties. *Scott Felsen.*

vacated by Rodman the 8th Connecticut was attacked and driven back by Toombs, Kemper, Drayton, and a part of Branch, and the 23rd and 30th Ohio forced to retreat from the stone fence, by the advance of Toombs, Archer and Branch on their front and Gregg on their left flank. Ferrero's Brigade, nearest Cox, advanced to the position vacated by Fairchild, and about this time Durell's and Clark's batteries, having fired their last round of ammunition, retired and Coffin's two guns retreated under the fire of Richardson's Battery and Toombs' musketry.

The 35th Massachusetts on Ferrero's right, was ordered forward by Cox in person. It was lying down 100 yards in rear of the ridge. It rose to its feet and moved a short distance, when Coffin's section came dashing back at full speed, breaking the line for a moment, but the men closed up, obliqued a little to the left, then charged with a hurrah, on the double quick over the hill from which the 9th New York had charged, and down the slope, passing some broken commands, to the rail fences of Otto's lane, where it halted in a very exposed position, laid its rifles on the fence rails and opened fire. In front was a plowed field through which ran a deep ravine, sloping up to a stone wall 300 yards distant, behind which were the enemy, and on the left front, 150 to 250 yards distant, was the 40 acre cornfield. Beyond the stone wall on rising ground, and at a distance varying from 600 to 1200 yards were Confederate batteries. The first fire of the 35th was a rattling volley, then at will. The 21st Massachusetts, 51st New York, and 51st Pennsylvania advanced on the left of the 35th, and, having more experience in war, did not descend the west slope of the ridge, but laid down just under its crest, a few yards back from the lane, and the entire brigade line came under heavy artillery fire, and a rattling fire of musketry from the stone fence and cornfield in front and on the left. A portion of the 4th Rhode Island rallied on the left of the 51st Pennsylvania. An officer of the brigade says: "It was now nearly dark and the enemy jumped the fence with their colors and endeavored to advance but were driven back." This refers to the 37th North Carolina or Archer's Brigade, probably both.

Of Nagle's Brigade, on the left, the 2nd Maryland and 6th New Hampshire were held in reserve near the bridge; the 48th Pennsylvania was in rear, as second line to the 51st Pennsylvania, and the 9th New Hampshire, which had been in the rear, near Muhlenberg's Battery, was now advanced nearly to the left of the 51st Pennsylvania, overlooking the cornfield and on the right of the 12th Ohio, which was still engaged. Here it laid down to avoid the heavy artillery fire poured upon it. It was covered by Muhlenberg's Battery a few yards in its rear, Muhlenberg being supported by the 11th Connecticut of Harland's Brigade, the other regiments of the brigade returning to their bivouac beyond the Antietam. Soon the ammunition of the 51st Pennsylvania gave out, and the 48th, crawling forward, relived it, and it fell back to the position from which the 48th had

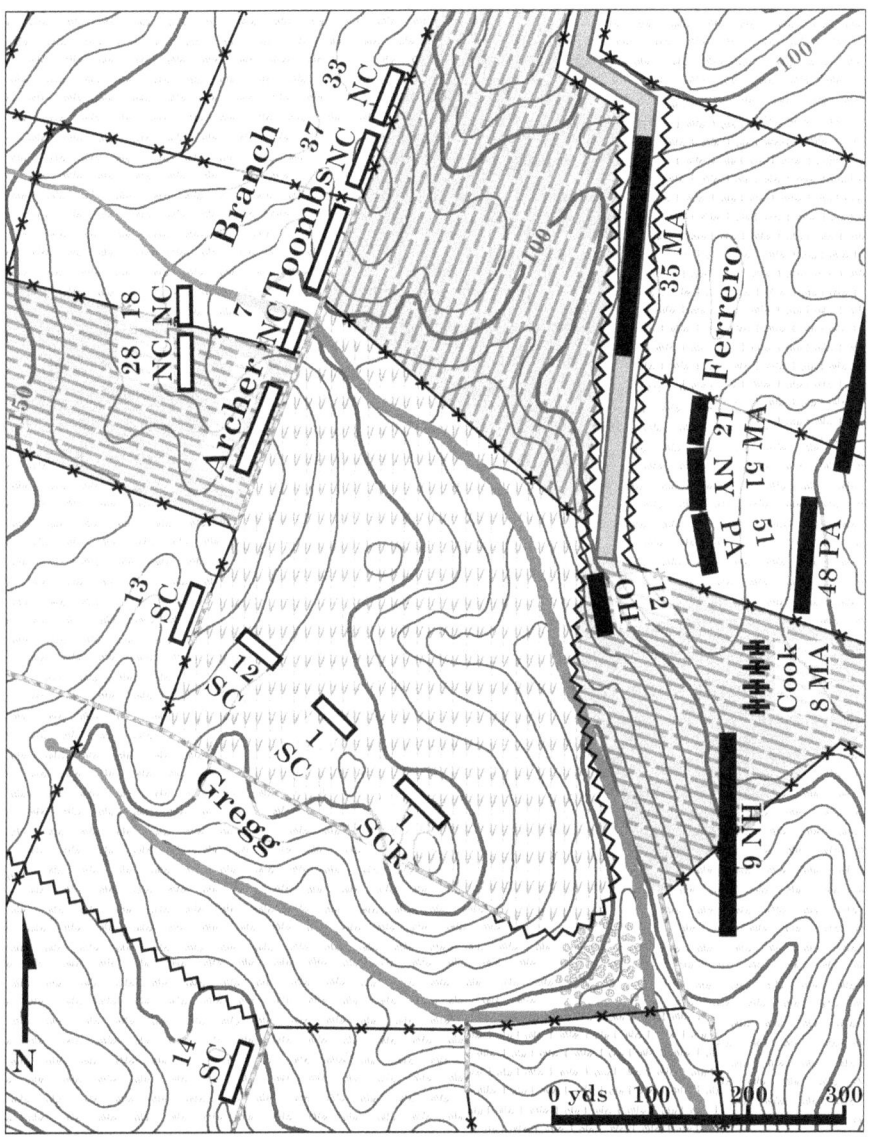

The Confederates line up along the stone wall and fences and engage Ferrero's brigade and other Union units to the south. The fighting continues until dusk.

advanced and replenished ammunition. Very soon after this, about sunset, the 12th Ohio fell back and the 9th New Hampshire soon followed, both under a heavy artillery fire from the batteries in front and from the three guns of Pegram and Braxton near Snavely's, the 9th New Hampshire went back in some disorder, most of it men recrossing the Antietam by the ford below the bridge, the remainder being rallied about half way between the cornfield and the bridge. It was now dark and the 2nd Maryland and 6th New Hampshire were sent forward as skirmishers on the left, overlooking the corn, and remained all night. On the right of the division line the 35th Massachusetts, though exposed to a most terrific fire of artillery and musketry, during which it lost 3 officers and 45 men killed and 160 wounded, remained until near dark, when, under orders, it fell back, under a shower of musketry, went down to the bridge, then up the road to the left and bivouacked. The 51st Pennsylvania, having replenished ammunition again went forward and occupied that point of the ridge beyond which the 35th Massachusetts had fought, and the 51st New York was relieved by an Ohio regiment of Crook's Brigade, now taking position to relive Sturgis, who was massing his division on the left. The 21st Massachusetts, after seeing everything on its right fall back and the 51st New York, on its left, relieved, fell back to the high ground just above the ridge and joined its brigade. Ferrero says of his brigade: "firing every round they had in their boxes, they quietly placed themselves on the ground in their position, and remained until other regiments had formed in front to relieve them, when by my orders they retired in good order from the field, and again marched to the banks of the creek." In marching to the banks of the creek Ferrero joined the other brigade of the division, which formed the extreme left resting on the creek below the bridge, and the troops relieving him and forming the center of the line were Crook's regiments supported by Ewing's rallied command.

It was under cover of Sturgis' advance to the ridge vacated by Rodman that Willcox and Crook were withdrawn. It was half past 4; Willcox was about out of ammunition, for the wagons had not been able to accompany the forward movement, and his advance was halted "partly in the town and partly on the hills," to allow his men to take some breath and to fetch up some cartridges, when he received Cox's order to fall back, upon which he sent an order to Fairchild, on his left, as we have seen, to withdraw to the ravine near Otto's. Here Fairchild, with the 11th Ohio of Crook's Brigade, faced to the left to meet the advance of Toombs and Archer, but these being held back by Sturgis, who had now formed on the ridge, Fairchild soon moved down the road to the bridge and halted in the roadway.

Willcox then withdrew to the position from which he had made his final advance, every regiment marching back in perfect order, Crook's Brigade which had remained at the stone fence in advance of Otto's and was about

View from the 35th Massachusetts toward the 33rd and 37th North Carolina. The Confederate line is on the crest of the hill in front of the wood line. *Author's collection.*

to advance when Willcox was ordered to withdraw, now fell back and relieved Sturgis, who fell back to the left; and the line, as thus established, covered the Burnside bridge, Sturgis' Division in front, on the left, supported by Fairchild; the Kanawha Division, under Colonel Scammon, in the center, Crook's large brigade in front, supported by Ewing, and Willcox's Division on the right. Muhlenberg's Battery and the 11th Connecticut recrossed the Antietam and bivouacked with the other three regiments of Harland near Rohrbach's. The 4 guns of Cook's Battery, which had been halted in the road, when Coffin went forward with his section, counter-marched about 4 p.m., went up the road to the left of the bridge and opened fire near the cornfield, where they were subjected to a cross fire from the enemy's batteries and infantry. The fire from the corn was very severe. After firing several rounds, while Sturgis was taking his position on the left, the approach of darkness compelled the cessation of operations, but the guns were charged with canister and the men lay with them.

Cox expressed his satisfaction with the manner in which his divisions were handled: "The movements were accurate as those of a parade, and the systematic order with which they were executed made the spectacle in the heat of the battle a grand and inspiring one." No corps commander on the field displayed more tactical ability than Cox, both in the attack and the dispositions quickly made when reverse, for which he was not responsible, came to his left.

Cox reports that these dispositions were made "shortly before dark," and elsewhere says: "The men of the Ninth Corps lay that night upon their arms, the line being one which rested with both flanks near the Antietam, and curved outward upon the rolling hill tops which covered the bridge and commanded the plateau between us and the enemy. With my staff I lay upon the ground behind the troops, holding our horses by the bridles as we rested, for our orderlies were so exhausted that we could not deny them the same chance for a little broken slumber."

An instance of comradeship and thoughtful devotion to duty may here be noted. As the sun was setting, a regimental commissary sergeant, of 18 years, who had remained with the trains in camp, east of the Antietam, approached the Burnside bridge with a loaded wagon. Loaded ammunition wagons were going forward, as far as the bridge, and empty ones were returning; empty ambulances were going and loaded ones were coming back, wounded men were finding their way to the rear, shells were exploding, and he was cautioned of danger and advised not to proceed, and a general officer, passing to the rear, ordered him to turn back but, when he had passed by, the young soldier crossed the bridge, went up the road to the left, turned to the right, and, halting at the bivouac of the 23rd Ohio, under the artillery fire, distributed to his comrades cooked rations and coffee.

The William McKinley monument near the Lower Bridge. *Author's collection.*

There was no finer exhibition of thoughtful duty than that given by this youthful soldier—William McKinley. It was recognized by promotion and was the beginning of a brilliant career.

The Confederates did not venture an attack upon Cox's position but, content with having repulsed him, kept up a brisk artillery and musketry fire until dark, when it gradually ceased and the battle of Antietam was ended.

A. P. Hill's Division rested for the night along the stone fences running northerly from the large cornfield to the Burnside bridge road; Kemper and Drayton in its rear, in the position occupied earlier in the day. Toombs was on Cemetery hill on Hill's left; Jenkins' Brigade again advanced to the apple orchard and threw out skirmishers beyond Sherrick's lane, and Garnett's small command re-occupied Cemetery hill. At dark Carter's Battery was sent by General Lee to occupy the hill and guard the road leading from the middle bridge.

The loss of the Ninth Corps was 24 officers and 414 men killed; 98 officers and 1,698 men wounded; 2 officers and 113 men missing, an aggregate of 2,349. Rodman's Division suffered the most severely, and the heaviest percentage of loss was Fairchild's Brigade. Crook's Brigade suffered least, it had 73 killed, wounded, and missing.

The loss in A. P. Hill's Division, in its short, sharp, and successful encounter, was 66 killed, 332 wounded, and 6 missing, an aggregate of 404. The loss in D. R. Jones' Division, the day alone, and including the loss in its engagement with the regular infantry on the Keedysville road, was about 75 killed, 450 wounded, and 40 missing, an aggregate of 565; or a total loss in the two divisions of 969. The loss of the artillery not belonging to these divisions would increase the loss to over 1,000.

The conduct of the battle on the Union left has given rise to much heated discussion, in which McClellan, Fitz-John Porter and Burnside have been severely condemned, McClellan and his friends contending that for Burnside's tardiness, "the victory might have been much more decisive." In this chapter we have given in some detail, Burnside's movements; in the preceding chapter we have treated of Porter's, it remains to say a few words of McClellan, who has been criticized for his failure in uniting what he could spare from Franklin's corps to Porter's, and supporting Burnside's attack by a movement along the Keedysville road directly towards Sharpsburg.

McClellan passed nearly the entire day on the high ground at Pry's house, where he had his headquarters and where, Palfrey says, he "had some glasses strapped to the fence, so that he could look in different directions." Early in the day Colonel Sackett, of his staff, was sent with an order to Burnside to push across the bridge, and Sackett was directed to remain with Burnside, to see that the order was promptly executed and to give him assistance. Other messengers went from headquarters to Burnside urging

William Fitzsimons, Company B, 35th Massachusetts Infantry
Library of Congress.

haste in the execution of this movement. Before noon McClellan sent Pleasonton across the Antietam by the middle bridge to support Sumner's fight at the Sunken Road and, about noon, sent two batteries of Porter's corps and some of Porter's infantry to support them and drive back the Confederate skirmishers, who had been annoying Pleasonton's guns. Sykes says these were sent against his (Sykes) judgment and Porter complained that the infantry were diverted from the service of supporting the batteries and were "employed to drive the enemy's skirmishers to their reserves." At 1 o'clock information was received that the bridge had been carried, and there was a lull along the whole line from right to left, the fighting on the extreme right had ceased, and that at the Sunken Road was confined to artillery.

A short time before the bridge was carried McClellan sent Colonel Key of his staff to inform Burnside that he desired him to push forward with the utmost vigor, take the bridge with the bayonet, and carry the enemy's position on the heights; that the movement was vital to success; that this was the time he must not stop for loss of life, if a great object could thereby be accomplished, that if, in his judgment, the attack would fail, to inform him so at once, that his troops might be withdrawn and used elsewhere on the field. The bridge was now carried, and Key quickly returned with Burnside's reply that he would soon advance and go up the hill as far as a battery of the enemy, on the left, would permit. Key was immediately sent back to Burnside with preemptory orders to advance at once. "At this time," says W. F. Biddle," Colonel Key carried an order in McClellan's handwriting relieving Burnside on the spot and placing General Morell in command, to be used if Burnside did not instantly advance and fight."

Captain Hiram Dryer was now ordered across the middle bridge with additional battalions of regular infantry, with directions to take command of all of Porter's troops there. After sending Key on the second mission to Burnside, McClellan "towards the middle of the afternoon, proceeding to the right, found that Sumner's, Hooker's and Mansfield's corps had met with serious losses,...and the aspect of affairs was anything but promising." McClellan says: "At the risk of greatly exposing our center, I ordered two brigades from Porter's corps, the only available troops, to reinforce the right." Franklin was chafing to attack with the Sixth Corps, but Sumner had forbidden it and expressed to McClellan "the most decided opinion against another attempt during that day to assault the enemy's position in front, as portions of our troops were so much scattered and demoralized. In view of these circumstances," says McClellan, "after making changes in the positions of some of the troops, I directed the different commanders to hold their positions, and, being satisfied that this could be done without the assistance of the two brigades from the center, I countermanded the order, which was in course of execution."

Eli Franklin of Company B, 1st South Carolina Infantry
Library of Congress.

While McClellan was absent on the right, where there was no fighting, and where he had determined that his own part, so far as he could prevent, there should be none, Porter and Sykes were discontinuing movements that would have helped Burnside. We have already stated, in the preceding chapter that, about 3 p.m. Pleasonton asked McClellan for more infantry. He received this reply:

> HEADQUARTERS ARMY OF THE POTOMAC,
> September 17, 1862 3.30 p. m.
> Brigadier-General PLEASONTON:
>
> GENERAL: General McClellan directs me to say he has no infantry to spare.
> Confer with Major-General Porter, and if he cannot support your batteries, withdraw them.
> I am, general, very respectfully, your obedient servant,
>
> R. B. MARCY,
> Chief of Staff.[5]

The tenor of the dispatch and the surrounding circumstances indicate that it was not dictated by McClellan, who was absent, but that it was made upon the responsibility of the chief of staff, who had remained at headquarters, for certainly it would be very singular that McClellan, if present, would have referred Pleasonton to Porter, when Porter, himself, was at headquarters, a word to whom would have decided the matter, without having the reply go to Pleasonton and then another message to Porter, all of which would have consumed nearly an hour of very precious time; and it is still more singular that either McClellan, Porter or Marcy would consent to the withdrawal of the batteries at the very moment Burnside was advancing; the natural conclusion would be that all would have united in supporting them strongly to assist Burnside. But it was not so; both Porter and Sykes had very reluctantly sent their artillery and infantry across the Antietam, they were not disposed to do more; and a half an hour later Pleasonton was ordered by McClellan to send some of his cavalry to the right, where it was employed in gathering stragglers of the First Corps.

---

[5] *OR*, vol. 51, part I, p. 845.

Cemetery Hill and the area where Willcox's division fought from Fairchild's line. Looking north from the stone wall they captured from Drayton and Kemper. The National Cemetery is visible. *Author's collection.*

HEADQUARTERS ARMY OF THE POTOMAC,

September 17, 1862—p.m.

Brigadier-General PLEASONTON:

GENERAL: General McClellan directs you to send two squadrons of cavalry to report to Brigadier-General Meade. He will probably be found near the Pennsylvania Reserves, on our right.
I am, general, very respectfully, your obedient servant,

GEO. D. RUGGLES,
Colonel and Aide-de-Camp.[6]

    Pleasonton saw the weakness of the Confederate line in his front, and the advance of Burnside on Sharpsburg and believing that there was a good opening for him to advance his batteries to Cemetery Hill and ridge and there assist Burnside, acted upon the suggestion made by the chief of staff, in his note of 3:30 p.m.; and, at 4 p.m. sent a request to Porter for a division to support his advance. Porter says he did not receive the request until after Burnside had been repulsed, that he did not have the division and could not, under his orders, imperil the success of the day by diminishing his small command. Not only were troops withheld from Pleasonton, but, soon after this, Sykes, who saw the regulars, under Dryer, advancing in fine style upon Cemetery Hill and ridge, and making close connection with Burnside's right, withdrew them and reprimanded their commander for exceeding his instructions. In justice to Porter it may be stated that at 5 p.m. he sent this dispatch to Sykes, elsewhere quoted: "Burnside is driving the enemy. Please send word to the command you sent to Pleasonton to support his batteries, and let him drive them."
    Colonel Sackett, who had been directed to remain with Burnside waited until his troops were well under way up the heights and then returned to headquarters, where he found Porter, McClellan being away on the right and it was past 4 o'clock in the afternoon, and it was not long after this that the check and repulse of was witnessed.
    Soon after Sackett's arrival at headquarters McClellan returned from the right and was a quiet witness to the check given Burnside and his withdrawal to the bridge, and at this time General R. E. Lee was rallying his broken commands in the streets of Sharpsburg. McClellan made such

---

[6] *OR*, vol. 51, part I, p. 845.

The Isaac P. Rodman mortuary cannon along Fairchild's line. *Author's collection.*

dispositions of the troops on the right as to satisfy him that it "was safe without the assistance" of Porter's two brigades from the center, and under these circumstances one would suppose he could have spared some of Porter's troops to assist Burnside, who was seen to be hard pressed, but he did not use a man of them, and, when Burnside called for assistance, replied that he had no infantry to give him. There was at this time a correspondent of the *New York Tribune* at McClellan's headquarters, who wrote that evening that, while Burnside was being checked and then falling back:

> McClellan's glass for the last half hour has seldom been turned from the left. He sees clearly enough that Burnside is pressed—needs no messenger to tell him that. His face grows darker with anxious thought. Looking down into the valley where 15,000 (about 10,000) troops are lying, he turns a half-questioning look on Fitz-John Porter, who stands by his side, gravely scanning the field. They are Porter's troops below, are fresh and only impatient to join in this fight. But Porter slowly shakes his head, and one may believe that the same thought is passing through the minds of both generals, 'They are the only reserve of the army; they cannot be spared.' McClellan mounts his horse, and with Porter and a dozen officers of his staff, rides away to the left in Burnside's direction. Sykes meets them on the road, a good soldier, whose opinion is worth taking. The three generals talk briefly together. Burnside's messenger rides up. His message is, 'I want troops and guns. If you do not send them, I cannot hold my position half an hour.' McClellan's only answer for the moment is a glance at the western sky. Then he turns and speaks very slowly. 'Tell General Burnside this is the battle of the war. He must hold his ground at any cost. I will send him Miller's Battery. I can do nothing more. I have no infantry.' Then as the messenger was riding away, he called him back. 'Tell him if he cannot hold his ground, then the bridge, to the last man! Always the bridge! If the bridge is lost, all is lost.' The sun is already down; not half an hour of daylight is left.

McClellan did not go to Burnside. Miller's Battery was sent and took position with Benjamin, east of the Antietam, to guard the bridge, and this order was sent to Burnside:

HEADQUARTERS ARMY OF THE POTOMAC,
September 17, 1862—6.10 p.m.
Major-General BURNSIDE:

> GENERAL: General McClellan directs me to say that whatever the result of your affair to-night may be, you must so guard the bridge

Brigadier General George Sykes
Library of Congress

with infantry and artillery as to make it impossible for the enemy to cross it.

I am, general, very respectfully, your obedient servant,

R. B. MARCY,
Chief of Staff.[7]

Five minutes after this, upon a report that the enemy was retreating, this dispatch was sent:

HEADQUARTERS ARMY OF THE POTOMAC,
September 17, 1862—6.15 p. m.
Major-General BURNSIDE:

GENERAL: General McClellan directs me to enclose the accompanying dispatch from signal officer, and to say that if there is any truth in it, he desires you to push the enemy vigorously. Let the general know if the enemy is retreating, and he will push forward with the center.

I am, general, very respectfully, your obedient servant,

R. B. MARCY,
Chief of Staff.[8]

McClellan's reasons for not using Porter's corps, are given in his official report:

This corps filled the interval between the right wing and General Burnside's command, and guarded the main approach from the enemy's position to our trains of supply. It was necessary to watch this part of our line with the utmost vigilance, lest the enemy should take advantage of the first exhibition of weakness here to push upon us a vigorous assault for the purpose of piercing our center and turning our rear, as well as to capture or destroy our supply trains. Once having penetrated this line, the enemy's passage to our rear could have met with feeble resistance, as there were no reserves to reinforce or close up the gap...Continually under the vigilant watch of the enemy, this corps guarded a vital point.

---

[7] *OR*, vol. 51, part I, p. 844.
[8] Ibid.

The Otto farm from the high ground across the bridge road. *Indiana at Antietam.*

Porter shared McClellan's views as to the great importance of his position, in guarding the trains, and that any diminution of his force, for offensive operations, would endanger their safety and imperil the army. It is inconceivable that these two soldiers could seriously suppose that Lee would think of putting a column of attack against McClellan's center, snugly ensconced behind the Antietam and a bold bluff bordering it, a position approached only over open ground for nearly a mile, covered by a direct and cross-fire of 80 guns, of 120, if necessary, then by head of column, cross a narrow bridge, so entirely commanded by the heights looking down upon it, from either side of the road, that an officer of ordinary spirit with 2,000 men, could have successfully have defended it against 20,000 men of the very best Lee had in his army; it is conceivable only upon the theory that they supposed Lee had such an overwhelming force that he could afford a great sacrifice for the desperate venture. In fact Lee never entertained a thought of McClellan's trains and, in striking contrast to McClellan, cared for and defended his own by putting every man on the fighting line.

One of the defects of McClellan as a commander was his overestimate of his adversary's numbers. It began with his campaign in western Virginia, it was with him on the Peninsula, and he had been not a week on his Maryland campaign that we find (sic) estimating Lee's army at 120,000, and at Antietam he believed that he was greatly outnumbered. If he had substantial reasons for this belief at all: "prudence of the commonest kind would have forbidden any attack at all": especially is it true that, after Sedgwick's repulse on the right and Franklin's enforced inaction, the persistent urging of Burnside to advance from the high ground at the bridge, without supporting him on the line of the Sharpsburg road, was a stupendous crime. If it had any justification it was that such a movement was necessary to save the right from a disastrous defeat, and this is the view taken by General Cox, who, as commander of the 9th Corps on the field, was in a position to know, and has thus written of Porter's reserve and the failure of McClellan to use it:

> As troops are put in reserve, not to diminish the army, but to be used in a pinch, I am deeply convinced that McClellan's refusal to use them on the left was the result of his continued conviction through all the day after Sedgwick's defeat, that Lee was overwhelmingly superior in force, and was preparing to return a crushing blow upon our right flank. He was keeping something in hand to cover a retreat, if that wing should be driven back. Except in this way, also, I am at a loss to account for the inaction of our right during the whole of our engagement on the left. Looking at our part of the battle as only a strong diversion to prevent or delay Lee's following up his success

The Sherrick farm from the front yard of the Otto house across the bridge road. *Library of Congress.*

against Hooker and the rest it is intelligible. I certainly so understood it at the time, as my report witnesses, and McClellan's report supports this view. If he had been impatient to have our attack delivered earlier, he had reason for double impatience that Franklin's fresh troops should assail Lee's left simultaneously with ours, unless he regarded action there as hopeless, and looked upon our movement as a sort of forlorn-hope to keep Lee from following up his advantages.

Longstreet says McClellan's plan of battle was not strong, "the handling and execution were less so. Battles by the extreme right and left, divided by a river, gave us the benefit of interior lines, and it was that that saved the Confederate army, for it became manifest early in the day that his reserves were held at the bridge No. 2, which gave us freer use of our inner lines." He also says: "We were so badly crushed that at the close of the day 10,000 fresh troops could have come in and taken Lee's army and everything it had."

The battle was a succession of disjointed attacks and stubborn resistance to them. It began with the advance of the First Corps at daybreak and the fighting of this corps was over when the Twelfth Corps became engaged at 7:30 a.m., and this corps, without any assistance from the First, except Patrick's small brigade, fought alone and drove the enemy across the Hagerstown road a little before 9 o'clock. At 9 o'clock Sumner came up with one division, went forward and was repulsed with great loss. Palfrey says this one division (Sedgwick) "might as well have been another county for any direct aid it received from the rest of the Army of the Potomac," but Palfrey is in error, for support and aid was given it by the greater part of the Twelfth Corps. The other two divisions of Sumner became engaged later, and not simultaneously, and not in close connection with Sedgwick, and not until this fighting was nearly over on the right did Burnside become seriously engaged. General Sumner testified before the Committee on the Conduct of the War:

> I have always believed that, instead of sending these troops into that action in details, as they were sent, if General McClellan had authorized me to march these 40,000 men on the left flank of the enemy, we could not have failed to throw them right back in our front of the other divisions of our army on our left. Burnside's, Franklin's and Porter's corps, as it was, we went in, division after division, until even one of my divisions was forced out. The other two drove the enemy and held their positions.

Franklin's Sixth Corps arrived near Keedysville a little after 10 a.m. and "it was first intended to keep this corps in reserve on the east of the

Confederate dead on the battlefield. Although the image is labelled "Antietam, Maryland. Battlefield near Sherrick's house where the 79th N.Y. Vols. fought after they crossed the creek." Its definitive location has not been established. *Library of Congress.*

Antietam to operate on either flank or on the center, as circumstances might require; but on nearing Keedysville the strong opposition on the right, developed by the attacks of Hooker and Sumner, rendered it necessary at once to send this corps to the assistance of the right wing." Had Franklin's entire corps, or one division of it, been pushed across the middle bridge, and seized the ridge overlooking Sharpsburg, as it could have done, Lee would have had his hands full in guarding his center, without any offensive operations against McClellan's right. It is futile, however, to speculate on what might have done. McClellan was content that he had handled his army with great skill.

Both McClellan and Lee considered Antietam their greatest battle. In a home letter written the day after, McClellan says, "Those in whose judgment I rely tell me that I fought the battle splendidly, and that it was a master piece of art." History will not accept this view of a battle in the conduct of which more errors were committed by the Union commander than in any other battle of the war: it will accept the opinion of the Confederate historian:

> Whatever may be thought or said of the strategy which led to the battle of Sharpsburg, the conduct of that battle itself by Lee and his principal subordinates seems absolutely above criticism. Had Lee known all that we know now of the Federal plans and forces, it is difficult to see how he could have more wisely disposed or more effectively used the means he had at hand. The utmost tension existed at different points of his lines during the day. He had no reserves, but so judiciously were the Confederate troops handled that their obstinate courage was sufficient everywhere to prevent any serious loss of position.

Between daybreak and the setting sun of September 17, 1862, was the bloodiest day of American history. Ninety three thousand men of kindred blood (56,000 Union and 27,000 Confederate), and 520 guns engaged in the desperate struggle, and when the sun went down and mercifully put an end to the strife, 3,654 were dead, and 17,292 wounded. About 1,779 were missing, some of whom were dead, but most of whom were carried as prisoners from the field. Every state from the great lakes on the north to the Gulf of Mexico, on the south; from the Atlantic to the Mississippi, and, with the exception of Iowa and Missouri, every state watered by the Mississippi, contributed to this carnival of death and suffering.

Palfrey has most beautifully written:

> As the sun sank to rest on the 17th of September, the last sounds of battle along Antietam Creek died away. The cannon could at last grow

Dead on the Antietam battlefield. Location unknown. *Library of Congress.*

cool, and unwounded men and horses could enjoy rest and food, but there were already thousands sleeping the sleep that knows no waking, and many times as many thousands were suffering all the agonies that attend on wounds. The corn and trees, so fresh and green in the morning, were reddened with blood and torn by bullet and shell; and the very earth was furrowed by the incessant impact of lead and iron. The blessed night came, and brought with it sleep and forgetfulness and refreshment to many, but the murmur of the night wind, breathing over fields of wheat and clover, was mingled with the groans of the countless sufferers of both armies. Who can tell, who can imagine, the horrors of such a night, while the unconscious stars shone above, and the unconscious river went rippling by?

Appendix 1[9]

Order of Battle

Union

Army of the Potomac 55,956[10]
Major General George B. McClellan

General Headquarters

Escort
Independent Company Oneida (New York) Cavalry
4th United States Cavalry, Companies A and E

Provost Guard
Major William F. Hood
2nd United States Cavalry, Companies E, F, H, and K
8th United States, Companies A, D, F, and G
19th United States, Company H

Headquarters Guard
93rd New York

---

[9] Carman published an order of battle as Appendix 1 and unit strength calculations as Appendix 2. However, since I have modified it slightly to include only those units engaged in battle or on the field by September 17th, this chapter is not as Carman published it, but a new representation.

[10] Unit strengths listed as Carman presented them in his manuscript and appendixes with little clarification except using the *Official Records* to separate the strengths of attached artillery batteries from their infantry brigades where necessary. Carman calculated engaged strengths and not present for duty. Still, he's just as likely to be as accurate as other sources.

First Army Corps 9,438
Major General Joseph Hooker

1st Division 3,425
Brigadier General Abner Doubleday

<u>1st Brigade</u> 425
Colonel Walter
Phelps Jr.
22nd New York
24th New York
30th New York
84th New York*
2nd United States
Sharpshooters
*Also known as the
14th Brooklyn

<u>2nd Brigade</u> 750
Lt. Colonel J.
William Hoffman
7th Indiana
76th New York
95th New York
56th Pennsylvania

<u>3rd Brigade</u> 829
Brigadier General
Marsena R. Patrick
21st New York
23rd New York
35th New York
80th New York

<u>4th Brigade</u> 971
Brigadier General John Gibbon
19th Indiana
2nd Wisconsin
6th Wisconsin
7th Wisconsin

<u>Artillery</u> 450
1st New Hampshire Battery
Battery D, 1st Rhode Island
Battery L, 1st New York
Battery B, 4th United States

2d Division 3,158
Brigadier General James B. Ricketts

<u>1st Brigade</u> 1,100
Brigadier General
Abram Duryée
97th New York
104th New York
105th New York
107th Pennsylvania

<u>2nd Brigade</u> 937
Colonel William A.
Christian
26th New York
94th New York
88th Pennsylvania
90th Pennsylvania

<u>3rd Brigade</u> 1,000
Brigadier General
George L. Hartsuff
12th Massachusetts
13th Massachusetts
83rd New York
11th Pennsylvania

<u>Artillery</u> 121
Battery F, 1st Pennsylvania
Battery C, Pennsylvania Light

3rd Division 2,855
Brigadier General George G. Meade

<u>1st Brigade</u>
Brigadier General Truman Seymour
1st Pennsylvania Reserves
2nd Pennsylvania Reserves
5th Pennsylvania Reserves
6th Pennsylvania Reserves
13th Pennsylvania Reserves

<u>2nd Brigade</u>
Colonel Albert L. Magilton
3rd Pennsylvania Reserves
4th Pennsylvania Reserves
7th Pennsylvania Reserves
8th Pennsylvania Reserves

<u>3rd Brigade</u>
Lt. Colonel Robert Anderson
9th Pennsylvania Reserves
10th Pennsylvania Reserves
11th Pennsylvania Reserves
12th Pennsylvania Reserves

<u>Artillery</u> 248
Battery A, 1st Pennsylvania
Battery B, 1st Pennsylvania
Battery C, 5th United States

Second Army Corps 16,065
Major General Edwin V. Sumner

1st Division 4,275
Major General Israel B. Richardson

<u>1st Brigade</u> 1,339
Brigadier General John C. Caldwell
5th New Hampshire
7th New York
61st & 64th New York
81st Pennsylvania

<u>2nd Brigade</u> 1,340
Brigadier General Thomas F. Meagher
29th Massachusetts
63rd New York
69th New York
88th New York

<u>3rd Brigade</u> 1,336
Colonel John R. Brooke
2nd Delaware
52nd New York
57th New York
66th New York
53rd Pennsylvania

<u>Artillery</u> 246
Battery B, 1st New York
Batteries A & C, 4th United States

2nd Division 5,681
Major General John Sedgwick

1st Brigade 1,691
Brigadier General
Willis A. Gorman
15th Massachusetts
1st Minnesota
34th New York
82nd New York
Massachusetts Sharpshooters, 1st Company
Minnesota Sharpshooters, 2nd Company

2nd Brigade 1,800
Brigadier General
Oliver O. Howard
69th Pennsylvania
71st Pennsylvania
72nd Pennsylvania
106th Pennsylvania

3rd Brigade 1,946
Brigadier General
Napoleon J. T. Dana
19th Massachusetts
20th Massachusetts
7th Michigan
42nd New York
59th New York

Artillery 244
Battery A, 1st Rhode Island
Battery I, 1st United States

3rd Division 5,740
Brigadier General William H. French

1st Brigade 1,751
Brigadier General
Nathan Kimball
14th Indiana
8th Ohio
132nd Pennsylvania
7th West Virginia

2nd Brigade 2,191
Colonel Dwight
Morris
14th Connecticut
108th New York
130th Pennsylvania

3rd Brigade 1,798
Brigadier General
Max Weber
1st Delaware
5th Maryland
4th New York

Unattached Artillery 369
Battery G, 1st New York
Battery B, 1st Rhode Island
Battery G, 1st Rhode Island

Fifth Army Corps
Major General Fitz John Porter

1st Division
Major General George W. Morell

<u>1st Brigade</u>
Colonel James Barnes
2nd Maine
18th Massachusetts
22nd Massachusetts
1st Michigan
13th New York
25th New York
118th Pennsylvania
Massachusetts Sharpshooters, 2nd Company

<u>2nd Brigade</u>
Brigadier General Charles Griffin
2nd District of Columbia
9th Massachusetts
32nd Massachusetts
4th Michigan
14th New York
62nd Pennsylvania

<u>3rd Brigade</u>
Colonel Thomas B. W. Stockton
20th Maine
16th Michigan
12th New York
17th New York
44th New York
83rd Pennsylvania
Michigan Sharpshooters, Brady's Company

<u>Unassigned</u>
1st United States Sharpshooters

<u>Artillery</u>
Battery C, Massachusetts Light
Battery C, 1st Rhode Island
Battery D, 5th United States

2nd Division
Brigadier General George Sykes

<u>1st Brigade</u>
Lt. Colonel Robert C. Buchanan
3rd United States
4th United States
12th United States, 1st Battalion
12th United States, 2nd Battalion
14th United States, 1st Battalion
14th United States, 2nd Battalion

<u>2nd Brigade</u>
Major Charles S. Lovell
1st & 6th United States
2nd & 10th United States
11th United States
17th United States

3rd Brigade
Colonel Gouverneur K. Warren
5th New York
10th New York

Artillery
Batteries E & G, 1st United States
Battery I, 5th United States
Battery K, 5th United States

Artillery Reserve
Battery A, 1st Battalion New York
Battery B, 1st Battalion New York
Battery C, 1st Battalion New York
Battery D, 1st Battalion New York
5th New York Battery
Battery K, 1st United States
Battery G, 4th United States

Sixth Army Corps
Major General William B. Franklin

1st Division
Major General Henry W. Slocum

1st Brigade
Colonel Alfred T. A. Torbert
1st New Jersey
2nd New Jersey
3rd New Jersey
4th New Jersey

2nd Brigade
Colonel Joseph J. Bartlett

5th Maine
16th New York
27th New York
96th Pennsylvania

3rd Brigade
Brigadier General John Newton
18th New York
31st New York
32nd New York
95th Pennsylvania

Artillery
Battery A, Maryland Light
Battery A, Massachusetts Light
Battery A, New Jersey Light
Battery D, 2nd United States

2nd Division
Major General William F. Smith

<u>1st Brigade</u>	<u>2nd Brigade</u>	<u>3rd Brigade</u> 1,684
Brigadier General	Brigadier General	Colonel William H.
Winfield S. Hancock	William T. H. Brooks	Irwin
6th Maine	2nd Vermont	7th Maine
43rd New York	3rd Vermont	20th New York
49th Pennsylvania	4th Vermont	33rd New York
137th Pennsylvania	5th Vermont	49th New York
5th Wisconsin	6th Vermont	77th New York

<u>Artillery</u>
Battery B, Maryland Light
1st New York Light Battery
Battery F, 5th United States

Ninth Army Corps 12,765
Major General Ambrose E. Burnside
Brigadier General Jacob D. Cox

1st Division 3,248
Brigadier General Orlando B. Willcox

<u>1st Brigade</u> 1,395	<u>2nd Brigade</u> 1,623	<u>Artillery</u> 246
Colonel Benjamin C. Christ	Colonel Thomas Welsh	8th Battery Massachusetts Light
28th Massachusetts	8th Michigan	Battery E, 2nd United States
17th Michigan	46th New York	
79th New York	45th Pennsylvania	
50th Pennsylvania	100th Pennsylvania	

2nd Division 3,254
Brigadier General Samuel D. Sturgis

<u>1st Brigade</u> 1,412	<u>2nd Brigade</u> 1,601	<u>Artillery</u> 241
Brigadier General James Nagle	Brigadier General Edward Ferrero	Battery D, Pennsylvania Light
2nd Maryland	21st Massachusetts	Battery E, 4th United States
6th New Hampshire	35th Massachusetts	
9th New Hampshire	51st New York	
48th Pennsylvania	51st Pennsylvania	

3rd Division 2,914
Brigadier General Isaac P. Rodman

<u>1st Brigade</u> 943
Colonel Harrison S. Fairchild
9th New York
89th New York
103rd New York
Co. K, 9th New York Infantry (Battery)

<u>2nd Brigade</u> 1,848
Colonel Edward Harland
8th Connecticut
11th Connecticut
16th Connecticut
4th Rhode Island

<u>Artillery</u> 123
Battery A, 5th United States

Kanawha Division 3,154
Colonel Eliakim P. Scammon

<u>1st Brigade</u> 1,026
Colonel Hugh B. Ewing
12th Ohio
23rd Ohio
30th Ohio
Gilmore's Company West Virginia Cavalry
Harrison's Company West Virginia Cavalry
1st Battery Ohio Light Artillery

<u>2nd Brigade</u> 2,128
Colonel George Crook
11th Ohio
28th Ohio
36th Ohio
Kentucky Light Artillery

<u>Unattached</u>
6th New York Cavalry
Ohio Cavalry, 3d Independent Co.

<u>Unattached Artillery</u> 195[11]
Batteries L & M 3rd United States
Battery L, 2nd New York

---

[11] Clemens, 582.

Twelfth Army Corps 7,631
Brigadier General Joseph K. Mansfield

1st Division 4,735
Brigadier General Alpheus S. Williams

<u>1st Brigade</u> 2,525
Brigadier General
Samuel W. Crawford
10th Maine
28th New York
46th Pennsylvania
124th Pennsylvania
125th Pennsylvania
128th Pennsylvania

<u>3rd Brigade</u> 2,210
Brigadier General George H. Gordon
27th Indiana
2nd Massachusetts
13th New Jersey
107th New York
3rd Wisconsin

2nd Division 2,504
Brigadier General George S. Greene

<u>1st Brigade</u> 1,191
Lt. Colonel Hector Tyndale
5th Ohio
7th Ohio
66th Ohio
28th Pennsylvania

<u>2nd Brigade</u> 536
Colonel Henry J. Stainrook
3rd Maryland
102nd New York
111th Pennsylvania

<u>3rd Brigade</u> 777
Colonel William B. Goodrich
3rd Delaware
Purnell Legion
60th New York
78th New York

<u>Artillery Battalion</u> 392
4th Maine Battery
6th Maine Battery
Battery M, 1st New York
10th New York Battery
Battery E, Pennsylvania Light
Battery F, Pennsylvania Light
Battery F, 4th United States

Cavalry Division 4,320
Brigadier General Alfred Pleasonton

<u>1st Brigade</u>
Major Charles J. Whiting
5th United States Cavalry
6th United States Cavalry

<u>2nd Brigade</u>
Colonel John F. Farnsworth
8th Illinois Cavalry
3rd Indiana Cavalry
1st Massachusetts Cavalry
8th Pennsylvania Cavalry

<u>3rd Brigade</u>
Colonel Richard H. Rush
4th Pennsylvania Cavalry
6th Pennsylvania Cavalry

<u>4th Brigade</u>
Colonel Andrew T. McReynolds
1st New York Cavalry
12th Pennsylvania Cavalry

<u>5th Brigade</u>
Colonel Benjamin F. Davis
8th New York Cavalry
3rd Pennsylvania Cavalry

<u>Artillery Battalion</u>
Battery A, 2nd United States
Batteries B & L, 2nd United States
Battery M, 2nd United States
Batteries C & G, 3rd United States

Army of Northern Virginia 37,351
General Robert E. Lee

Longstreet's Command 17,646
Major General James Longstreet

McLaw's Division 2,961
Major General Lafayette McLaws

<u>Kershaw's Brigade</u> 858
Brigadier General
Joseph B. Kershaw
2nd South Carolina
3rd South Carolina
7th South Carolina
8th South Carolina

<u>Barksdale's Brigade</u> 858
Brigadier General
William Barksdale
13th Mississippi
17th Mississippi
18th Mississippi
21st Mississippi

<u>Semmes' Brigade</u> 709
Brigadier General
Paul J. Semmes
10th Georgia
53rd Georgia
15th Virginia
32nd Virginia

<u>Cobb's Brigade</u> 398
Lt. Colonel Christopher C. Sanders
16th Georgia
24th Georgia
Cobb's Legion
15th North Carolina

<u>Cabell's Battalion</u>
Manly's North Carolina Battery
Pulaski Georgia Battery
Richmond Fayette Artillery
1st Richmond Howitzers
Troup Georgia Battery

Anderson's Division 4,000
Major General Richard H. Anderson

Wilcox's Brigade
Colonel Alfred Cumming
8th Alabama
9th Alabama
10th Alabama
11th Alabama

Mahone's Brigade
Colonel William A. Parham
6th Virginia
12th Virginia
16th Virginia
41st Virginia

Featherston's Brigade
Colonel Carnot Posey
12th Mississippi
16th Mississippi
19th Mississippi
2nd Mississippi Bn.

Armistead's Brigade
Brigadier General Lewis A. Armistead
9th Virginia
14th Virginia
38th Virginia
53rd Virginia
57th Virginia

Pryor's Brigade
Brigadier General Roger A. Pryor
14th Alabama
2nd Florida
8th Florida
3rd Virginia

Wright's Brigade
Brigadier General Ambrose R. Wright
44th Alabama
3rd Georgia
22nd Georgia
48th Georgia

Saunders' Battalion
Donaldsonville Louisiana Battery
Norfolk Virginia Battery
Lynchburg Virginia Battery
Grimes's Virginia Battery

Jones' Division 1,540
Brigadier General David R. Jones

Garnett's Brigade 261
Brigadier General Richard B. Garnett
8th Virginia
18th Virginia
19th Virginia
28th Virginia
56th Virginia

Jenkins' Brigade 755
Colonel Joseph Walker
1st South Carolina
2nd South Carolina
5th South Carolina
6th South Carolina
4th South Carolina Bn.
Palmetto Sharpshooters

Kemper's Brigade 443
Brigadier General James L. Kemper
1st Virginia
7th Virginia
11th Virginia
17th Virginia
24th Virginia

Artillery 81
Wise Virginia Battery

Toomb's Division (temporary)* 1,852
Brigadier General Robert Toombs

<u>Toombs' Brigade</u> 638
Colonel Henry L. Benning
2nd Georgia
15th Georgia
17th Georgia
20th Georgia

<u>Drayton's Brigade</u> 465
Brigadier General Thomas F. Drayton
50th Georgia
51st Georgia
15th South Carolina
3rd South Carolina Bn.
Phillip's Legion

<u>Anderson's Brigade</u> 749
Brigadier General George T. Anderson
1st Georgia Regulars
7th Georgia
8th Georgia
9th Georgia
11th Georgia

*This temporary division, split from D. R. Jones', was created at the onset of the campaign at Leesburg, Virginia.

Walker's Division
Brigadier General John G. Walker

<u>Walker's Brigade</u> 2,279
Colonel Van H. Manning

3rd Arkansas
27th North Carolina
46th North Carolina
48th North Carolina
30th Virginia
French's Virginia Battery

<u>Ransom's Brigade</u> 1,715
Brigadier General Robert Ransom Jr.
24th North Carolina
25th North Carolina
35th North Carolina
49th North Carolina
Branch's Virginia Battery

Hood's Division 2,304
Brigadier General John B. Hood

<u>Hood's Brigade</u> 854
Colonel William T. Wofford
18th Georgia
Hampton Legion
1st Texas
4th Texas
5th Texas

<u>Law's Brigade</u> 1,146
Colonel Evander M. Law
4th Alabama
2nd Mississippi
11th Mississippi
6th North Carolina

<u>Artillery Battalion</u> 304
German South Carolina Battery
Palmetto South Carolina Battery
Rowan North Carolina Battery

<u>Evans's Brigade</u> 399
Brigadier General Nathan G. Evans*
Colonel Peter. F. Stevens
17th South Carolina
18th South Carolina
22nd South Carolina
23rd South Carolina
Holcombe Legion
Macbeth South Carolina Battery
*Believed he was a division commander and had Col. Stevens command the brigade.

Corps Artillery

<u>Lee's Battalion</u> 318
Ashland Virginia Battery
Bedford Virginia Battery
Brook's South Carolina Battery
Eubanks' Virginia Battery
Madison Louisiana Battery
Parker's Virginia Battery

<u>Washington Artillery Bn.</u> 278
1st Company
2nd Company
3rd Company
4th Company

Jackson's Command 14,584
Major General Thomas J. Jackson

Ewell's Division 4,127
Brigadier General Alexander R. Lawton

<u>Lawton's Brigade</u> 1,250
Colonel Marcellus Douglass
13th Georgia
26th Georgia
31st Georgia
38th Georgia
60th Georgia
61st Georgia

<u>Early's Brigade</u> 1,331
Brigadier General Jubal A. Early
13th Virginia
25th Virginia
31st Virginia
44th Virginia
49th Virginia
52nd Virginia
58th Virginia

<u>Trimble's Brigade</u> 761
Colonel James A. Walker
15th Alabama
12th Georgia
21st Georgia
21st North Carolina

Hay's Brigade 598
Brigadier General Harry T. Hays
5th Louisiana
6th Louisiana
7th Louisiana
8th Louisiana
14th Louisiana

Artillery 223
Johnson's Virginia Battery
Louisiana Guard Artillery
First Maryland Battery
Staunton Virginia Battery

A. P. Hill's Light Division 2,568*
Major General Ambrose P. Hill

Branch's Brigade
Brigadier General Lawrence O. Branch
7th North Carolina
18th North Carolina
28th North Carolina
33rd North Carolina
37th North Carolina

Gregg's Brigade
Brigadier General Maxcy Gregg
1st South Carolina Prov. Army
1st South Carolina Rifles
12th South Carolina
13th South Carolina
14th South Carolina

Field's Brigade
Colonel John M. Brockenbrough
40th Virginia
47th Virginia
55th Virginia
22nd Virginia Bn.

Archer's Brigade
Brigadier General James J. Archer
5th Alabama Battalion
19th Georgia
1st Tennessee Provisional Army
7th Tennessee
14th Tennessee

Pender's Brigade
Brigadier General William D. Pender
16th North Carolina
22nd North Carolina
34th North Carolina
38th North Carolina

Artillery Battalion 337
Crenshaw's Virginia Battery
Fredericksburg Virginia Battery
Pee Dee South Carolina Battery
Purcell Virginia Battery

*Does not include the Field's or Pender's Brigades, as they were not actively engaged.

Jones' Division 2,094
Brigadier General John R. Jones

Stonewall Brigade 489
Colonel Andrew J. Grigsby
4th Virginia
5th Virginia
27th Virginia
33rd Virginia

Taliaferro's Brigade 543
Colonel James W. Jackson
47th Alabama
48th Alabama
23rd Virginia
37th Virginia

Jones's Brigade
Cpt. John E. Penn
21st Virginia
42nd Virginia
48th Virginia
1st Virginia Bn.

Stark's Brigade 706
Brigadier General William E. Starke
1st Louisiana
2nd Louisiana
9th Louisiana
10th Louisiana
15th Louisiana
Coppens' Battalion

Andrew's Battalion 310
Alleghany Virginia Battery
Brockenbrough's Maryland Battery
Danville Virginia Battery
Lee Virginia Battery
Rockbridge Virginia Battery

D. H. Hill's Division 5,795
Major General Daniel H. Hill

Ripley's Brigade 1,349
Brigadier General Roswell S. Ripley
4th Georgia
44th Georgia
1st North Carolina
3rd North Carolina

Garland's Brigade 756
Colonel Duncan K. McRae
5th North Carolina
12th North Carolina
13th North Carolina
20th North Carolina
23rd North Carolina

Anderson's Brigade 1,174
Brigadier General George B. Anderson
2nd North Carolina
4th North Carolina
14th North Carolina
30th North Carolina

Rodes' Brigade 850
Brigadier General Robert E. Rodes
3rd Alabama
5th Alabama
6th Alabama
12th Alabama
26th Alabama

Colquitt's Brigade 1,320
Colonel Alfred H. Colquitt
13th Alabama
6th Georgia
23rd Georgia
27th Georgia
28th Georgia

<u>Artillery Battalion</u> 346
Hardaway's Alabama Battery
Jefferson Davis Alabama Battery
Jones' Virginia Battery
King William Virginia Battery

Artillery Reserve 621
Brigadier General William N. Pendleton

<u>Cutts's Artillery Battalion</u>
Blackshear's Georgia Battery
Irwin's Georgia Battery
Patterson's Georgia Battery
Ross' Georgia Battery

<u>Jones' Artillery Battalion</u>
Morris Virginia Battery
Orange Virginia Battery
Turner's Virginia Battery
Wimbish's Virginia Battery

<u>Miscellaneous Artillery</u>
Cutshaw's Virginia Battery
Dixie Virginia Battery
Magruder Virginia Battery
Rice's Virginia Battery

Cavalry 4,500
Major General J.E.B. Stuart

<u>Hampton's Brigade</u>
Brigadier General Wade Hampton
1st North Carolina Cavalry
2nd South Carolina Cavalry
Cobb's Georgia Legion
Jeff Davis Legion

<u>Robertson's Brigade</u>
Colonel Thomas T. Munford
2nd Virginia Cavalry
7th Virginia Cavalry
12th Virginia Cavalry

<u>Fitz-Hugh Lee's Brigade</u>
Brigadier General Fitz-Hugh Lee
1st Virginia Cavalry
3rd Virginia Cavalry
4th Virginia Cavalry
5th Virginia Cavalry
9th Virginia Cavalry

<u>Horse Artillery</u>
Chew's Virginia Battery
Hart's South Carolina Battery
Pelham's Virginia Battery

Bibliography

A Committee of the Regimental Association. *History of the Thirty-Fifth Regiment Massachusetts Volunteers, 1862-1865.* Boston: Mills, Knight, & Co., Printers, 1884.

Albert, Allen D. ed. *History of the Forty-Fifth Regiment Pennsylvania Veteran Volunteer Infantry 1861-1865.* Williamsport: Grit Publishing Company, 1912.

Carman, Ezra A. *The Maryland Campaign of September 1862: Vol. II: Antietam.* Edited by Thomas G. Clemens. El Dorado Hills: Savas Beatie LLC, 2012.

Carman, Ezra A. and Emmor B. Cope. "Atlas of the Battlefield of Antietam, prepared under the direction of the Antietam Battlefield Board, Lieut. Col. Geo. W. Davis, U.S.A., president, Gen. E.A. Carman, U.S.V., Gen. H Heth, C.S.A. Surveyed by Lieut. Col. E.B. Cope, engineer, H.W. Mattern, assistant engineer, of the Gettysburg National Park. Drawn by Charles H. Ourand, 1899. Position of troops by Gen. E. A. Carman. Published by authority of the Secretary of War, under the direction of the Chief of Engineers, U.S. Army, 1908.", 1904, Revised Edition 1908, Library of Congress.

Croffut, W. A. and John M. Morris. *The Military and Civil History of Connecticut During the War of 1861-65: Comprising a Detailed Account of the Various Regiments and Batteries, Through March, Encampment, Bivouac, and Battle: Also Instances of Distinguished Personal Gallantry, and Biographical Sketches of Many Heroic Soldiers: Together With Record of the Patriotic Action of Citizens at Home, and of the Liberal Support Furnished by the State in its Executive and Legislative Departments.* Boston: Geo. C. Rand & Avery Stereotypers and Printers, 1868.

Cunningham, D. and W. W. Miller. *Antietam: Report of the Ohio Antietam Battlefield Commission*. Springfield: Springfield Publishing Company, State Printer, 1904.

Frassanito, William A. *Antietam: The Photographic Legacy of America's Bloodiest Day*. Gettysburg: Thomas Publications, 1978.

Gottfried, Bradley M. *The Maps of Antietam: An Atlas of the Antietam (Sharpsburg) Campaign, Including the Battle of South Mountain, September 2-20, 1862*. El Dorado Hills: Savas Beatie LLC, 2012.

Johnson, Curt and Richard C. Anderson Jr. *Artillery Hell: The Employment of Artillery at Antietam*. College Station: Texas A&M University Press, 1995.

Lord, A. M., Edward O. *History of the Ninth Regiment New Hampshire Volunteers in the War of the Rebellion*. Concord: Republican Press Association, 1895.

Pickerill, W. N. ed. *Indiana at Antietam: Report of the Indiana Antietam Monument Commission and Ceremonies at the Dedication of the Monument*. Indianapolis: The Aetna Press, 1911.

Pierro, Joseph, ed. *The Maryland Campaign of September 1862: Ezra A. Carman's Definitive Study of the Union and Confederate Armies at Antietam*. New York: Taylor & Francis Group, LLC, 2008.

Sid Meier's Antietam!. Firaxis Games, 1999.

U. S. War Department. *The War of the Rebellion: A Compilation of the Official Records of the Union and Confederate Armies*. 128 vols. Washington D. C.: Government Printing Office, 1880-1901.

Index

Anderson, George B., 103
Anderson, George T., 3, 10, 17, 59, 100
Anderson, Richard H., 99
Anderson, Robert, 91
Anderson, Thomas M., 20, 21
Archer, James J., 61, 67, 68, 69, 70, 71, 102
Armistead, Lewis A., 99
Ashby, Philip S., 45
Avey Farm, 45, 49, 50, 53, 55
Baker, W. L., 38
Barksdale, William, 98
Barnes, Dixon, 62, 63, 69
Barnes, James, 93
Bartlett, Joseph J., 94
Beach, Francis, 61, 63, 64
Bell, Thomas S., 37
Benning, Henry L., 29, 38, 39, 45, 60, 66, 67, 69, 70, 100
Betts, W. H., 13, 14
Biddle, William F., 24, 79
Bingham, Seth D., 60
Blackford House, 46, 53, 58, 61, 62, 66, 72
Blackford's Ford, 58, 61
Blunt, M. M., 6, 16, 21
Boonsboro Turnpike, 10
Boyce, Robert, 19, 51
Branch, Lawrence O., 61, 71, 102
  Killed, 71

Brockenbrough, John M., 61, 102
Brooke, John R., 91
Brooks, William T. H., 95
Brown, Caleb T., 64
Brown, Harvey W., 8
Brown, J. S., 54
Brown, J. Thompson, 20
Buchanan, Robert C., 20, 21, 93
Burnside Bridge, 8, 16, 23, 28, 31, 32, 33, 34, 36, 37, 38, 45, 50, 53, 69, 77, 78
Burnside, Ambrose E., 14, 18, 21, 23, 25, 26, 27, 29, 30, 31, 34, 40, 43, 47, 78, 79, 80, 81, 82, 84, 95
Cabell, George C., 15, 17
Caldwell, John C., 91
Carlton, C. H., 9, 12, 13, 14, 15, 16, 17
Carter, T. H., 50
Cemetery Hill, 3, 4, 8, 9, 10, 11, 16, 30, 37, 44, 45, 48, 49, 50, 51, 57, 69, 71, 72, 78, 81
Childs, James H., 3, 4
Christ, Benjamin C., 43, 47, 49, 50, 95
Christian, William A., 90
Clark Jr., Joseph C., 38
Clark, William S., 35, 36
Clarke, Melvin, 51
Clement, Adam, 54
Coffin, J. H., 48, 50, 70, 77
Coleman, Augustus H., 32
Colquitt, Alfred H., 13, 14, 103

Comly, J. M., 65, 68
Confederate Army Units
   Alabama
      10th Alabama Infantry, 99
      11th Alabama Infantry, 99
      12th Alabama Infantry, 103
      13th Alabama Infantry, 103
      13th Alabama Infantry, 13, 14
      14th Alabama Infantry, 99
      15th Alabama Infantry, 101
      26th Alabama Infantry, 103
      3rd Alabama Infantry, 103
      44th Alabama Infantry, 99
      47th Alabama Infantry, 103
      48th Alabama Infantry, 103
      4th Alabama Infantry, 100
      5th Alabama Bn. Infantry, 102
      5th Alabama Infantry, 103
      6th Alabama Infantry, 103
      8th Alabama Infantry, 99
      9th Alabama Infantry, 99
      Hardaway's Alabama Battery, 104
      Jefferson Davis Alabama Battery, 104
      Jefferson Davis Battery, 11
   Arkansas
      3rd Arkansas Infantry, 100
   Florida
      2nd Florida Infantry, 99
      8th Florida Infantry, 99
   Georgia
      10th Georgia Infantry, 98
      11th Georgia Infantry, 45, 59, 100
      12th Georgia Infantry, 101
      13th Georgia Infantry, 101
      15th Georgia Infantry, 45, 59, 70, 100
      16th Georgia Infantry, 98
      17th Georgia Infantry, 29, 45, 59, 60, 100
      18th Georgia Infantry, 100
      19th Georgia Infantry, 67, 102
      1st Georgia Regular Infantry, 3, 100
      20th Georgia Infantry, 29, 39, 59, 60, 70, 100
      21st Georgia Infantry, 101
      22nd Georgia Infantry, 99
      23rd Georgia Infantry, 103
      24th Georgia Infantry, 98
      26th Georgia Infantry, 101
      27th Georgia Infantry, 103
      28th Georgia Infantry, 103
      2nd Georgia Infantry, 29, 38, 39, 59, 100
      31st Georgia Infantry, 101
      38th Georgia Infantry, 101
      3rd Georgia Infantry, 99
      44th Georgia Infantry, 103
      48th Georgia Infantry, 99
      4th Georgia Infantry, 103
      50th Georgia Infantry, 29, 41, 100
      51st Georgia Infantry, 54, 100
      53rd Georgia Infantry, 98
      60th Georgia Infantry, 101
      61st Georgia Infantry, 101
      6th Georgia Infantry, 103
      7th Georgia Infantry, 100
      8th Georgia Infantry, 100
      9th Georgia Infantry, 100
      Blackshear's Georgia Battery, 104
      Cobb's Georgia Legion Cavalry, 104
      Cobb's Georgia Legion Infantry, 98
      Irwin's Georgia Battery, 104
      Patterson's Georgia Battery, 104
      Pulaski Georgia Battery, 73, 98
      Ross' Georgia Battery, 104
      Troup Georgia Battery, 98
   Louisiana
      10th Louisiana Infantry, 103
      14th Louisiana Infantry, 102
      15th Louisiana Infantry, 103
      1st Louisiana Infantry, 103
      2nd Louisiana Infantry, 103
      5th Louisiana Infantry, 102
      6th Louisiana Infantry, 102
      7th Louisiana Infantry, 102
      8th Louisiana Infantry, 102
      9th Louisiana Infantry, 103
      Coppens' Battalion Infantry, 103

Donaldsonville Louisiana Battery, 99
Louisiana Guard Artillery, 102
Madison Louisiana Battery, 11, 12, 15, 16, 45, 48, 50, 69, 101
Washington Artillery Battalion
    1st Company, 9, 10, 11, 12, 16, 45, 47, 49, 72, 101
    2nd Company, 30, 37, 45, 52, 54, 66, 69, 70, 75, 101
    3rd Company, 9, 45, 72, 101
    4th Company, 30, 42, 45, 72, 101

Maryland
    Brockenbrough's Maryland Battery, 103
    First Maryland Battery, 72, 102

Mississippi
    11th Mississippi Infantry, 100
    12th Mississippi Infantry, 99
    13th Mississippi Infantry, 98
    16th Mississippi Infantry, 99
    17th Mississippi Infantry, 98
    18th Mississippi Infantry, 98
    19th Mississippi Infantry, 99
    21st Mississippi Infantry, 98
    2nd Mississippi Infantry, 99, 100
    Jeff Davis Legion, 104

North Carolina
    12th North Carolina Infantry, 103
    13th North Carolina Infantry, 103
    14th North Carolina Infantry, 103
    15th North Carolina Infantry, 98
    16th North Carolina Infantry, 102
    18th North Carolina Infantry, 71, 102
    1st North Carolina Cavalry, 104
    1st North Carolina Infantry, 103
    20th North Carolina Infantry, 103
    20th North Carolina Infantry, 11
    21st North Carolina Infantry, 101
    22nd North Carolina Infantry, 102
    23rd North Carolina Infantry, 103
    24th North Carolina Infantry, 100
    25th North Carolina Infantry, 100
    27th North Carolina Infantry, 100
    28th North Carolina Infantry, 70, 71, 102
    2nd North Carolina Infantry, 103
    30th North Carolina Infantry, 103
    33rd North Carolina Infantry, 71, 102
    34th North Carolina Infantry, 102
    35th North Carolina Infantry, 100
    37th North Carolina Infantry, 58, 59, 66, 67, 70, 71, 74, 75, 102
    38th North Carolina Infantry, 102
    3rd North Carolina Infantry, 103
    46th North Carolina Infantry, 100
    48th North Carolina Infantry, 100
    49th North Carolina Infantry, 100
    4th North Carolina Infantry, 103
    5th North Carolina Infantry, 103
    5th North Carolina Infantry, 10, 13
    6th North Carolina Infantry, 100
    7th North Carolina Infantry, 58, 59, 66, 67, 70, 71, 74, 102
    Manly's North Carolina Battery, 98
    Rowan North Carolina Battery, 45, 47, 52, 54, 72, 100

South Carolina
    12th South Carolina Infantry, 62, 63, 64, 69, 71, 102
    13th South Carolina Infantry, 62, 63, 69, 71, 102
    14th South Carolina Infantry, 62, 102
    15th South Carolina Infantry, 45, 48, 51, 54, 57, 100
    17th South Carolina Infantry, 4, 10, 12, 45, 48, 101
    18th South Carolina Infantry, 10, 14, 101
    1st South Carolina Infantry, 99
    1st South Carolina Provisional Army Infantry, 62, 63, 64, 102
    1st South Carolina Rifles, 62, 64, 68, 73, 102
    22nd South Carolina Infantry, 10, 13, 101

23rd South Carolina, 101
23rd South Carolina Infantry, 10
2nd South Carolina Cavalry, 104
2nd South Carolina Infantry, 98, 99
3rd South Carolina Bn. Infantry, 54, 100
3rd South Carolina Infantry, 98
4th South Carolina Bn. Infantry, 99
5th South Carolina Infantry, 99
6th South Carolina Infantry, 99
7th South Carolina Infantry, 98
8th South Carolina Infantry, 98
Brook's South Carolina Battery, 11, 101
German South Carolina Battery, 9, 11, 45, 73, 100
Hampton Legion, 100
Hart's South Carolina Battery, 104
Holcombe Legion, 10, 45, 48, 101
Macbeth South Carolina Battery, 9, 10, 11, 14, 19, 20, 51, 101
Palmetto Sharpshooters, 99
Palmetto South Carolina Battery, 11, 16, 45, 47, 49, 100
Pee Dee South Carolina Battery, 53, 58, 59, 60, 61, 62, 66, 72, 102
Phillip's Legion, 100
Tennessee
  14th Tennessee Infantry, 67, 68, 102
  1st Tennessee Provisional Army Infantry, 67, 102
  7th Tennessee Infantry, 67, 68, 102
Texas
  1st Texas Infantry, 100
  4th Texas Infantry, 100
  5th Texas Infantry, 100
Virginia
  11th Virginia, 54
  11th Virginia Infantry, 99
  12th Virginia Cavalry, 104
  12th Virginia Infantry, 99

13th Virginia Infantry, 101
14th Virginia Infantry, 99
15th Virginia Infantry, 98
16th Virginia Infantry, 99
17th Virginia Infantry, 54, 55, 56, 99
18th Virginia Infantry, 15, 17, 99
19th Virginia Infantry, 15, 99
19th Virgninia Infantry, 15
1st Richmond Howitzers, 98
1st Virginia Battalion Infantry, 103
1st Virginia Cavalry, 104
1st Virginia Infantry, 54, 99
21st Virginia Infantry, 103
22nd Virginia Bn. Infantry, 102
23rd Virginia Infantry, 103
24th Virginia Infantry, 45, 99
25th Virginia Infantry, 101
27th Virginia Infantry, 103
28th Virginia Infantry, 15, 99
2nd Virginia Cavalry, 104
30th Virginia Infantry, 100
31st Virginia Infantry, 101
32nd Virginia Infantry, 98
33rd Virginia Infantry, 103
37th Virginia Infantry, 103
38th Virginia Infantry, 99
3rd Virginia Cavalry, 104
3rd Virginia Infantry, 99
40th Virginia Infantry, 72, 102
41st Virginia Infantry, 99
42nd Virginia Infantry, 103
44th Virginia Infantry, 101
47th Virginia Infantry, 102
48th Virginia Infantry, 103
49th Virginia Infantry, 101
4th Virginia Infantry, 103, 104
52nd Virginia Infantry, 101
53rd Virginia Infantry, 99
55th Virginia Infantry, 102
56th Virginia Infantry, 12, 15, 99
57th Virginia Infantry, 99
58th Virginia Infantry, 101
5th Virginia Infantry, 103, 104
6th Virginia Infantry, 99
7th Virginia Cavalry, 104

7th Virginia Infantry, 45, 52, 53, 60, 99
8th Virginia Infantry, 15, 99
9th Virginia Cavalry, 104
9th Virginia Infantry, 99
Alleghany Virginia Battery, 103
Ashland Virginia Battery, 101
Bedford Virginia Battery, 11, 14, 101
Branch's Virginia Battery, 100
Chew's Virginia Battery, 73, 104
Crenshaw's Virginia Battery, 61, 72, 102
Cutshaw's Virginia Battery, 73, 104
Danville Virginia Battery, 103
Dixie Virginia Battery, 104
Eubanks' Virginia Battery, 26, 30, 37, 45, 101
Fredericksburg Virginia Battery, 61, 62, 72, 76, 102
French's Virginia Battery, 100
Grimes's Virginia Battery, 99
Johnson's Virginia Battery, 102
Jones' Virginia Battery, 104
King William Virginia Battery, 104
Lee Virginia Battery, 103
Lynchburg Virginia Battery, 99
Magruder Virginia Battery, 104
Morris Virginia Battery, 104
Norfolk Virginia Battery, 99
Orange Virginia Battery, 104
Parker's Virginia Battery, 11, 20, 101
Pelham's Virginia Battery, 104
Purcell Virginia Battery, 61, 62, 72, 73, 76, 102
Rice's Virginia Battery, 104
Richmond Fayette Artillery, 98
Rockbridge Virginia Battery, 103
Staunton Virginia Battery, 102
Turner's Virginia Battery, 104
Wimbish's Virginia Battery, 104
Wise Virginia Battery, 37, 38, 45, 47, 52, 54, 56, 58, 99
Corse, M. D., 54, 55, 56
Cox, Jacob D., 24, 26, 27, 28, 30, 31, 33, 35, 39, 40, 41, 43, 47, 73, 74, 75, 77, 84, 95
Crawford, Samuel W., 97
Crook, George R., 27, 31, 32, 33, 35, 37, 74, 96
Cumming, Alfred, 99
Cummings, John B., 29
Curtis, George E., 64
Curtis, Joseph B., 64, 65
Dana, Napoleon J. T., 92
Davis, Benjamin F., 98
Dennison, W. N., 3
DeSaussure, W. D., 45, 54, 57
Doubleday, Abner, 90
Douglass, Marcellus, 101
Drayton, Thomas F., 50, 54, 57, 70, 100
Dryer, Hiram, 6, 8, 9, 11, 12, 13, 15, 16, 17, 18, 19, 20, 21, 22, 79, 81
Dunker Church, 1, 24, 27
Durham, S. A., 10
Duryea, J. E., 33
Duryée, Abram, 90
Duval, H. F., 46
Early, Jubal A., 101
East Woods, 27
Edwards, E. O., 62, 71
Elliott, William, 51
Eshleman, B. F., 45
Evans, Nathan G., 11, 20, 101
Ewing, Hugh B., 41, 68, 73, 96
Fairchild, Harrison S., 40, 49, 52, 53, 54, 58, 59, 60, 75, 76, 96
Farnsworth, John F., 98
Fellows, Enoch A., 33
Ferrero, Edward, 95
Franklin, William B., 23, 24, 79, 94
French, William H., 92
Furbay, Reese R., 68
Gailbraith, J. M., 72
Garden, Hugh P., 11
Garnett, Richard B., 9, 15, 50, 57, 70, 99
Gibbon, John, 90
Goodrich, William B., 97
Gordon, George H., 97
Gorman, Willis A., 92

Graham, M. J., 52
Greene, George S., 97
Gregg, Maxcy, 60, 61, 62, 64, 68, 74, 102
Griffin, Charles, 18, 93
Griffin, S. S., 33
Grigsby, Andrew J., 103
Hagerstown Turnpike, 9, 10, 11, 14, 19, 85
Hains, Peter C., 18
Hamilton, D. H., 62
Hampton, Wade, 104
Hancock, Winfield S., 17, 95
Harland, Edward, 40, 41, 42, 57, 58, 63, 64, 96
Harper's Ferry Road, 44, 45, 52, 53, 54, 55, 56, 57, 58, 59, 60, 61, 62, 66, 70, 71, 72, 73, 74
Harper's Ferry Road, 44
Hartranft, John F., 35, 36
Hartsuff, George L., 90
Hawley, T. H., 60
Hays, Harry T., 102
Haywood, Edward S., 66
Henry Rohrbach Farm, 26, 27, 32, 33, 77
Hildt, George H., 68
Hill, Ambrose P., 46, 51, 57, 58, 61, 70, 72, 102
Hill, Daniel H., 1, 8, 9, 10, 13, 14, 17, 103
Hilton, H., 10
Hoffman, J. William, 90
Hoke, Robert F., 71
Holmes, William R., 29, 38
Hood, John B., 100
Hood, William F., 89
Hooker, Joseph, 23, 90
Howard, Oliver O., 92
Irwin, William H., 95
Iverson, Alfred, 11, 13
Jackson, James W., 103
Jackson, Lyman J., 32, 56
Jackson, Thomas J., 101
Jardine, Edward E., 51
Jones, David R., 46, 56, 61, 99
Jones, John R., 103
Jones, Theodore, 65, 68, 69

Kearse, Francis, 29
Keedysville, 1, 2, 7, 18, 78, 85
Kemper, James L., 50, 54, 57, 58, 99
Kershaw, Joseph B., 98
Kimball, Edgar A., 51, 55, 56
Kimball, Nathan, 92
Kingsbury, Henry W., 28, 31
Lane, James H., 70, 71
Law, Evander M., 100
Lawton, Alexander R., 101
Le Baire, Adolphus, 55
Leahy, Lawrence, 55
Lee, Fitz-Hugh, 104
Lee, Robert E., 5, 10, 11, 46, 51, 57, 61, 72, 73, 78, 81, 84, 86, 98
Lee, Stephen D., 11, 12, 15, 20, 50
Lion, Thomas W., 57
Little, F. H., 59
Little, F. W., 45
Longstreet, James, 85, 98
Lovell, Charles S., 93
Lutheran Church, 15, 51
Magilton, Albert L., 91
Manning, Van H., 100
Mansfield, Joseph K. F., 97
Marcy, Randolph B., 80
McClellan, George B., 2, 6, 8, 20, 23, 24, 25, 26, 27, 29, 31, 43, 47, 78, 79, 80, 81, 82, 83, 84, 86
McClellan, George G., 89
McComb, William A., 67, 68
McCook, Asa M., 44
McCorkle, W. H., 69, 71
McGregor, J. A., 45, 60
McIntosh, David G., 58, 59, 72
McKibbin, D. B., 7, 14
McKinley, William, 78
McLaws, Lafayette, 98
McMaster, F. W., 10
McRae, Duncan K., 103
McReynolds, Andrew T., 98
Meade, George G., 91
Meagher, Thomas F., 91
Merkel, C. F., 38
Middle Bridge, 2, 22, 23, 43, 45, 46, 78, 79, 86

Millican, W. T., 45, 60, 70
Montgomery, W. J., 71
Morell, George W., 79, 93
Morris, Dwight, 92
Morris, W. G., 66, 71
Morrison, David, 46
Muhlenberg, Charles P., 40
Munford, Thomas T., 46, 104
Myers' Ford, 42
Nagle, James, 95
Neal, James H., 67
Neikirk Farm, 7
Newcomer Farm, 4, 7
Newcomer Mill, 20
Newton, John, 94
Otto 40-acre Cornfield, 38, 45, 51, 52, 53, 57, 59, 60, 62, 63, 65, 67, 68, 71, 74, 75
Otto Farm, 51, 56, 69, 76
Otto Lane, 37
Otto's Lane, 51, 53, 75
Palmer, W. H., 54
Parham, William A., 99
Patrick, Marsena R., 90
Pender, William D., 61, 72, 74, 102
Pendleton, William N., 46, 104
Penn, John E., 103
Pennington, A. C. M., 8
Perrin, James M., 62
Phelps Jr., Walter P., 90
Piper Farm, 8, 17, 18
Pleasonton, Alfred, 2, 4, 5, 6, 8, 17, 18, 21, 22, 43, 79, 80, 81, 98
Poland, John S., 6, 7, 8, 9, 12, 13, 15, 16, 17, 48
Porter, Fitz John, 2, 8, 16, 18, 20, 22, 78, 79, 80, 81, 82, 83, 93
Porterstown Road, 28
Posey, Carnot, 99
Potter, Robert B., 35, 36
Powell, W. H., 16, 21
Pringle, S. M., 49
Pry House, 78
Pryor, Roger A., 99
Purdie, Thomas J., 71
Ramsay, J. A., 72

Randol, A. M., 6, 8
Ransom Jr., Robert, 100
Richardson, Israel B., 91
Richardson, John B., 72
Ricketts, James B., 90
Ringold, Benjamin, 51
Ripley, Roswell S., 103
Rodes, Robert E., 103
Rodman, Isaac P., 28, 33, 40, 41, 42, 47, 52, 57, 58, 63, 96
    Mortally Wounded, 60, 61
Rohrbach Road, 31, 32, 33, 34, 35, 36
Rohrersville, 28
Rohrersville Road, 29, 41
Roulette House, 60
Rush, Richard H., 98
Sackett, Delos B., 27, 78, 81
Sanders, Christopher C., 98
Scammon, Eliakim P., 77, 96
Sedgwick, John, 92
Semmes, Paul J., 98
Seymour, Truman, 91
Sharpsburg, 1, 3, 5, 8, 10, 12, 13, 14, 16, 18, 19, 20, 23, 30, 36, 37, 38, 42, 43, 44, 45, 46, 47, 48, 49, 50, 51, 52, 54, 55, 58, 60, 61, 67, 70, 72, 74, 78, 81, 84, 86
Shepherdstown Ford, 46
Sheppard, S. G., 67
Sherrick Farm, 12, 37
Sherrick Lane, 15, 16
Sherrick's Lane, 10, 12, 49, 78
Sigfried, Joshua K., 33
Simmonds
    Seth J., 32
Simpson, W. D., 62
Slocum, Henry W., 94
Smith, William F., 95
Snavely Farm, 72, 76
Snavely's Ford, 29, 31, 37, 38, 40, 41, 72
Snook, John M., 73
Squires, Charles W., 72
Stainrook, Henry J., 97
Starke, William E., 103
Steere, W. H. P., 63
Steere, William H. P., 64, 65

Stevens, Peter F., 10, 14, 19, 101
Stockton, Thomas B. W., 18, 93
Stuart, J. E. B., 104
Sturgis, Samuel D., 24, 32, 33, 34, 35, 43, 74, 76, 77, 95
Sumner, Edwin V., 18, 23, 85, 91
Sunken Road, 1, 2, 9, 10, 13, 27, 50, 57, 72, 79
Sykes, George, 6, 8, 15, 16, 18, 19, 20, 21, 22, 79, 80, 81, 82, 93
Tanner, Thomas B., 64
Thatcher, Horace K., 7, 14
Toombs, Robert, 100
Toombs, Robert A., 30, 33, 45, 57, 59, 60, 66, 67, 68, 69, 70, 72
Torbert, Alfred T. A., 94
Turney, Peter, 67
Twiggs, H. D. D., 3, 4, 10, 45, 49
Tyndale, Hector, 97
Union Army Units
   Connecticut
      11th Connecticut Infantry, 28, 31, 32, 33, 40, 75, 77, 96
      14th Connecticut Infantry, 92
      16th Connecticut Infantry, 40, 42, 57, 58, 60, 61, 63, 64, 65, 69, 96
      8th Connecticut Infantry, 40, 41, 42, 57, 58, 59, 60, 61, 66, 67, 69, 70, 71, 74, 75, 96
   Delaware
      1st Delaware Infantry, 92
      2nd Delaware Infantry, 91
      3rd Delaware Infantry, 97
   District of Columbia
      2nd District of Columbia Infantry, 93
   Illinois
      8th Illinois Cavalry, 4, 7, 98
   Indiana
      14th Indiana Infantry, 92
      19th Indiana Infantry, 90
      27th Indiana Infantry, 97
      3rd Indiana Cavalry, 4, 7, 98
      7th Indiana Infantry, 90
   Kentucky
      Kentucky Light Artillery, 24, 32, 34, 35, 37, 96
   Maine
      10th Maine Infantry, 97
      20th Maine Infantry, 93
      2nd Maine Infantry, 93
      4th Maine Battery, 97
      5th Maine Infantry, 94
      6th Maine Battery, 97
      6th Maine Infantry, 95
      7th Maine Infantry, 18, 95
   Maryland
      2nd Maryland Infantry, 33, 34, 35, 75, 76, 95
      3rd Maryland Infantry, 97
      5th Maryland Infantry, 92
      Battery A, Maryland Light, 94
      Battery B, Maryland Light, 95
      Purnell Legion, 97
   Massachusetts
      12th Massachusetts Infantry, 90
      13th Massachusetts Infantry, 90
      15th Massachusetts Infantry, 92
      18th Massachusetts Infantry, 93
      19th Massachusetts Infantry, 92
      1st Massachusetts Cavalry, 4, 5, 7, 98
      20th Massachusetts Infantry, 92
      21st Massachusetts Infantry, 24, 35, 36, 37, 75, 76, 95
      22nd Massachusetts Infantry, 93
      28th Massachusetts Infantry, 95
      28th Massachusetts Infantry, 43, 47, 50
      29th Massachusetts Infantry, 91
      2nd Massachusetts Infantry, 97
      32nd Massachusetts Infantry, 93
      35th Massachusetts Infantry, 33, 35, 36, 37, 44, 47, 70, 75, 76, 95
      8th Battery Massachusetts Light, 24, 28, 48, 77, 95
      9th Massachusetts Infantry, 93
      Battery A, Massachusetts Light, 94
      Battery C, Massachusetts Light, 93
      Massachusetts Sharpshooters, 1st Company, 92
      Massachusetts Sharpshooters, 2nd

Company, 93
Michigan
   16th Michigan Infantry, 93
   17th Michigan Infantry, 17, 43, 47, 50, 95
   1st Michigan Infantry, 93
   4th Michigan Infantry, 93
   7th Michigan Infantry, 92
   8th Michigan Infantry, 43, 47, 48, 53, 95
   Michigan Sharpshooters, Brady's Company, 93
Minnesota
   1st Minnesota Infantry, 92
   Minnesota Sharpshooters, 2nd Company, 92
New Hampshire
   1st New Hampshire Battery, 90
   5th New Hampshire Infantry, 91
   6th New Hampshire Infantry, 33, 34, 35, 37, 75, 76, 95
   9th New Hampshire Infantry, 33, 34, 35, 37, 75, 76, 95
New Jersey
   13th New Jersey Infantry, 97
   1st New Jersey Infantry, 94
   2nd New Jersey Infantry, 94
   3rd New Jersey Infantry, 94
   4th New Jersey Infantry, 94
   Battery A, New Jersey Light, 94
New York
   102nd New York Infantry, 97
   103rd New York Infantry, 40, 42, 51, 52, 55, 56, 96
   104th New York Infantry, 90
   105th New York Infantry, 90
   107th New York Infantry, 97
   108th New York Infantry, 92
   10th New York Battery, 97
   10th New York Infantry, 94
   12th New York Infantry, 93
   13th New York Infantry, 93
   14th New York Infantry, 93
   16th New York Infantry, 94
   17th New York Infantry, 93
   18th New York Infantry, 94
   1st New York Cavalry, 98
   1st New York Light Battery, 95
   20th New York Infantry, 95
   21st New York Infantry, 90
   22nd New York Infantry, 90
   23rd New York Infantry, 90
   24th New York Infantry, 90
   25th New York Infantry, 93
   26th New York Infantry, 90
   27th New York Infantry, 94
   28th New York Infantry, 97
   30th New York Infantry, 90
   31st New York Infantry, 94
   32nd New York Infantry, 94
   33rd New York Infantry, 95
   34th New York Infantry, 92
   35th New York Infantry, 90
   42nd New York Infantry, 92
   43rd New York Infantry, 95
   44th New York Infantry, 93
   46th New York Infantry, 43, 47, 48, 95
   49th New York Infantry, 95
   4th New York Infantry, 92
   51st New York Infantry, 35, 36, 37, 38, 41, 44, 75, 76, 95
   52nd New York Infantry, 91
   57th New York Infantry, 91
   59th New York Infantry, 92
   5th New York Battery, 1, 20, 35, 94
   5th New York Infantry, 94
   60th New York Infantry, 97
   61st & 64th New York Infantry, 91
   63rd New York Infantry, 91
   66th New York Infantry, 91
   69th New York Infantry, 91
   6th New York Cavalry, 96
   76th New York Infantry, 90
   77th New York Infantry, 95
   78th New York Infantry, 97
   79th New York Infantry, 95
   79th New York Infantry, 17, 43, 46, 48
   7th New York Infantry, 91

80th New York Infantry, 90
82nd New York Infantry, 92
83rd New York Infantry, 90
84th New York Infantry, 90
88th New York Infantry, 91
89th New York Infantry, 40, 42, 51, 52, 53, 55, 56, 96
8th New York Cavalry, 98
93rd New York Infantry, 89
94th New York Infantry, 90
95th New York Infantry, 90
97th New York Infantry, 90
9th New York Infantry, 40, 41, 47, 48, 51, 52, 53, 54, 55, 56, 70, 75, 96
    Company K (Whiting's Battery), 41, 42, 96
Battery A, 1st Battalion New York, 1, 94
Battery B, 1st Battalion New York, 1, 94
Battery B, 1st New York, 91
Battery C, 1st Battalion New York, 1, 94
Battery D, 1st Battalion New York, 1, 94
Battery G, 1st New York, 92
Battery L, 1st New York, 90
Battery L, 2nd New York, 28, 96
Battery M, 1st New York, 97
Independent Company Oneida (New York) Cavalry, 89
Ohio
    11th Ohio Infantry, 32, 34, 51, 76, 96
    12th Ohio Infantry, 40, 65, 68, 73, 75, 76, 96
    1st Battery Ohio Light Artillery, 24, 28, 96
    23rd Ohio Infantry, 40, 65, 66, 68, 69, 70, 71, 73, 75, 77, 96
    28th Ohio Infantry, 32, 34, 35, 37, 51, 96
    30th Ohio Infantry, 40, 41, 65, 68, 69, 70, 71, 73, 75, 96
    36th Ohio Infantry, 96
    36th Ohio Infantry, 32, 33, 37, 46, 51
    5th Ohio Infantry, 97
    66th Ohio Infantry, 97
    7th Ohio Infantry, 97
    8th Ohio Infantry, 92
    Ohio Cavalry, 3d Independent Co., 96
Pennsylvania
    100th Pennsylvania Infantry, 44, 47, 48, 49, 95
    106th Pennsylvania Infantry, 92
    107th Pennsylvania Infantry, 90
    111th Pennsylvania Infantry, 97
    118th Pennsylvania Infantry, 93
    11th Pennsylvania Infantry, 90
    124th Pennsylvania Infantry, 97
    125th Pennsylvania Infantry, 97
    128th Pennsylvania Infantry, 97
    12th Pennsylvania Cavalry, 7, 98
    130th Pennsylvania Infantry, 92
    132nd Pennsylvania Infantry, 92
    137th Pennsylvania Infantry, 95
    28th Pennsylvania Infantry, 97
    3rd Pennsylvania Cavalry, 98
    45th Pennsylvania Infantry, 43, 47, 48, 49, 75, 95
    46th Pennsylvania Infantry, 97
    48th Pennsylvania Infantry, 33, 34, 35, 36, 37, 42, 60, 75, 95
    49th Pennsylvania Infantry, 95
    4th Pennsylvania Cavalry, 3, 4, 7, 98
    50th Pennsylvania Infantry, 95
    50th Pennsylvania Infantry, 43, 47, 50
    51st Pennsylvania Infantry, 35, 36, 37, 38, 41, 44, 65, 75, 76, 95
    53rd Pennsylvania Infantry, 91
    56th Pennsylvania Infantry, 90
    62nd Pennsylvania Infantry, 93
    69th Pennsylvania Infantry, 92
    6th Pennsylvania Cavalry, 8, 18, 98
    71st Pennsylvania Infantry, 92
    72nd Pennsylvania Infantry, 92
    81st Pennsylvania Infantry, 91

83rd Pennsylvania Infantry, 93
88th Pennsylvania Infantry, 90
8th Pennsylvania Cavalry, 4, 7, 98
90th Pennsylvania Infantry, 90
95th Pennsylvania Infantry, 94
96th Pennsylvania Infantry, 94
Battery A, 1st Pennsylvania, 91
Battery B, 1st Pennsylvania, 91
Battery C, Pennsylvania Light, 90
Battery D, Pennsylvania Light, 1, 24, 37, 38, 42, 44, 51, 52, 65, 75, 95
Battery E, Pennsylvania Light, 97
Battery F, 1st Pennsylvania, 90
Battery F, Pennsylvania Light, 97
Pennsylvania Reserves
   10th Pennsylvania Reserve Infantry, 91
   11th Pennsylvania Infantry, 91
   12th Pennsylvania Reserve Infantry, 91
   13th Pennsylvania Reserve Infantry, 91
   1st Pennsylvania Reserve Infantry, 91
   2nd Pennsylvania Reserve Infantry, 91
   3rd Pennsylvania Reserve Infantry, 91
   4th Pennsylvania Reserve Infantry, 91
   5th Pennsylvania Reserve Infantry, 91
   6th Pennsylvania Reserve Infantry, 91
   7th Pennsylvania Reserve Infantry, 91
   8th Pennsylvania Reserve Infantry, 91
   9th Pennsylvania Reserve Infantry, 91
Rhode Island
   4th Rhode Island Infantry, 40, 42, 57, 58, 60, 63, 64, 65, 75, 96
   Battery A, 1st Rhode Island, 92
   Battery B, 1st Rhode Island, 92
   Battery C, 1st Rhode Island, 2, 93
   Battery D, 1st Rhode Island, 90
   Battery G, 1st Rhode Island, 92
United States Regular Army
   11th United States Infantry, 93
   12th United States Infantry, 93
   12th United States Infantry, 3, 6, 8, 16
   14th United States Infantry, 7, 8, 9, 13, 93
   17th United States Infantry, 93
   19th United States Infantry, 89
   1st & 6th United States Infantry, 93
   1st United States Sharpshooters, 93
   2nd & 10th United States Infantry, 4, 6, 8, 48, 93
   2nd United States Cavalry, 89
   2nd United States Sharpshooters, 90
   3rd United States Infantry, 93, 96
   4th United States Cavalry, 8, 18, 89
   4th United States Infantry, 8, 9, 12, 13, 16, 20, 57, 89, 93
   5th United States Cavalry, 4, 8, 18, 98
   6th United States Cavalry, 4, 98
   8th United States Infantry, 89
   Batteries A & C, 4th United States, 91
   Batteries B & L, 2nd United States, 3, 4, 6, 8, 98
   Batteries C & G, 3rd United States, 3, 4, 6, 8, 98
   Batteries E & G, 1st United States, 2, 6, 8, 94
   Battery A, 2nd United States, 3, 4, 6, 8, 17, 18, 98
   Battery A, 5th United States, 24, 28, 40, 65, 75, 77, 96
   Battery B, 4th United States, 90
   Battery C, 5th United States, 91
   Battery D, 2nd United States, 94
   Battery D, 5th United States, 1, 93

Battery E, 2nd United States, 1, 24, 27, 28, 32, 37, 44, 54, 82, 95
Battery E, 4th United States, 24, 35, 37, 38, 42, 44, 51, 52, 53, 54, 65, 74, 75, 95
Battery F, 4th United States, 97
Battery F, 5th United States, 2, 95
Battery G, 4th United States, 2, 82, 94
Battery I, 1st United States, 92
Battery I, 5th United States, 1, 4, 20, 24, 94
Battery K, 1st United States, 2, 6, 94
Battery K, 5th United States, 2, 6, 8, 18, 94
Battery M, 2nd United States, 3, 4, 6, 18, 98
Vermont
  2nd Vermont Infantry, 95
  3rd Vermont Infantry, 95
  4th Vermont Infantry, 95
  5th Vermont Infantry, 95
  6th Vermont Infantry, 95
West Virginia
  7th West Virginia Infantry, 92
  Gilmore's Company West Virginia Cavalry, 96
  Harrison's Company West Virginia Cavalry, 96
Wisconsin
  2nd Wisconsin Infantry, 90
  3rd Wisconsin Infantry, 97
  5th Wisconsin Infantry, 95
  6th Wisconsin Infantry, 90
  7th Wisconsin Infantry, 90
Upham, C. L., 41, 59, 66
Van Reed, William E., 6
Vincent, Albert O., 6
Walker, James A., 101
Walker, John G., 100
Walker, Joseph, 11, 19, 49, 50, 51, 99
Wallace, William, 10, 14
Warren, Gouverneur K., 94
Watts, George H., 64
Webb, Alexander S., 7
Weber, Max, 92
Welsh, Thomas, 43, 47, 48, 49, 51, 55, 95
West Woods, 27
White, C. B., 73
Whiting, Charles J., 98
Whiting, J. R., 40, 42, 43
Willcox, Orlando B., 44, 47, 48, 52, 74, 77, 95
Williams, Alpheus S., 97
Winthrop, Frederick, 6
Wofford, William T., 100
Wright, Ambrose R., 99
Young, S. B. M., 3, 7

ABOUT THE AUTHORS

Ezra A. Carman was born in 1839 and served as colonel of the 13th New Jersey Infantry regiment from 1862 to 1864, moving on to brigade command during Sherman's March to the Sea. After the war, he served as chief clerk of the United States Department of Agriculture, historical expert for the Antietam National Battlefield, and Chairman of the Chickamauga-Chattanooga National Battlefield Commission. He passed away in 1909.

Brad Butkovich has a Bachelor of Arts degree in history from Georgia Southern University. He has published several books on the American Civil War including studies on the Battle of Pickett's Mill and Allatoona Pass. He has always had a keen interest in Civil War history, photography and cartography, all of which have come together in his current projects.

Available Now

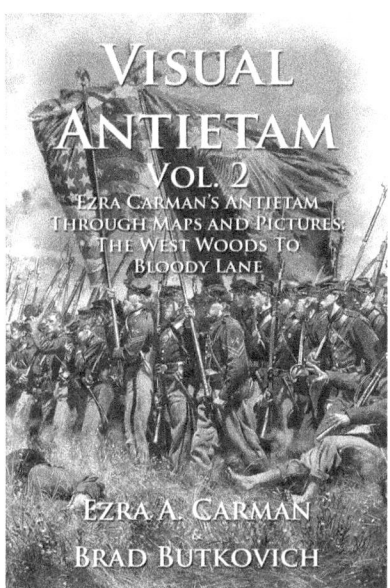

Available Now

www.ingramcontent.com/pod-product-compliance
Lightning Source LLC
Chambersburg PA
CBHW071435080526
44587CB00014B/1856